THE SHADOW OF ATLANTIS

By

COLONEL A. BRAGHINE

With 25 Illustrations

NEW YORK

E. P. DUTTON & CO., INC.

1940

STATUETTES FOUND IN SAN SALVADOR
Have we here an archaic Egyptian style?

THIS WORK IS DEDICATED, AS A SIGN OF MY
GRATITUDE AND PROFOUND ESTEEM, TO
THE COMPANION OF MY LONG AND STRENUOUS
VOYAGES AND MY FAITHFUL ASSISTANT
AND INSPIRER, MY BELOVED WIFE.

I met a traveller from an antique land
    Who said : " Two vast and trunkless legs of stone
Stand in the desert.   Near them on the sand
Half sunk, a shattered visage lies, whose frown
    And wrinkled lip and sneer of cold command
Tell that its sculptor well those passions read
    Which yet survive, stamped on those lifeless things,
The hand that mocked them and the heart that fed.
And on the pedestal these words appear :
    ' My name is Ozymandias, king of kings :
Look on my works, ye mighty, and despair ! '
    Nothing beside remains.   Round the decay
Of that colossal wreck, boundless and bare,
    The lone and level sands stretch far away."

SHELLEY.

TABLE OF CONTENTS

7

LIST OF ILLUSTRATIONS

AUTHOR'S PREFACE

AS far as the evolution of the historic process is concerned the scientific outlook which became crystallized during the last century is at present apparently undergoing a radical revision. History and archæology are assisted now by other branches of science, which formerly had little community with them; anthropology, ethnology, toponymy, and even paleontology frequently furnish new information which alters the picture of the life of mankind during the remotest epochs. During recent years archæological discoveries have become much more numerous: ancient cities are unearthed from beneath mighty millenarian layers of alluvium, philologists decipher the inscriptions in tongues long dead, while the students of languages are tracing the bonds between these dead idioms and contemporary ones. The researches of scientists have removed the primitive periods of the life of organized mankind far more remotely into past millenniums. Epochs which not long ago were considered absolutely prehistoric, now, under the light of modern synthesis, are featuring more and more in the realm of actual history.

If poetical metaphors are permitted here, I would compare the contemporary epoch with that period of any youth when he first begins to take interest in his own origin as hidden behind a misty veil of childish reminiscence. So the mankind of the twentieth century is striving to call to its mind its origin and something that was thoroughly forgotten during its 'childhood.' Certain rambling remembrances of our common past live still in the collective conscience of mankind. . . . We take them for myths or legends. But time passes on and suddenly some unexpected discovery, some archæological find or deciphered inscription, confirms that which seemed to be a fairy story of past millenniums. Then the myth becomes clothed with the flesh of reality and we 'recollect' the event masked by the legend.

The last hundred years have been especially rich in research concerning the mysterious continent or the great island with a highly cultured population which, according to Plato and other classical authors, existed long ago in the Atlantic Ocean. Little by little there has arisen around this problem an enormous literature and even a new branch of prehistoric archæology which has been baptized by certain authors as 'atlantology': the atlantological literature (or bibliography) consists now of more than 25,000 volumes. Both in America and Europe have been created societies of students of atlantology and special reviews dealing with the subject have begun to be published.

It is difficult enough for one to orientate oneself in this spate of atlantological literature: besides the knowledge of many ancient and modern languages one requires a wide acquaintance with history, archæology, ethnology, mythology, and even geology and astronomy.

I would like to touch on quite a different source of information concerning Atlantis, i.e. the so-called 'revelations' of theosophists, anthroposophists, etc. Personally I am not on the side of the materialists who consider all such revelations to be merely the imagery of disordered minds: on the contrary, I think that occult methods of obtaining knowledge, such as by clairvoyance, may enable us sometimes to perceive something that ordinarily escapes our five very elementary senses. But unfortunately those methods have failed up to the present in producing fresh scientific knowledge on any subject, be it a phenomenon of nature or the history of mankind, and until now such sources have not provided more than quite ordinary and trivial information. A true description of events which occurred some millenniums ago would be a feat completely beyond the range of occult possibilities, at any rate for the present. . . . Therefore I cannot attach great importance to the information received by hypothetical 'White Lodges,' or by clairvoyants, mystics, mediums, etc. From this point of view I consider the works concerning Atlantis of such authors as H. P. Blavatsky, Scott Elliot, Leadbeater, and other similar writers as more or less successful fictions, since they do not supply any information capable of scientific control. I base my theories only upon facts concerning which one is allowed to make a certain number of more or less plausible conjectures. Moreover, it is to be regretted that various visionaries and novelists have exploited the subject of Atlantis, and their activity has alienated it from the attention of many serious truth-seekers and created around it an atmosphere of fancy and fiction. Therefore the public has become unable to separate the fact from the fiction and remains ignorant of those conquests of true knowledge that are painstakingly collected by serious investigators such as, for instance, Lewis Spence, Mrs. Whishaw and others. A solution of the problem of Atlantis, whether positive or negative, would be immensely useful for science in general: it entails numerous excursions into the realms of various sciences, and the search for pros and cons has already brought a very rich harvest. Thanks to these attempts our knowledge of the remotest epochs is now incomparably larger than it was two centuries ago.

In order to help students of the problem of Atlantis we will examine in this book some material concerning it, together with my own conjectures.

* * *

Should the critical reader notice unusual forms of expression in my writings, I should be most grateful if he would remember that English is not my mother tongue and read my book for the facts it contains rather than for its literary style.

A. BRAGHINE.

THE SHADOW OF ATLANTIS

CHAPTER I

UNTIL comparatively recent days serious academical science has absolutely disregarded the legends concerning Atlantis. If geologists mentioned the continent which existed long ago between Europe and America they relegated its existence to very remote periods, distant from the present epoch by millions of years. Moreover, their boundaries for this ancient continent did not correspond with the boundaries of Plato's Atlantis. All hypotheses concerning the latter the scientists left to novelists, poets, theosophists and other dreamers.

But unexpectedly the researches made in the last few years by various specialists, archæologists and others, begin, it seems, to create a necessity to infer the existence in an epoch not too distant from our times of a mighty centre of unknown prehistoric culture in the Atlantic Ocean. It now appears that Plato and other ancient writers were probably right when they treated as facts the misty legends which circulated in their time among the Mediterranean peoples.

The French scientist Glotz speaks in his *History of Greece* of the role of myths in historical research as follows: ' it is a well-known fact that legend comes before history, but an attentive and rigorous analysis of any myth gives us the opportunity to detect historical data even in a myth. The comparative method is very useful in these cases.'

Professor P. Gaffarel in his work about Atlantis affirms that the Atlanteans played an important role in the history of mankind, and we cannot deny the influence of their culture on the subsequent development of our species. According to the opinion of Professor Gauthier (see his work on the Sahara Desert, p. 166) the solution of the problem of Atlantis is very important.

Before starting my account of various aspects of this problem, I have considered it necessary to discuss the copious information contained in the famous Dialogues of Plato, *Timaeus* and *Critias*. *Timaeus* represents a colloquy between Socrates, Timaeus, Hermocrates and Critias. Critias tells Socrates a very remarkable story, which he regards as authentic.

'I heard this story,' declares Critias, 'from my great grandfather who had it from Solon, the famous philosopher. In the Delta of the Nile stands the city of Sais, formerly the capital of the Pharaoh Amasis. It was founded by the goddess Neith, called by the Greeks Athena. The inhabitants of Sais are friends of the Athenians because they believe they had a common origin. Therefore Solon was received by the population of Sais with great honour. The wisest priests of the temple of the goddess Neith initiated Solon into the most ancient traditions concerning the history of mankind, and particularly the history of Sais. It dawned upon Solon that neither he nor his compatriot-Greeks had the slightest idea concerning the remotest epochs of history. The priests explained this ignorance by the fact that various catastrophes, such as floods and earthquakes, had destroyed the memory of the past. " Moreover," added the priests, " sometimes much more dreadful catastrophes occur, owing to the action of the heavenly fire. For instance, the story of Phaeton who appropriated the flaming chariot of his father, Phoebus, and through his inability set on fire half the world, is a very true one, although it seems improbable. Certain perturbations in the movement of heavenly bodies occur periodically, causing the destruction of millions of lives. After these cataclysms mankind lapses again into barbarity and forgets the art of writing. The Athenians remember, for instance, only one world-deluge, whilst there have been several. You do not know even your own origin, and you ignore that you are a feeble offshoot of a great and famous race." '

Further, the priests informed Solon that their knowledge of the history of Sais covered 8,000 years. ' These manuscripts contain the description of a war between the Athenians and an ancient nation which inhabited a great island in the Atlantic Ocean. In the neighbourhood of that island there were others and beyond them, at the limit of the ocean, a great continent. This island, called Poseidonis, or Atlantis, was ruled by kings to whom also belonged the neighbouring islands. Moreover, they were the masters of Lybia and of the lands around the Tyrrhenian Sea. When Europe was invaded by the Atlantean army, the valour of the head of a Greek coalition, the city of Athenae, saved Greece from the Atlanteans' yoke. These events were soon followed by a dreadful catastrophe : a violent earthquake tore the earth asunder and heavy and lasting rains flooded it. The Greek troops perished and Atlantis sank beneath the ocean.'

The other Dialogue of Plato, *Critias*, gives us the date of that remarkable event : it occurred about 9,000 years before Plato's time. Further, the philosopher gives the details of the government of Atlantis, and the earlier history of that country. It appears that the first king of Poseidonis was Atlas, the first son of Poseidon, and his brother Gadir became ruler of another part of the island, situated near the Pillars of Hercules, or the present Gibraltar. Therefore all that country was called Gadirique and we can discern a survival of the word ' Gadir ' in the name of the modern Cadiz. Atlantis was a very rich country : it possessed forests of valuable trees, fertile plains, mines of various metals and multi-coloured stones. A metal, ' oreichalkos,' which glittered like gold, was renowned among the ancients.

The Dialogue of *Critias* explains the tragic end of the brilliant civilization of Atlantis by the wrath of gods : they were indignant at the Atlanteans' pride. Other classical texts tell us that the gods were displeased at the Atlanteans practising Black Magic, and decided to exterminate the sinful race. So Atlantis sank for ever in the ocean's abyss.

A commentator on Plato's works, the classical writer Proclus, tells us about the voyage of a certain Krantor : the latter visited Sais 300 years after Solon's trip, and the priests of Neith's temple showed him columns with hieroglyphic inscriptions. These ancient texts contained the story of Atlantis and its population : according to Krantor's report, this story was identical with that related by Plato. All the ancient authors, save Aristotle, believed Plato's Dialogues to be a truthful description of events which had taken place in the Atlantic ocean some millenniums earlier.

Various ancient and medieval authors, novelists as well as scientists, tried to resolve the problem of Atlantis. An erudite Jesuit, Father Kircher, in the seventeenth century came nearer than others to the solution of this historic riddle : in his very interesting work, *The Subterranean World*, he placed the sunken continent westward of Gibraltar. According to Father Kircher, the Azores and Canaries represent the summits of the uplands of Atlantis. This author left us also a hypothetical map of Plato's island : its outlines resemble a pear, whose narrow end is pointed southwards. In the island's centre stood a mountain wherefrom issued five rivers and, more southwards from another mount, came a sixth one.

Plato gives the dimensions of the island as 3,000 stadia in length and 2,000 stadia in width; so that the whole island's surface should be equal to approximately 78,800 square miles. But the contemporary scientist, Abbé Moreux, deems these figures exaggerated and supposes that the Greek philosopher made a mistake while converting the Egyptian measures into Greek. The same hypothesis was advanced by a German archæologist, Dr. A. Herrmann : later on we shall have an opportunity to examine the discoveries of that scientist in detail. At the moment we can only say that the Moreux hypothesis seems to us absolutely unfounded, because Plato definitely says : Atlantis was larger than North Africa (Lybia) and Asia Minor together. Therefore the dimensions of Atlantis, as given by the Greek philosopher, seem to us rather an understatement : in our opinion Atlantis must have been a real continent, like Australia, or Greenland.

According to the famous naturalist Buffon (see his *Proofs of Earth's Sphericity*, Chap. XIX), the narrative of Plato does not contain anything improbable. Perhaps, says Buffon, America was once connected by a comparatively narrow strip of land with the Azores group and Ireland. We find the proof of this assertion in the following fact : the remains of certain fossil animals and shells peculiar to America have been discovered also in Ireland, but nowhere else in Europe. In this Buffon's opinion agrees with the work of the scientist Lamettrie, published at the end of the eighteenth century.

Further, the Abbé Moreux mentions the interesting researches of the scientist Bory de Saint Vincent, who undertook in 1803 the first investigation of the Atlantic Ocean, near the Canary Islands. According to Moreux this investigation confirmed the reports of the ancient authors concerning the difficulties of navigation in those regions : the islands of Madeira, Azores, the Cape Verde

group, the Savages, the Steer-Ground rocks and other islets
scattered there, give the impression of being the remains of an
ancient continent submerged by the sea. According to the
hypothesis of Bory de Saint Vincent, the fractions of a continent
in this region were more numerous in the past, but in consequence
of the action of various natural agents they have disappeared little
by little. The same scientist cites the account of Diodorus of
Sicily : this writer affirmed that in North Africa there once
existed a large lake, called by the ancients the ' Triton's Lake,'
which disappeared simultaneously with Atlantis. The same
earthquake which sank Plato's continent destroyed the narrow
band of land which separated the lake from the sea.

Another scientist, the Bishop Tollerat, contemporary of Bory
de Saint Vincent, adds that the same earthquake also destroyed
the European–African isthmus, and simultaneously the waters of
the Mediterranean Sea rushed upon unhappy Atlantis. According
to Bishop Tollerat, the Triton's Lake at one time covered the
entire surface of the Sahara and the present desert was formed
only after this catastrophe.

The Abbé Moreux does not doubt the truth of Plato's account,
but considers the date of the catastrophe as given by the Greek
philosopher to be wrong : according to Moreux, it is probable
that it may have occurred earlier than ten thousand years ago.
Probably Atlantis existed in the beginning of our present
geological age (the Quaternary Epoch) and perhaps the story of
its tragic fate was still talked about by Solon's contemporaries.

*   *   *

As I stated before, many facts mentioned in this book lead to
the belief that during some remote epoch, somewhere on the
Earth's surface there lived a race which developed a high, even
refined, culture. Some facts I will discuss later on permit us to
suppose that the bloom of this culture took place in the XIVth
or XVth millenary. As to its tragic end, following some stupendous catastrophe, I have reason to believe this occurred 11,000
years ago, i.e. about 9,000 years B.C. Otherwise, taking into
consideration certain indications and conjectures, we should
place the catastrophe much later, namely about 4,000 years B.C.

Was the culture to which I have referred the development of
the great Atlantean race ? Was Plato's continent the centre of

the above-mentioned civilization, from which the cultural influences ran as mighty currents far away to the peripheries of the world of that time ? It is difficult to give a precise answer to these questions, but I feel inclined to affirm that it was so.

The geographical boundaries of this culture can be outlined also only conjecturally : on the north, the latitude of Brittany, on the west, the meridian of Guatemala City in Central America, in the south, the parallel of the ruins of Tihuanaco in Bolivia, and on the east, the meridian of Cairo in Egypt. These wide limits are taken on the ground of the similarity of various archæological finds, legends, linguistic material, anthropological resemblances, historical survivals and other ethnological data. This data was either discovered in our time, or has been handed down by the nations which inhabited those regions during remote epochs. Later, I will describe the eastward migrations of the prehistoric races and tribes from some unknown land in the ocean to Europe, and westward migrations from Europe to America of the European tribes.

If we recognize the Azores and the Canary Islands as the remaining vestiges of Atlantis, we will immediately establish that it occupied almost the central position in the above-outlined region. But we cannot say yet if Atlantis was the political centre of the hypothetical ancient culture and its irradiation, or if it was only a dominion of that highly-developed race which flourished thirteen to fifteen millenniums ago. . . . Perhaps the progress of archæology and the deciphering of the Mayan manuscripts will give us in the near future a chance to answer these questions. The material concerning this problem is really enormous and continues to grow. At present we can only affirm that all researches and finds lead us to the same conclusion : a tremendous catastrophe annihilated the centre of an unknown mighty culture which dominated an area almost equal to the area of the modern Aryan culture. Moreover, this hypothetical cataclysm played havoc, it seems, with the zone of the Atlantic Ocean, with the most mischievous consequences for the Western hemisphere, and the effect was felt throughout the entire world.

Geology has established positively enough that in the period of the present Quaternary Epoch the Earth's surface was a theatre of various tremendous processes. They were of orogenic character and the Abbé Moreux thinks that mankind witnessed some of those cataclysms. This is proved by the following find : in the Auvergne's hills (in the Department of the High Loire), among the ancient lavas of the volcano Denize (near Le Puits), was found a petrified human skeleton. The activity of the Auvergnian volcanoes developed at the beginning of the present geological epoch. In particular the geological age of the lavas in Le Puits is equal to about 60,000 years. Certainly it is very questionable whether the primeval inhabitants of Auvergne had advanced enough in their culture to be considered as a part of the population of the empire of Atlantis. My aim is to prove that the eye-witnesses of the Atlantis catastrophe belonged to tribes already comparatively civilized.

But I think that certain information concerning the mysterious prehistoric culture in Central and South America allows us to conclude that the refinement of that culture was due to Atlantean influences : the great age of the former permits us to admit the great age of the latter.

It seems that the Atlantean culture reached even the shores of Northern and North-Western Africa : the famous German archæologist, Leo Frobenius, found in the neighbourhood of the mouth of the Niger, in Jorubaland, a bronze statue of the god Olokun, the African Poseidon. Jorubaland was actually the Ufa kingdom, occupying the whole Gold Coast of Guinea, and some authorities believe that Ufa was in the past nothing more than an Atlantean colony. One must remember that Poseidon's cult was preponderant in Atlantis and its colonies. Leo Frobenius also found on the Gold Coast marvellous prehistoric monuments belonging to an architecture of an unknown type.

The cultural influence of the Atlanteans seems to have flourished luxuriantly on both extremities of the above-outlined region in America and in the Nile valley. Later on we shall have an opportunity to treat this question in detail in a special chapter. hapter.

Speaking about the diffusion of the Atlantean culture on the African continent I shall mention the researches of the German archæologists, Drs. A. Herrmann and Borchard. The first is a representative of that group of scientists which is very sceptical as regards to Plato's story, and I dedicate to his finds and theories a special chapter. At the moment I will mention only those conjectures of both scientists which attest to the vestiges of the

Atlanteans in North Africa. For instance, we see such vestiges in present Tunisian territory. The salt-marshes of Shott-el-Djerid in Tunis represent, according to Professor Borchard, the dried bottom of the Triton's Lake, mentioned by Diodorus of Sicily, and we see on the maps of the Arab medieval geographers the name of this region : ' Bahr Attalà,' i.e. ' The Great Atlanteans' Water.' Borchard even thinks that Bahr-Attalà was, in fact, the Atlantean Sea, in which Plato placed his Poseidonis or Atlantis. The classical historians tell about a tribe of ' Atarants,' which inhabited the original Tunis ; it is difficult not to recognize in this word a simple alteration of the word ' Atlanteans.' The later geographers, particularly Ptolemy, call this tribe ' Attalà,' and the hills in this part of Lybia are even to-day called the ' Mountains of Talàe.' The inhabitants of this region still regard a certain Poseidon as their forefather, although surely they have not the slightest idea of the Dialogues of Plato, in which the Greek philosopher tells about the origin of the Atlanteans from the god Poseidon.

Contrary to Bishop Tollerat's opinion (see the preceding pages), the German scientists suppose that the Triton's Lake on the northern shore of Africa was definitely dried up in 1250 in consequence of a tremendous earthquake. In any case, the fact of the existence until not long ago of large water-surfaces in North Africa is beyond any doubt. Some years ago a French expedition bored an artesian well at Fort Lasaire in the Sahara : when the depth of 100 yards had been reached the water spouted up many fish, molluscs, and crabs. These animals inhabit the subterranean water reservoirs, which probably were filled during the epoch when the Sahara was a large interior sea. This must have disappeared in consequence of a cataclysm, and the misty legends about this catastrophe has lived long among the nations of the Mediterranean basin. However, it is necessary to add that certain geologists suppose that the fish and other animals penetrate into the subterranean reservoirs of the Sahara from the superterrene basins of Algeria and Morocco.

It is interesting to connect the conjectures of the atlantologists concerning the universality of the Atlantean culture with the recent discovery of Professor Geras (University of Bombay) in Sind (India). This archæologist found there the vestiges of a very highly developed culture, which flourished in the VIIth millenary. The unknown race which then inhabited the region of Sind apparently reached a profound knowledge in the field of astronomy, but this mysterious race had nothing to do with the Aryans. Professor Geras supposes that this prehistoric culture was the source of all the successive Old World cultures. Was not this culture of Sind the most distant echo of the great Atlantean civilization?

The archæologist, Hans Fischer, thinks that the Atlanteans' cultural influences reached at one time even remotest China : this German researcher deduces the presence of these influences in Chinese hieroglyphic writing and in the misty legends of the remotest Chinese past.

We are surprised also by the resemblance between some American sacred symbols and the corresponding symbols of the ancient Europeans. We see, for instance, the sign of the swastika not only on the most ancient Aryan monuments, but also on the prehistoric American ones ; the head of the Gorgon, the symbol of divine knowledge, we can meet with not only on the classical monuments, but also in the Mexican ruins and on the inscrutable Stone of Chavin, a magnificent relic of the Tihuanaco culture. The so-called ' false vault ' of primeval architecture is to be found in the old monuments of Central America as well as in the Etruscan monuments and in the cyclopean buildings of pre-historic Greece. Lord Kinsborough tells us in his works on ancient Mexico that the Mexicans, the Cherokees and the Indian tribes of Michoacan and Honduras used in their religious cere-monies a Holy Ark, like that of the ancient Jews and, like the Jews, they did not allow anybody, save the priests, to approach or to touch the Ark. The religious rituals of these Indians resemble those of the ancient Bretons and Irish.

Professor Leo Frobenius has established some resemblances between the mysterious Etruscans and certain Indian tribes. It seems likely that a great deal of ancient European folk-lore was borrowed by the prehistoric Europeans from certain ancient American races, the Atlanteans in this case serving as a bridge between the Europeans and Americans. In this respect the analogies, which we find in the legends concerning the world's creation, are very interesting, for instance the Great Flood, as also are the methods of popular occultism employed by the ancient Greeks, Celts, Scandinavians, and Indians, as well as by such ancient Asiatic races as the Sumers, Jews, Phœnicians, and African Egyptians.

The myth of Atlas (Atlan ?), that giant who supported by his mighty shoulders the entire universe, seems to be a kind of poetical hyperbole, or a symbol of the political and spiritual power of the Atlanteans: the prehistoric world was once sub-jugated not only by the Atlanteans' weapons but also by their cultural superiority. The mythical Quetzal-Coatl, Mexican leader and first teacher, was also represented on the ancient Aztec paintings as a giant supporting the universe, so also was the enlightener of the Chibchas, the old Bochica. It is important to note that according to the ancient Mexican legends, Quetzal-Coatl arrived on the upland of Anahuac from the far east. We can find allusions to the same idea of Atlas in the sculptural remains among the ruins of ancient harbours disseminated along the Brazilian shores and on the islands of the Azores and Canaries.

The Atlanteans probably bequeathed to their heirs, the Mediterranean as well as American races, some elements of mathematics, astronomy, and also occult knowledge : according to some researchers, the hermetism of the mystagogs of ancient Egypt was inherited from the Atlanteans. In the course of their penetration into various European and Asiatic countries the Atlanteans came in contact with some tribes whose languages were exceedingly primitive, and the necessities of their relations and trade forced the backward nations to adopt certain Atlantean words. Needless to say, most of those words were of a com-mercial, diplomatic, and religious nature. As a result of such a process of assimilation we sometimes see even to-day a striking resemblance between certain synonymous words in the languages of nations very widely separated. Although, in the absence of more solid proofs, the linguistical resemblances alone are not sufficient for the demonstrating of the ethnical bonds, I find it advisable to mention some salient examples of these resemblances.

For instance, the ancient Greek word *Theos* (God) sounds in the Toltec and Mayan languages *teo ;* the Arab word *malkà* (king, or tribal chief) reappears as *melek* in Hebraic and startlingly enough as *malko* amongst some Indian tribes ; to the Uzbek (a Centralasian tribe) the word *tepè* (mountain, or hill) corresponds to the *tepek* of the Central American Zapotecs, etc. These examples are very numerous : Le Plongeon found that one-third of all

Mayan words correspond to the synonymous ancient Greek words and the Chiapenecs of Yucatan use many words similar to Hebraic. The same similarity with the Hebrew language was found by some American philologists in the dialects of various Indian tribes of South America.

While the similarity between certain American and Semitic languages might be conceivable as a very strange ' coincidence,' the similarity of the ancient Greek and some American idioms is for the present writer absolutely inexplicable except by the hypothesis of contact : we must not forget that Greek belongs to the family of Indo-Germanic tongues and apparently derives from the Sanskrit.

The myths of the Mediterranean races have preserved for us vague information about the technical progress of a certain prehistoric nation and analogous legends live in the memory of some American tribes. The folk-lore of various nations contain even to-day tales about flying horses, flying carpets, etc. The old Greek myth concerning Icarus is the most striking example of such legends.

Some thirty years ago Sir Authur Evans discovered on the island of Crete the vestiges of the highly-developed Minoan culture which flourished there six or seven thousand years ago. Besides magnificent frescoes and majestic ruins, we have inherited some myths of the Cretan primeval population, one of which tells us about Icarus, who built a flying apparatus in order to reach the resplendent Phœbus, i.e. the sun. But Icarus committed a fatal mistake : he consolidated the parts of his apparatus with wax.   Therefore, when he had ascended to a considerable height, the angry god melted the wax by his mighty beams, the wings of the apparatus became detached, and Icarus, like Humpty-Dumpty, fell down and was smashed to pieces. May we not see in this tale a reminiscence of some prehistoric attempt at aviation ? Certain ancient traditions mention that the Atlanteans used some kind of a flying machine. Perhaps Crete constituted one of the eastern provinces of the Atlantean empire and its mysterious civilization was nothing but an inheritance of the great Atlantean culture.

In addition to this conjecture I may mention one very interesting archæological find : I have seen in a private collection in San Salvador (a Central American Republic) a clay dish with drawings. These drawings represent men flying over the palms on curious machines, exhaling flame and smoke. Unless these drawings are nothing more than an illustration of some local tale, we have to recognize that some unknown prehistoric race in America witnessed the first flying attempts of mankind.

Should we deny a certain cultural inheritance received by the ancient Egyptians, Mayas, and Toltecs from the Atlanteans, we must admit that their cultures arose suddenly in some inconceivable way, without a previous long barbaric period; but the history of civilization does not know such incomprehensible jumps. Moreover, we do not know any other civilization in Europe or America which could be credited with the origin of all the above-mentioned cultures. Although we may consider that both American cultures derived from the mysterious Tihuanaco civilization, some features of the latter demonstrate its affinities with the old Egyptian culture. Thus, not having a better hypothesis at our disposal, we are forced to suppose that all these three cultures and, perhaps, the Egyptian and Creto-Minoan also, proceeded from the Atlantean. The reader can find in this book much other information which sustains the hypothesis concerning the existence in a very remote epoch of a mighty cultural centre somewhere in the middle of the Atlantic Ocean.

*   *   *

Some prehistoric Mexican hieroglyphs are strikingly similar to the old Egyptian ones and to the so-called ' trigrams ' of the legendary Chinese emperor Fo-Hi, which we can see on the oldest Chinese monuments. How can we explain such a similarity? Is their existence a proof that the writings of Chinese, Egyptians, and prehistoric Americans derived from a common source? Or, perhaps, the explanation of that fact is much more simple : the psychological process of the symbolization of fundamental ideas was the same everywhere among the primeval nations.

This last hypothesis is sustained, as it seems, by a very common and well-known archæological fact : the so-called ' ideograms ' scattered as petroglyphs over the whole Earth's surface. These mysterious drawings and ideograms of an hieroglyphoid character are to be found everywhere : on the rocks bordering the Siberian rivers Irtysh, Lena, and Ienissey, on the rocks of the Onega-Lake in European Russia, on the islands of Cyprus and Crete, in Manchuria, in Corea, in India, on the famous Zimbabwe ruins in South Africa, in Algeria, in the Brazilian jungles and so on. Perhaps the newly-discovered inscriptions in Mohenjo-Daro (Northern India) and the analogous mysterious 'speaking boards' of Easter Island in the Pacific should be included in this category also.

Those inscriptions and drawings are carved deeply in the hard stone and some of them are filled with a certain red matter. The scientist Strahlenberg discovered such inscriptions also in Iceland, but they are there of a Runic character. It is wonderful that this dye-stuff has persisted during many thousands of years in spite of the various destructive influences of nature.

The Brazilian forests are full of these ideograms and primitive drawings in particular in the states of Bahia and Piauhy. On the Marajo island (in the Amazonic delta) we see ideograms resembling the old Mexican and Egyptian hieroglyphs, on Fo-Hi trigrams and on the enigmatical inscriptions of Cyprus. Humboldt first drew attention to the resemblance between the old Chinese trigrams and certain Mayan hieroglyphs.

In the United States of North America such ideograms are found along the migration routes of the mysterious 'Mounds-Builders' tribe. The mysterious tribe of Tchud marked its sojourn in North-Western Russia with analogous ideograms on the rocks and shores of Lake Onega. In the Atlas Mountains, in Algeria, and in the country of the Tuaregs and Berbers we find many ideograms and petroglyphs which by the natives are called 'tifinars.' These ancient inscriptions are numerous in South Africa, in the countries of the Bushmen and Kaffirs.

The character of the inscriptions is mostly uniform. The Brazilian scientist, Dr. Gustavo Barroso (see his work *Aquem da Atlantida*), filled some pages with reproductions of various inscriptions of this kind, found in all countries. The texts represent irregular and tortuous lines, composed of drawings, symbols, or letters of an unknown alphabet. The drawings are mostly roughly planned and show animals, human hands, feet, and heads, heavenly stars, flowers, and plants. Sometimes there are phallic signs. The letters, or symbols, are mostly of a hieroglyphic character and represent combinations of the same drawings with straight or curved lines of wavy type, or with points, circumferences, etc.

This uniformity is very puzzling. When we have established that the ideograms of the Onega rocks, for instance, and the inscriptions on rocks in the virgin forests of Bahia (Brazil) express the same style of thought-expression, the researcher is involuntarily inclined to suppose them to be from the same source, of the authorship of the same race. As an example of this uniformity I mention, for instance, the famous stone of Vodla River (European Russia) : it is covered with ideograms absolutely analogous with those of Brazil.

However, this uniformity is, perhaps, nothing more than an illusion. The apparent identity of these ideograms is, very likely, due to our inability to decipher them. . . . But, if this resemblance of style in the ideograms is everywhere a fact, I am forced to a conclusion of a rather revolutionary character : in a very remote epoch, possibly even before the last Glacial Period, the Earth was inhabited by a world-wide race. This race enjoyed a great influence on posterity. I do not consider that the Atlanteans were this unknown race, because it is probable they already possessed a hieroglyphic writing which later on was adopted by their heirs, the old Egyptians, the Mayas and perhaps the Phœnicians, who created the true alphabet. In this direction, however, only conjectures are possible : at present we do not possess any proof concerning the hypothetical inheritance of Atlantean culture by the above-mentioned nations. But, meditating on these problems, one involuntarily remembers Breal's words : ' The world is much older than we usually think and we see in human progress much more consequentialness and continuity in its development than is customarily recognized.'

Concerning the Mexican hieroglyphic texts I would recall the rather questionable discoveries of the French investigators, Brasseur de Bourbourg and Le Plongeon.

A valuable treasure, the so-called Codex Troanus of the Mayas, one of the very few manuscripts of that great race which we have inherited from the epoch of the Conquest, is preserved in the British Museum. Brasseur de Bourbourg claimed to have deciphered one fragment of this Codex : according to him it contains a striking testimonial concerning the catastrophe that overtook Plato's continent. It relates that a certain tremendous cosmic cataclysm at a remote epoch overtook certain unknown lands of Mu and Moud. Further, the manuscript affirms that this cataclysm happened 8,060 years before the compilation of the Codex Troanus. But the interpretation of Brasseur de Bourbourg has been met by scientists with considerable scepticism. Here is the translation : ' On the Sixth year of Can, in the Eleventh Muluc of the month of Zac, occurred dreadful earthquakes and continued until the Thirteenth Chuen. The Land of Clay Hills Mu and the Land Moud were victims. They were shaken twice and in the night suddenly disappeared. The earth-crust was continually raised and lowered in many places by the subterranean forces until it could not resist such stresses, and many countries became separated one from another by deep crevices. Finally both provinces could not resist such tremendous stresses and sank in the ocean together with 64,000,000 inhabitants. It occurred 8,060 years ago.'

The translation of the hieroglyphic inscription on the famous pyramid of Xochicalco, in Mexico, made by another Frenchman, Le Plongeon, seems to be as questionable as the ' discovery ' of Brasseur de Bourbourg. Le Plongeon stated that he employed the methods of the old Egyptian hieratic writing in order to decipher this inscription. It consists of a rectangle inside which we see a human face with a wide open mouth and six hieroglyphs, and below that some animal features. The hieroglyph ' ppay ' Le Plongeon takes to signify ' transformed into dust ' and the whole inscription is translated by him as follows : ' a land in the ocean is destroyed and its inhabitants killed in order to transform them into dust.'

Le Plongeon asserts that the Mayas of the Oldest Empire used a phonetic alphabet, but later on introduced hieroglyphic writing, in which thirteen signs are absolutely identical with the corresponding old Egyptian ones. This fact, if true, is very perplexing : for what reason did the Indians exchange a simple phonetic alphabet for a more complicated hieroglyphic one ?

*   *   *

The legends of the American races and tribes concerning great reformers, leaders, and missionaries who from time to time appeared among the natives, also sustain our hypothesis of the cultural mission of the Atlanteans in the prehistoric world. There were, it seems, eight such reformers : in Peru, Manco

Capac, Viracocha, and Pachacamac; in Columbia, Bochica, among the Tupis, Tupan; in Yucatan, It-Zamna, or Zamna; in Mexico, Quetzal-Coatl (called in Guatemala ' Gucumatz,' and in Yucatan, ' Cuculcan '); and in Brazil and Paraguay, Zume (called by the Caribs ' Tamu,' by the Arovacs ' Camu,' and by the Carayas ' Caboy '). The Peruvian myth concerning Viracocha resembles the Columbian myth concerning Bochica.

All these men, or gods, were sages, all came from some unknown land situated to the East of America, all wore long beards, all were white-skinned and their end was everywhere the same : their mission fulfilled, the sages mysteriously disappeared, promising to return to their beloved people later on. In all these Central and South American legends are hidden, it seems, the same facts : from time to time Atlantean missionaries appeared in America and their activity was clothed later on by poetry and religion. I can mention in favour of this hypothesis the following fact : one of above-named reformers, Quetzal-Coatl, introduced into Mexico the cult of Tlaloc, or the Mexican Poseidon, who was the god of the sea, water, and rains. We know that the cult of Poseidon was the most important in Atlantis, or Poseidonis.

The legends of the Mayas relate that Quetzal-Coatl came to the Anahuac uplands from a certain land ' Tlapallan,' which name means ' The Land of the Rising Sun.' He later became the principal deity of the Toltecs, and after the invasion of the Nahoa tribe was adopted in the same degree by them also. His name in Mexico, as well as in Guatemala (' Gucumatz ') and in Yucatan (' Cuculcan '), signifies ' The Feathered Serpent.' The Aztec myth relates that the god Tezcatlipoca by means of charms exiled Quetzal-Coatl from Mexico and he returned to Tlapallan. Other myths affirm that Quetzal-Coatl burnt himself on a funeral pyre, but that his heart ascended to heaven and was transformed into the Morning Star.

Quetzal-Coatl wore a long white cloth and had a beard. His images often present a pilgrim with a pastoral staff and in addition sometimes the solar disk or half-disk. The latter circumstance indicates the Oriental origin of Quetzal-Coatl. His arrival on the Anahuac upland was entirely unexpected and nobody saw his disembarkation on the Mexican shores. Immediately after his arrival Quetzal-Coatl started to preach a new religion and new morals. He was infinitely kind-hearted, abhorred every violence and stopped his ears with cotton when the conversation touched on war or war-deeds. He introduced into Mexico a better social order, taught the natives the useful arts and trades and contributed largely to the gentleness of manners.

Evidently the cult of Tlaloc-Poseidon in the course of millenniums suffered many modifications for the worse and the humanitarian precepts of Quetzal-Coatl were forgotten by new generations. The cruel and barbarous ritual called ' the wedding of Tlaloc,' which was celebrated among the Aztecs, is a proof of it. Yearly the prettiest girl and youth among the population were chosen and consecrated to Tlaloc. This newly-married couple enjoyed three days of every possible care and comfort : they were placed in a sumptuous apartment, ate of the best dishes and drank the best beverages, but after these three days they were thrown in their festival attire by the priests of Tlaloc into a bottomless pit near the temple, where they died in torture from hunger and thirst. When in Teotihuacan I visited in the ruins of that temple this place of torture : the pit is very deep and is supposed to be full of human bones. When I threw into it a stone, the sound of the fall came to my ears only after a considerable interval. Its irregular configuration permits one to conjecture that it was probably a canal from some ancient geyser. It is improbable that the benign Quetzal-Coatl established such a cruel ritual as that of the ' Wedding of Tlaloc.'

It is at present impossible to ascertain the time of Quetzal-Coatl's arrival in Mexico : opinions concerning this date are rather divergent. Some Catholic authors suppose that Quetzal-Coatl was a certain unknown Christian missionary and came to Mexico in A.D. 544, and others even think that he was nobody else than the apostle Thomas, who preached everywhere and also in Mexico. But the majority suppose that Quetzal-Coatl's arrival happened at least a few millenniums B.C.

The Peruvian legends concerning Manco Capac relate that once upon a time in the region of the lake Titicaca lived a highly-cultured nation. They were probably the forefathers of the modern Aymara Indians, or, perhaps, the legends are inherited from the mysterious Tihuanaco race. The myths of the Aymara relate that the unknown nation referred to was ruled by *tupacs* (kings). A mysterious foreigner, Manco Capac, together with his sister Mama-Oello, who was also his wife, suddenly appeared on a certain island of the above-named lake. Manco Capac soon seized the power and from this mysterious couple later derived all the dynasties of *tupacs*. The first one began about 1300 B.C. under the name of Pirua-Pacari-Manco. The *tupac* Capac VII was the most remarkable ruler of this dynasty. The second dynasty consisted of the mysterious ' Amauta,' a word which in the Quichua idiom signifies ' the Sages.' The Incas appeared much later, after the extinction of the Amauta.

It would be impossible to presume the Atlantean origin of Manco Capac if 1300 B.C., as the date of his arrival, is correct. But perhaps he was a representative of one of the numerous Atlantean colonies which survived the catastrophe. He and his wife claimed their origin directly from the sun itself. But it is highly probable that the original version of this claim meant the arrival of Manco Capac and Mama-Oello from the country ' where the sun comes into the world,' and the successive versions of the myth have added fancy to the truth. Consequently the Bolivian, Ecuadorian, and Peruvian tribes adopted the solar cult.

Manco Capac organized the priests' hierarchy, founded a religious system, and taught the arts and trades to the Andean highlander tribes. The Peruvian scientist Francisco Loaisa offers a rather interesting hypothesis concerning the founder of the prehistoric dynasties of *tupacs :* he suggests that Manco Capac came from the ' Land of the Rising Sun,' i.e. Japan. According to Loaisa the ignorant subjects of the new *tupac* took their ruler's assertion literally. But we must note that Manco Capac was bearded and white-skinned, while the Japanese belong to the yellow race and rarely have beards. I am rather inclined to think that the Japanese race itself lived at one remote epoch somewhere to the east of its present dwelling-place and in the denomination ' The Land of the Rising Sun ' we have only a remembrance of the previous Japanese dwelling-place. It is clear that the sun rises for Japan from the American side.

Another Peruvian hero, Pachacamac, whose name signifies ' The Earth's Father,' was a great enlightener of his people and a rival of the third Peruvian reformer Viracocha whom finally he overcame. In the course of millenniums Pachacamac was transformed into a god of earthquakes and his temple at Pachacamac-

City became a kind of Peruvian Delphi : listening to the subterranean rumbles the priests took them for the speech of the
god himself.

Yucatan's enlightener Itzamna, or Zamna, is recognized by
the Mayan Indians as founder of their civilization and ' Master
of the Dawn.' This last name permits us to think that there
was a certain eastern land wherefrom he originated.

The god and hero Zume, recognized throughout South
America as a great reformer, came also from the East. The
scientist Ehrenreich in his book concerning the Caraya tribes
(see p. 39) sees in this expression ' came from the East ' an
indication of the solar origin of all analogous myths, but I prefer
to suppose it to express nothing more than a remembrance of
the Atlantean origin of all these reformers and missionaries.

Zume is the Paraguayan name of this famous enlightener, but
the Caribs call him Tamu, the Arovacs, Camu, and the Carayas,
Caboy. The latter affirm that Caboy brought them out the
Subterranean World : perhaps in this vague myth is hidden
an indication of a great seismic cataclysm witnessed by the
forefathers of the Carayas? The Brazilian Caribs relate that
Tamu, or Zume, was white-skinned and came from the East.
He taught his people agriculture and later on disappeared in an
easterly direction.

The god Tupan, worshipped by the Tupis, taught them and
other Brazilian tribes agriculture and the use of fire. Later I
shall give a more detailed account of the origin of the Tupan
cult, which is a very interesting branch of South American
mythology.

Now I will dedicate a few words to the enlightener of the
Chibcha (Muisco) race in Columbia. The culture of this race
was an absolutely independent one, and the Columbian historian,
Miguel Triana, thinks that only the Spanish invasion handicapped
its further brilliant progress.

The legends of the Chibchas relate that a certain mysterious
and venerable man named Bochica was the reformer, preacher,
and founder of the civilization of this interesting race. Here is
the highly remarkable story, according to the account of
A. d'Orbigny.

Many millenniums ago, when the moon did not yet exist,
there suddenly came to Columbia from the east an old man with

a long white beard. He had three names : Bochica, Zukha, and Nemketaba. His handsome wife had also three names : Chia, Huitaca, and Ubecaihuara. Both came riding camels. Chia was a very wicked enchantress, a true contrast to her infinitely kind-hearted husband : she tried to hinder him in everything that he undertook to help his people. At one time she created a dreadful inundation : obeying her charms, the Funza river came out of its bed and inundated the whole Bogotà valley. A multitude of Chibchas perished and only those who succeeded in climbing the mountains in time remained safe. Bochica became very angry with his handsome wife Chia for such a misdeed, and threw her heavenwards, transforming her into the moon. After that Bochica destroyed the rocks which impeded the flow of the Funza and drained the Bogotà valley.

Bochica enlightened the Bogotà upland tribes, organized their government, ordered them to build cities, introduced the solar cult, and appointed two rulers : one religious with the title of ӡakè, and one civil, subordinated to the first. According to the legend, the first ӡakè ruled the Chibchas for 250 years. His mission fulfilled, Bochica retired to a lonely place named Iraca, where he lived for 2000 years under the name of the anchorite Idacansas. During all this period he fasted and prayed for his beloved people. The end of Bochica was as mysterious as his arrival in Columbia : he disappeared. Later on he was transformed into the sun-god.

Many centuries after his disappearance, approximately in the second century A.D., there came from the far east to the country of the Chibchas a priest named Nemketeba. He claimed to be sent by the great Bochica-Nemketaba to help the further progress of his beloved people. Nemketeba taught the natives agriculture, the weaving of fine cloths, astronomy, and weather-forecasting, he introduced some reforms in the priests' organization, built a temple to the Sun, and preached elevated morals. According to M. Triana, the Chibchas still retain a vivid memory of this apostle of Bochica.

The Spanish conquistadores were amazed by the high level of culture of the Chibchas : this Indian tribe produced artistic copper and gold work, carved magnificent bas-reliefs in stone, wove elegant cloths and decorated them with fine paintings, possessed a monetary system based of massive gold coins and a calendar. The Chibchas divided the year of 365 days into 12 months, and the day of the spring-equinox was their national feast. It was consecrated to the Sun with child-sacrifices : the nature of the rituals of this equinoctial feast is a clear indication of its agricultural meaning.

The state-system of the Chibchas consisted of a kind of despotic theocracy and the *zipas* (kings) were revered as sovereigns anointed by god himself. Before his accession to the throne the new *zipa* had to undergo a series of tests, and M. Triana says that those tests and ceremonies resemble the analogous rituals for the Egyptian Pharaohs and ancient Hindu rulers. The Chibchas' legislation was very severe : adultery was punished by the death of both criminals, the talon's law prevailed, luxury was pursued as a crime, inheritances were regulated by law, and cowards and traitors to the fatherland were subjected to an infamous death. The Chibchas used ideographic writing and we can find on the Columbian rocks petroglyphs of that remote epoch when an independent Chibcha state still existed. These Indians mostly selected for their inscriptions black rocks and, when obliged to adopt lighter ones, used coloured ideograms. Among them we can find almost all the signs of European, Asiatic, African, Brazilian, and other ideograms, and with particular frequency the swastika. This resemblance between Columbian petroglyphs and other similar inscriptions favours the hypothesis of the Atlantean origin of such writings. In the villages El Infernito, Tunja, and Ramiriki are to be found monoliths from the flourishing period of this peculiar South American culture : they are covered with a marvellous and fanciful carving, the meaning of which has not yet been deciphered.

The memory of the kind-hearted old Bochica, long-bearded and white-skinned reformer and preacher, still lives in the Andean valleys and gorges : when a traveller, lost in the mountains, sees suddenly in the fog his own shape magnified to giant's dimensions (a phenomenon known as ' Brocken's Ghost '), he thinks in fear that it is the spirit of the divine old man himself, who goes to visit his beloved people and help them in their present misfortunes. . . .

*　　　*　　　*

In many of the oldest inscribed monuments of the American natives and in the folklore of various tribes we can find more or less dim allusions to Atlantis and its tragic end.

The Toltec Codex Tira ('The Book of Migrations'), for instance, mentions the migration of eight tribes : they came to the Pacific shores from a certain eastern country called Aztlan. The Mexican legends mention a terrific catastrophe, a great inundation which forced the Nahoa and Quiché tribes to emigrate to the far west. The mysterious Toltec and Aztec fatherland, the country Aztlan, is represented on the ancient Mexican drawings as a mountainous island ; one of its mountains is encircled by a wall and a canal.

According to the scientist Clavigero, the Mexican Olmecs, or Ulmecs, have a legend which records the arrival of their ancestors from a distant eastern country.

The North American Indians also believe that their ancestors came from the east. Major Lind, known as an expert in Indian folklore, came across one legend in the states of Iowa and Dakota : it tells that all Indian tribes at one time inhabited an eastern island and formed one nation. Later on they launched a ship of peculiar form and navigated it for some weeks before they landed on the American shores.

It seems, however, that this legend makes a mistake in affirming that all Indian tribes once belonged to the same race : the difference of the colour of the skin among them is too great. We can find the most diverse shades of pigmentation : while the tribes of Menomines, Dacoits, Zuni, and others are almost white-skinned, the Caro tribe in Kansas and the Californian Indians (now almost extinct) are very dark. We can find also tribes with swarthy-red, olive-coloured, bright-yellow, and bronze-coloured skins. Professor Retzius considers that all primeval dolichocephalic tribes in America are very closely related to the Guanches of the Canary Islands and to the races which inhabit the Atlantic shores of Africa. All the above-mentioned races and the dolichocephalic Caribs possess a red-brown skin. It is interesting to mention here that the mysterious tribe of Masinti portrayed on the ancient Egyptian frescoes is depicted with the same shade of skin.

Moreover, we can occasionally find white Indian tribes in Venezuela and on the peninsula of Darien : they are even light-

haired, have blue eyes, and a few researchers suppose them to be
descendants of some Atlantean tribe. Usually American Indians
possess black hair, but the ancient Peruvians, for instance, were
auburn-haired, which fact is confirmed by the discoveries of
Short who found some modern Peruvian tribes with auburn
hair.

The Warrau tribe of Arovacs affirm that their ancestors long
ago inhabited a certain ' Heavenly Land ' : neither malicious men
nor pernicious animals existed there.

The Quichés of Guatemala possess a remarkable monument of
great antiquity, the famous Codex Popul-Vuh (' A Bouquet of
Leaves '). It is their sacred book and it was discovered in 1854
by Dr. Scherzer. The four volumes of this book, written in the
tongue of the Quichés, give the history and the mythology of
the Mayas. The Popul-Vuh asserts that the forefathers of the
Quiches came in a very remote epoch from a distant eastern
country situated in the ocean. Later on three sons of their king
visited this country of their origin and returned to Guatemala
with the knowledge of writing. This mysterious eastern country
is described by the Codex as a true paradise : Whites and Negroes
lived there in peace like brothers and spoke the same language.
Further on the Book of Popul-Vuh relates that the god Huracan
became angry with mankind and flooded the Earth. Simultaneously with this calamity a great conflagration was observed
in the heavens. Evidently the cataclysm on Earth was a consequence of some tremendous cosmic catastrophe and this
circumstance connects the Guatemalian myth with the Greek
one concerning Phæthon : thanks to his mistake one half of the
Earth was burnt by heavenly fire.

The last representatives of a strange white-skinned Indian
tribe are still living in Venezuela. They are called Paria, and
some years ago inhabited a village called Atlan, in the virgin
forests between the Apure and the Orinoco, but now are almost
extinct. They possessed traditions of a certain catastrophe which
destroyed their old fatherland, a large island in the ocean
inhabited by a prosperous and ' wonderful ' race. Some representatives of the latter reached Venezuela and thus survived the
cataclysm. Their descendants lived for a long time among the
Venezuelan Indians as a separate tribe. Their women were much
appreciated by other tribes and we can find an account in the

Spanish chronicles of the Conquest, to the effect that some caciques possessed in their harems white concubines. Their masters did not allow them to show themselves to anybody and thus these unfortunate women, remaining throughout their whole life in semi-darkened harems, finally became blind. Moreover, the Venezuelan writer, H. B. Nuñez, told me that in the Venezuelan forests there are many monoliths covered with hieroglyphs and strange carvings. They were earlier mentioned by the famous German naturalist Humboldt in his descriptions of Venezuela.

*   *   *

The fact of the existence of black races among the inhabitants of the lost continent mentioned in the Codex Popul-Vuh is of the greatest interest. Hitherto, ethnologists imagined that negroes appeared in the New World only during our own epoch, when they were imported as slaves; but the most recent researches demonstrate that they first came to America in a period very remote. The Popul-Vuh relates that, after the cataclysm befell the former fatherland of the Quichés, one part of its spared population emigrated westwards, i.e. to America, and the other, eastwards, presumably to Europe, or to Africa. Perhaps these latter emigrants were the forefathers of the Berbers and Tuaregs, but it is not improbable, that in the present African black population the descendants of some Atlantean black-skinned tribes still exist.

Quatrefages, Le Plongeon, and Bancroft have proved that certain aboriginal negro tribes inhabited America not so very long ago. Some statues of the Indian gods in Central America possess typical negro features and certain prehistoric monuments there undoubtedly represent Negroes. We have, for instance, such statues in Teotihuacan, in Palenque, and a gigantic negro's head carved in granite near the Mexican volcano of Taxila. I have seen a statuette of a negro in the archæological collection of Mr. Ernesto Franco in Quito (Ecuador) : according to the opinion of local archæologists, this statuette is at least 20,000 years old.

The autochthonous black races in America were either gradually mixed with the Indian ones, or became extinct, but in a very remote time Negroes, or Negroids, were numerous in the

New World. It is possible, however, that some black individuals were drifted to America by the strong currents existing in the ocean between Africa and the New World : that was the opinion of Quatrefages. O'Donnelly proposes the same hypothesis, affirming that plants, animals, and men were probably carried from one continent to another by strong sea-currents.

Once I had the opportunity of living for about a month in Oyapoc, a locality in a lonely situation among the equatorial forests of French Guiana. There I saw many representatives of the local negro tribe of Saramaccas, which lives all by itself and is ruled by its own chiefs. The Saramaccas are divided into several clans and each clan possesses a sort of a coat of arms tattooed on the faces of its members. The opinions of scientists concerning the origin of the Saramaccas vary: wilst some consider these Negroes to be an autochthonous American tribe, others think that the Saramaccas are none else than the progeny of ancient slaves imported into South America, who deserted from their masters in the forests of Guiana. The Saramacca tongue resembles the dialect of the African Gold Coast which is situated directly opposite the Guiana shores. My own view is that the latter hypothesis is wrong : clearly it would be very difficult to transport into slavery an entire tribe, and still more difficult for that tribe to escape together with its wives and children. The complement of the slaves' groups was always entirely casual, so that each group of slaves was composed of the representatives of various tribes. Furthermore, the Saramaccas of to-day are a very kind-hearted people, friendly to the whites, which would not have been the case if their ancestors had been slaves, subjected to the bestial cruelty of the planters. So I am inclined to believe that Saramaccas are the last aboriginal negro tribe preserved in America.

The most surprising thing about this tribe is its knowledge of sorcery methods, inherited, perhaps, from an unknown and peculiar culture which flourished on the globe in a very remote epoch. Concerning this hypothesis I mention Tilac's opinion concerning the antiquity of the Hindu Vedas. He thinks the Vedas were inherited by the Hindus from a certain civilized race which inhabited a country covered by glaciers. Therefore only two conjectures are possible : either the author (or authors ?) of the Vedas belonged to some unknown, cultured Arctic race, or he witnessed the last Glacial Period. This latter hypothesis certainly destroys all theories concerning the comparative youthfulness of our civilization : it is much older than we hitherto supposed. Primeval men witnessed many great cataclysms : for instance, the sixteenth chapter of the Bhagawat-Purana tells us that the wheels of Priawata's chariot dug out seven oceans, thus dividing the firm land into seven big parts. According to this legend the first part was apparently the Old Continent, the second, North America, the third South America, the fourth Australia, the fifth the Antarctic mainland, the sixth Atlantis, and the seventh Gondwana ('Lemuria'), or, perhaps, Greenland.

The scientists de Launay (see his *La Terre*, p. 136) and Dr. Hamy suppose the legend concerning the existence of Atlantis to be very likely based on fact, Dr. Hamy thinks Atlantis must have been situated between Spain, Ireland, and the North American shores : in the Tertiary Epoch Atlantis served as a bridge for the slow migrations of men, animals, and plants from the Old Continent westwards.

According to some Central American monuments, it seems that the continent of the New World in a remote epoch was much more extensive in its eastern part, but that a series of terrific cataclysms destroyed a large area of the mainland. The Breton legends tell us that millenniums ago Brittany stretched farther, and the Welsh possess a legend concerning three terrific catastrophes which destroyed a great island in the ocean.

* * *

The historian Timagenes wrote in the first century A.D. about the Gauls, recording that at least some of these tribes preserved legends concerning their remote fatherland in the middle of the ocean. It is clear, therefore, that certain of these tribes were emigrants from Atlantis. Apparently the ancients gave the name of 'Gauls' to three very different races : to the Aryan Gauls who came from Asia, to the descendants of the autochthons of Western Europe, and to the descendants of the colonists, who emigrated to Europe from a certain western country. Concerning the Gauls and Celts the terminology of the classical authors is often vague and I consider that the terms 'Gauls' and 'Celts' should be applied only to the refugees from Atlantis.

The following important indication, in addition to the discovery of Professor Baudouin (see below its description), favour my hypothesis.

According to Paul Gruyer (see his *Visites d'Art*), the Celtic buildings (dolmens, menhirs, and cromlechs) belong not to the Neolithic, but to the Bronze Age. Gruyer considers that these dolmens were sun-god temples and that the menhirs, usually arranged in the form of avenues, led to prehistoric tombs. In Quiberon (Brittany), for instance, these avenues of menhirs extend right into the ocean and disappear under the water. This is doubtless a proof of subsidence of the land, which must have happened very long ago. The avenues of these prehistoric buildings, which were considered by some authorities to be mausoleums and now are understood to be astronomical symbols, produce a strange mystic impression during the calm moonlight nights of Brittany. . . . Some investigators of the Breton culture and folklore ascribe to these mysterious buildings even a prophetic meaning.

It is well known that the sacrifices to the main Atlantean deity, Poseidon, consisted of horses, and the ancient images of this god represent him as driving six horses. Also the goddess Cybele, whose cult was considerable in prehistoric times, was sometimes represented as a horse. It is interesting to note in this connection that there is a roughly made stone horse-head in the Breton village Kervedal which itself is situated near Cap Penmark : this latter name signifies in Breton ' a horse-head.'

Paul Termier and Lewis Spence consider that the Cro-Magnon race originated from Atlantis and, arriving in Europe about 20,000 years ago, brought there the oldest Atlantean traditions. A. Meillet thinks that almost all European languages derived from the Atlantean tongue. The amazing discoveries of Mrs. Whishaw (see her *Atlantis in Andalusia*) corroborate the opinion that the primeval inhabitants of Southern Spain were Atlanteans.

All the above-mentioned facts and conjectures permit us to suppose that the so-called Celts and Gauls were nothing else than various tribes which emigrated from Atlantis before and also after its catastrophe.

The Celtic myths taught that the souls of the dead went to a remote western submarine country called Avalon. According to some traditions the famous King Arthur was taken in a boat to

Avalon where he will repose neither dead, nor alive, until the Day of Resurrection. This reference to the submarine location of Avalon may be a hint at the sunken fatherland of the Celts, the continent of Atlantis. The word ' Avalon ' signifies ' The Island of Apples ' and, perhaps, refers to the oranges which were probably common in Atlantis. The Greek myth relates that Hercules, in his wanderings westwards, visited the Gardens of the Hesperides, the daughters of Atlas, where he found golden apples. These gardens were situated in the far west, near the giant Atlas, who supported the universe on his mighty shoulders. Perhaps, the golden apples of the Hesperides were also nothing more than the oranges of Atlantis, the powerful State of antiquity?

According to Greek mythology the famous Elysium, abode of the beatified souls, was situated in the far west, and enjoyed a fine climate and rare fertility. Is not this belief an allusion to the beautiful island of Poseidon, almost forgotten in the time of Hellas, but kept as a dim remembrance by the Pelasgi, the forerunners of the Greeks and also the probable descendants of the Atlanteans?

The oldest Egyptian papyrus, the so-called ' Book of the Dead,' places the abode of the beatified souls also in the far west, in a certain mysterious Land of Amenti, which formed a part of the Kingdom of Osiris. The Book of the Dead was found in many Egyptian tombs and there is a considerable difference between various versions : the largest one, consisting of 165 chapters, is known under the name of the ' Turin ' papyrus. Some years ago the British Museum published the facsimile of Ani's version of this book.

Some Egyptian manuscripts give the name to this abode of the beatified souls as ' Aaru,' or ' Aalu.' The oldest Egyptian sources call it ' Sekhet-Hetep ' (' The Field of Peace '), or ' Sekhet-Aaru ' (' The Plants' Field '). It was described as a fertile and well-irrigated land with a mighty river called ' The Heavenly Nile.' In a very remote epoch of Egyptian history the Kingdom of Osiris was supposed to be in the Delta and the fertility of the latter undoubtedly gave the ancient Egyptians the idea of Aaru's fertility.

In Aaru the dead enjoyed the gods' society and were occupied in the same way as during their earthly life : they ploughed, sowed, hunted, and played various games. In the course of millenniums the site of Aaru gradually changed until finally it came to be placed in the constellation of Ursa Major. Some other sources place Aaru west of the mysterious land of Tuat. The latter was divided into twelve parts, corresponding to the hours of the night, and each part was separated from the next by a gate, guarded by serpents. Every night the sun-god Ra sailed in his boat through Tuat. ' The Extermination of Mankind,' a papyrus found in the tomb of the pharaoh Seti I (1366 B.C.), gives us a detailed description of Aaru. This manuscript specifies that Aaru was encircled by an iron wall with many gates, to which converged mysterious roads, leading to the sacred land.

The site of Arallu-land, the mysterious paradise of the Babylonians and the abode of beatified souls, is indicated in the Babylonian myths with more precision than we find in the Egyptian. According to the belief of the Babylonians Arallu was situated in the far west in the middle of the ocean. It was also the dwelling-place of Ut-Napishtim (the Babylonian Noah) and his wife.

*   *   *

The Greek historian Proclus cites an ancient writer Marcellus, who mentioned many islands beyond the Pillars of Hercules : probably, he meant the Azores and Canaries, but the important fact for us is, that Marcellus asserted in this connection that the inhabitants of those islands retained up to his own days a recollection of Atlantis and its tragic end. Marcellus, enumerating the Atlantic archipelagoes, says that one of them consists of three large and seven small islands : one of the largest measured 1000 stadia in length and was dedicated to Poseidon, while Proserpina's cult dominated the other islands.

The nymph Calypso, daughter of the giant Atlas, is mentioned in the *Odyssey* : Homer relates that the cunning Ulysses spent much time in Calypso's grotto on the island of Ogygia, which, probably, was one of the Canary Islands. According to Homer, in its middle stood a great mountain (the peak of Teneriffe?), and around the island raged strong sea-currents.

Diodorus of Sicily tells us that those universal seafarers, the Phœnicians, discovered some big island in the Atlantic Ocean. Probably, the Phœnicians landed in Cuba, or Jamaica.

Pausanias, that exact and scrupulous writer, mentions a group of islands in the Atlantic Ocean, probably the present Caribbean group, which he calls the ' Satyrides.' The same writer describes also the adventures of a certain Carian, Euthymus, who was obliged by a storm to land there and was met by some red-skinned people, who wore long hair similar to a horse's mane. Pausanias did not explain how Euthymus returned home and why his discovery did not give some practical results.

According to Strabon, many daring seafarers of his time ventured to go far westwards. Plutarch, in his biography of the Roman general Sertorius, says that the latter, in fleeing from the tyranny of Sulla, came to Southern Spain and met there some pirates, who had returned from some islands situated about 1000 miles from Spain. These adventurers so much exalted the climate, the fertility, and the beauty of these islands, that Sertorius decided to make them his refuge, but his companions declined to accompany him and he remained in Spain.

These islands (doubtless the Canary archipelago) were called by the Greeks ' Blessed,' and by the Romans ' Happy.' Horace (*Epod.* xvi, 41) writes :

> ' Nos manet Oceanus circum vagus : arva, beata
> Petamus arva, divites et insulas,
> Reddit ubi Cererem tellus inarata quotannis.'

(' The Ocean, which surrounds the Earth, calls us. We direct ourselves to the blessed fields of the Happy Islands, where every year the soil of Ceres gives the crop without being cultivated.')

Pliny (*Hist. Natur.* iv, 31–32) says, that these Happy Islands are situated 750 miles west from Hades (the present Cadiz), and that the Numidian king Uba (of Mauretania) visited these islands and intended to develop there the production of purple dye.

Besides the detailed description of Plato, we find mention of Atlantis in the works of Diodorus of Sicily, Pliny, Strabon, Timagenes, Homer, Aelian, Cosma Indicopleustes, Proclus, Posidonius, Plutarch, Arnobius, and Pomponius Mela. It is proved that the ancient nations of the Mediterranean basin were aware of the existence of a certain mainland beyond the ocean, but sometimes it is difficult to establish exactly whether these notions concerned Atlantis or America. However, in many cases we can be quite sure that a given text concerns the New World.

Seneca, for instance, even explicitly foretold the discovery of America :

> ' Venient annis saecula seris
> Quibus Oceanus vincula rerum
> Laxet, et ingens patebit tellus
> Thetisque novos deteget orbes
> Nec sit terris ultima Thule.'

('Medea,' 376-380.)

('After many centuries will come the time when the Ocean will tear the chains which bind the world, and will open an enormous continent. Then Thetis will open a new world and no mysterious Thule will remain on Earth.')

Certainly, the Phœnicians were in commercial relations with some American nations about 3000 years ago and certain classical authors, relying upon the Phœnicians' accounts, allude to America. Plato, for instance, relates in his Dialogues that beyond the Pillars of Hercules exist some archipelagoes, beyond them a vast continent, and beyond that a great sea. It is clear that Plato must have been aware of the existence of America and the Pacific. There is no doubt that he received this information either from the Phœnicians, or from the Egyptians : these latter, with their very ancient traditions, could know about America and the Pacific Ocean from the inhabitants of lost Atlantis. Moreover, as the reader will see later on, the hypothesis of the American origin of the Egyptians themselves is supported by certain archæologists.

The classical writer Ælian in his *Varia Historia* (III Book, Ch. XVIII), mentions the historian Theopompus, whose works are now lost. Ælian reports a legend, related by Theopompus, according to which Silen once told the Phrygian King Midas about the existence in the far west of a very extensive mainland, inhabited by 'Merops.' This mysterious nation was ruled by the Queen Meropa, the daughter of the Lybian giant Atlas, who supports the universe. Hercules, in the course of his distant voyages westwards, met Meropa's father. This visit of Hercules is confirmed also by Plutarch in his work, *On the Lunar Spots.*

Speaking about Atlas, Homer says : ' Atlas knows every sea-abyss and is the unique master of the High Columns (Gibraltar), which stand between heaven and earth.' We have to understand the expression 'Atlas supporting the universe' as a poetical hyperbole: the Atlantean Empire had been so powerful that it merited this description perfectly. The 'daughters of Atlas,' such as Calypso and Meropa, were evidently nothing else than various provinces and colonies of the Atlanteans. Since Atlantis no longer existed in Homer's time, it is clear that the famous rhapsodist mixed with his narrative the legends about Atlantis and its power which still circulated in his days as dim recollections of a remote past. However, it is possible that some fragments of the powerful Atlantean Empire, such as Tartessos, for instance, still existed at that time.

If Plutarch in his treatise, *On Lunar Spots*, meant by the term 'Meropa's kingdom' a certain American territory, it would be clear that the Atlanteans also possessed colonies in America. However, it is possible that Hercules did not visit America, and that the mysterious Merops inhabited some province of the Atlantean continent spared by the catastrophe. But the Brazilian philologist, Dr. Enrique Onffroy de Thoron, is of a different opinion. This authority discerns the origin of the word 'Merop' in the language of the Indian tribe of Quichua (not to be confounded with the Central American tribe Quiché), which inhabits the north-western corner of South America and numbers some three millions of souls. The Quichua language is very poor in sounds, of which, according to the linguist Tchudi, they possess only fourteen. E. O. de Thoron cites the Quichua substantive *maro* ('land, earth, country,' etc.); its genitive case *marop* is employed in the sense of 'native, aboriginal, born here in this country, etc,' and corresponds perfectly to the Greek *gheghen*. Probably, says E. O. de Thoron, whenever the Phœnicians asked the South American natives : ' Who are you ? Where you come from ? ' they invariably received the same answer : ' We are of these parts, we are *marop*.' So, returning to Europe, the Phœnicians remained under the impression that they had visited a land populated by *marops*, and this word, altered into ' Merops,' finally reached Theopompus and Plutarch. Later on we shall see that there is sufficient evidence for us to conclude that the wanderings of Hercules westwards should be placed at the end of the fifth millennium B.C., although Theopompus, relating the conversation between Midas and Silen, adds that it occurred after the destruction of Troy. I consider the dating of Theopompus an anachronism.

A STONE SLAB FOUND IN LIBERDAD. TEXT
UNKNOWN (SAN SALVADOR)

AT THE BASE OF THE PYRAMID OF SIHUATAN
(SAN SALVADOR)

Central American pyramids are built of rubble faced with stone,
like the step pyramid at Sakkara, Egypt.

A CLAY HEAD FOUND FIVE YARDS DEEP (FRONT)
(SAN SALVADOR)

Considered to be at least 8,000 years old.

THE SAME (PROFILE)

In the nineteenth century there was discovered in Panama an ancient vessel, full of Roman bronze coins of the third and fourth centuries A.D. This find provoked great scientific interest, but the sceptics, with a mystifying air, asked why this unknown traveller of the beginning of our era took with him for such a distant journey not gold, or silver, but worthless bronze? It is easy to answer that question : probably the traveller concerned landed accidentally in Panama, being brought there by a storm, and his money was destined for an object absolutely different to the paying of his expenses to the aborigines of Panama, who, probably, at that time did not yet understand the value of any coin. Some of these sceptics even claimed that they had discovered the antiquarian who had sold these ancient coins to an unknown mystery-monger. But why should the latter go as far as Panama merely to mystify the archæologists ?

Europeans were not the only bold or shipwrecked seafarers who in antiquity found occasionally the opposite American shores. We have at our disposal one account which even proves the inverse, i.e. the accidental arrival in Europe of inhabitants of the New World. Pomponius Mela in his *Chronographia* (iii, 5, viii), which is the oldest preserved geographical treatise, and Pliny (*Hist. Natur.*, ii, 67), both tell us, that in 62 B.C. a boat, full of red-skinned people of unknown origin, was thrown up by the sea-waves on the German coast. The king of the Suevians gave some of these men as slaves to Metellus Celerus, the Roman proconsul of Gaul. This occurred soon after the conquest of Gaul and the contemporaries, such as Pliny and Pomponius Mela, supposed at that epoch that the Caspian Sea had a communication through the Polar Ocean with the Baltic Sea : therefore the arrival of Indians on the German coasts was explained by the fact that they had made the tour around Northern Europe, coming from Asia. But later on it was concluded (Gomara, *Historia general de las Indias*, 1553; and Wytfliet, *Descriptionis Ptolemaicae argumentum*) that these new-comers in Germany had been Indians from Labrador.

The French king, Charles X, bought once for the Louvre an ancient bronze bust of one of those Indians of 62 B.C. from a certain Edmond Durand. The authenticity of this artistic bust is beyond doubt and its Roman origin was established by the archæologist Egger : it is a contemporary bronze effigy of one of the mysterious new-comers to Germany of 62 B.C. It represents the head of a slave with very large and outstanding ears and a sloping forehead. The skull is dolichocephalic, the supraciliary arches being very prominent; the lips are thick and the eagle-nose resembles perfectly an Indian one. In fact, it is nothing else but the head of an Indian.

*   *   *

The priests of the goddess Neith related to Solon how the Pelasgian city of Athenæ was invaded by the army of the Atlanteans. Certainly, we cannot determine whether that invasion was a war of conquest, or a simple punitive expedition from Atlantis in order to stifle insurrection among the population of such a remote colony as Peloponnessus. . . . This 'invasion' may even have been the last eddy of that migration wave of Atlanteans which, according to Lewis Spence, was the origin of the so-called Aurignac race and comprised those inhabitants of the unfortunate continent who survived the great catastrophe. Further, according to Plato, this Atlantean army, which invaded unsuccessfully Athenæ, Egypt, and Lybia, was finally destroyed by 'Athenians' (Pelasgi), Egyptians, and African Getuls.

Professor Ludwig Schwennhagen affirms that the invasion by the mysterious Ibers-Gerions of Tartessos and Gades, *circa* 1300 B.C., dealt a formidable blow to the prosperity of these colonial states and resulted in their decadence. Tartessos, a great and rich semi-independent Phœnician colony in Spain (near the mouth of the river Guadiana), was also apparently founded by Atlanteans : according to Strabon, the inhabitants of Tartessos possessed chronicles 6,000 years old. The classical authors affirm that Tartessos carried on a definite foreign policy and the inhabitants of this mighty colony were much given to expeditions beyond the high seas.

If the Phœnicians, Tartessians, and mysterious Carians were not kinsmen, they were doubtless closely bound by commercial relations, or even by political treaties. Side by side with Tartessos existed another colonial state, whose capital was Gades (presently Cadiz), which, according to the priests of Neith, was founded by Gadir, the second son of Poseidon, to whom belonged all the region around Gibraltar. This myth means that Gades was founded by Atlanteans, because Poseidon was the chief deity of Atlantis and, to a certain extent, its symbol. We possess information about Gades from 2,000 B.C.

Thus, it appears probable that the Atlanteans of both colonies, under pressure from the Ibers-Gerions, retreated hastily eastwards and invaded Hellas and Egypt, where they were finally defeated by the Getuls and by the pharaoh Rameses II.

As to the Pelasgi, who at that time inhabited the Peloponnese, it is probable that they, as well as Phœnicians, were some other branch of the great Atlantean race, who emigrated from the continent referred to by Plato many centuries before.

Apparently all the ancient Atlantean colonies, including those of North Africa, Etruria and the present Dalmatia and Albania (Illyria), aspired after the Atlantean catastrophe to form once more one powerful state. All these countries were mentioned by the priests of Sais as Atlantean dominions in the past.

The Brazilian philologist, E. Onffroy de Thoron, even supposes that the Atlanteans invaded Europe, together with the South American 'Antis' (now the Quichua tribe, which inhabits the Andean region). However, while such migrations and invasions of the American tribes were probably possible during the existence of Atlantis, by 1300 B.C. the continent-bridge between Europe and America had already disappeared.

The same gentleman believes that the study of South American languages might give a key to the whole problem of Atlantis (see his article in the *Annals of the State Archives of Para*, 1905, pp. 5-37). He analyses, for instance, the word 'Atlantis,' and finds that in Quichua and in old Egyptian it would signify 'the land of high valleys.' The word 'anti' means in old Egyptian 'highly situated valley.' According to Plato, the mountains of the sunken continent possessed many valleys, which were situated high above sea-level. A part of the Andean ridge in Quichua is still called 'anti' and its population are 'Antis.' Doubtless our geographical term 'Andes' derives from the Quichua 'Anti.' The word 'Atlas,' according to H. O. de Thoron, is composed of two words : of the old Egyptian 'atl' (country) and 'as,' which belongs to old Egyptian and to Quichua. This latter language uses 'as' in order to designate 'the property of . . .', or to express the idea of permanence. But we can analyse the word 'Atlas' also in another way :

'atl' signifies in the language of the Berbers 'water' and the same significance of this word pertains to the language of the Central American Quiché Indians (not to be confounded with Quichua).

As the reader sees, all these linguistical conjectures are built upon rather a shaky foundation and in no case can be taken as starting point for a truly scientific theory.

The main source of information concerning the existence of Atlantis, the Dialogues of Plato, suffer from a very important defect : the information which we received from the Greek sage originated with the priests of Sais and reached, through Solon, the ears of the great grandfather of Critias. Thus, only after three generations it came to Critias, who in his turn passed it on to Plato. So we see that the original information suffered six subsequent repetitions which undoubtedly altered the main story, omitting certain important details and adding embroidery which did not belong to the original tale of the priests of Neith.

In fact, as the Atlantean public order, which the Dialogues describe, resembles very much Plato's own political outlook, some scientists suspect that he simply invented the story of Atlantis in order to present a practical illustration of the fitness of his political ideas. It seems, however, that the traveller Crantor, 300 years after Plato, saw in Sais the story of Atlantis recorded on a hieroglyphic text and noted its full agreement with Plato's account.

We must keep in mind that, in spite of all these unfavourable factors, Plato's account, after 2,000 years of criticism, still remains a scientific problem, especially as modern investigations show that this account contains much probable truth. Here are some striking examples :

Describing the shores of Atlantis, Plato says their rocks were composed of white, black, and red stones, which were also used for the building of all the edifices in the Atlantean capital. The geological structure of the present Azores and Canary Islands corresponds with this description and any traveller can admire for himself the picturesqueness of their multi-coloured shores : these islands, which were probably the summits of the ridges of Atlantis, consist of white, black, and red calcareous and plutonic strata.

Plato says that Atlantis was a country of fertile plains, surrounded by high mountain ridges, rich in various metals, and mentions an interesting, mysterious metal called ' oreichalkos ' : probably it was some alloy now unknown and in my opinion nothing more than hardened brass, or bronze. It has been proved by archæological finds that the secret of the hardening of bronze was known to certain prehistoric nations.   Indians on the Caribbean Islands, and Aztecs also, knew this secret.   Some facts show that the natives of Mexico still possess a method of bronze-hardening, but jealously guard it from the whites.

According to the ancient descriptions, the Atlanteans did not know winter, the climate of Atlantis being very mild and the atmosphere pure and transparent, which is not surprising since it is a well-known fact that the climate of Madeira, the Azores, and the Canary Islands is still the healthiest in the world, as testified by the many climatic stations on these islands.

Some years ago a French investigator, M. Paul le Cour, visited the Azores in search of proofs that this group of islands is nothing else than a fragment of Atlantis. According to his opinion, certain details of the geological structure of the Azores, such as the basaltic rocks, the black sand, and the boiling streams, correspond perfectly with Plato's descriptions in the Dialogue *Timæus*. M. Paul le Cour even hazards the suggestion that the large ' Lake of Seven Cities ' of the island of São Miguel covers with its waters prehistoric ruins.

Further, the French investigator noted a very curious circumstance : the natives of the group of Azores never use wheeled carriages and, although snow is absolutely unknown in the Azores, employ sledges whose runners they grease to enable them to negotiate the roads of the islands. The latter are paved with pebble-stones smoothly polished by the sea-waves and the natives reach a considerable velocity on their sledges. As regards this peculiarity of local life, I must add that the Mayas of Yucatan also did not know the use of wheels until the Spanish invasion, and some legends and myths tell us that the Mayas came to Yucatan after the catastrophe of Atlantis. P. le Cour explains this peculiarity by the fact that the continent of Plato disappeared before the invention of wheels. According to M. P. le Cour, we have here an example of a millenary tradition which cannot be overcome even by modern technical progress.

The *Critias* dialogue tells how Poseidon's trident, striking the soil of Plato's island, created two springs : one hot and the other cold. We can see now in the Furnas valley on the island of São Miguel side by side two water-springs : one of them is remarkable for its low temperature and the other is boiling.

The Atlantean capital, the magnificent Poseidonis, is described in detail by the Greek sage, but I feel that the author is somewhat inclined to myth and fancy. For instance, I cannot easily trust Plato's account of many statues of pure gold, oreichalkos roofs, etc. However, this description of Poseidonis partly resembles the account of Cortez to the king of Spain concerning the old Mexican Tenochtitlan (now Mexico City). It is probable that the founders of Tenochtitlan, the Toltecs or Aztecs, when building their new capital, imitated the old one in Atlantis, their former fatherland. Many interior citadels with large central squares from which radiated streets, crossed by a multitude of canals ; all these existed in Tenochtitlan as well as in Poseidonis. The numerous dams across those canals served for interior communication and helped in the defence of the town during wartime.

The walls encircling Poseidonis were covered with copper, but the wall of the main interior citadel was lined with oreichalkos which glittered like gold. In the centre of the main citadel, situated on the three-headed mountain, stood the temple of Poseidon covered with gold plates. The interior of the temple was adorned with numerous gold and ivory statues. Plato affirms that elephants were very numerous on the island.

One gigantic statue represented Poseidon as driving six winged horses and stood very high : the god's head touched the cupola of the temple. Around it were many statues of Nereides mounting dolphins. The temple was surrounded by golden statues of the Atlantean kings and queens. Visits to Poseidon's sanctuary without special permission from the priests were forbidden and those who disobeyed were killed for this sacrilege.

The Atlantean capital was strongly fortified and surrounded by a triple rampart. The city was built on the slopes of three high mountains and such a situation was analogous to the traditional images of the god Poseidon, always represented with a trident, as a remembrance of the three peaks which crowned his main sanctuary in the island of Atlantis.

According to Plato and other authors, the state-system of the Atlantean empire was theocratic. This information corresponds to the political structure of certain American states before the Spanish invasion. It is probable that the latter inherited their public system from their ancient centre, Atlantis. Such were, for instance, the states of the Mayas, Toltecs, Aymaras, and Chibchas. All the enumerated states possessed the solar cult and sometimes, as for instance Maya and Mexico, also the cult of Tlaloc-Poseidon.

The king-priest of the Atlanteans enjoyed unlimited power, and his orders were tantamount to the will of the gods. A complicated hierarchy of numerous priests ruled the country. Sun-worship and the adoration of Poseidon were the mainstay of their religious cult.

We know that the catastrophe of Atlantis was preceded by great inundations and strong earthquakes, after which, according to Plato, ' during one ill night the continent sank in the ocean-abyss.' We find in many classical sources clear allusions to this catastrophe and some writers, as for instance Marcellus, give us valuable details concerning the subsequent events. He says that the spared Atlanteans emigrated to Western Europe. This is confirmed by Timagenes, who received his information from the Gaulic Druids.

According to the ancient authors, the collapse of Atlantis was followed by the appearance of so much slime that navigation was impossible for a long time. Many centuries later the Phœnicians, sent around Africa by the pharaoh Nechao, reported that ships could not move beyond the Pillars of Hercules because the water was too dense, and one or two classical authors saw in this a result of the Atlantis cataclysm. But to me the statement of the cunning Phœnician merchants seems somewhat suspicious : was it possible that sea-storms and strong currents could not, in fact, scatter, during many centuries, this slime-accumulation, however large ? Probably the Phœnicians simply sought to discourage possible Egyptian competition with their world-trade. In fact their attempt was so successful that for the next 4,000 years no other seafarer ventured to explore the Atlantic Ocean. It was called by medieval geographers ' Mare Tene-brosum ' (The Sea of Darkness), and until the memorable expedition of Vasco da Gama not a single ship dared to undertake a voyage across the open sea.

CHAPTER II

THE existence of a large continent between Europe and America and its catastrophic disappearance are, as I said before, generally admitted by geologists, but they talk in terms of millions of years. Such antiquity would place the trouble long before the appearance of mankind on our planet. My aim is to demonstrate that the catastrophe of Atlantis occurred much nearer to our own times and was witnessed by human beings well advanced in civilization.

Plato's story has been attacked by many scientists. I will mention here some modern adversaries of the Greek philosopher.

Recently A. Schulten advanced the supposition that Plato's description had in view not a continent or an island in the middle of the Atlantic Ocean, but the city of Tartessos already mentioned in this book. The ruins of Tartessos are situated in the estuary of the Guadiana in Spain and have attracted the attention of archæologists for many years. Their excavations have proved the high cultural level of the ancient inhabitants of Tartessos. The earlier-mentioned book of Mrs. Whishaw, *Atlantis in Andalusia*, gives much precious information concerning the culture of that prehistoric nation.

As Tartessos probably was nothing but a colony of Atlanteans, this high level of culture simply reflects the advanced civilization of the Atlantean nation. Tartessos was probably founded by Atlanteans either in the·days of their prosperity, or immediately after the catastrophe, when as refugees they were seeking a new home. The hypothesis of A. Schulten, assuming that Tartessos was the city of Poseidon described by Plato, cannot be`accepted because the calamities mentioned by the Greek philosopher never overtook this powerful colony : its ruins stand on firm land and give no indication whatsoever of having ever been submerged, or subjected to destructive earthquakes.

A French geographer, Berlioux, published some fifty years ago the *History of the Atlanteans*, aspiring to demonstrate that

Plato's Atlantis was situated among the Atlas mountains, in the north-western corner of the African Mediterranean shore. The work of Berlioux is worthy of consideration and is supported by many serious proofs. It is necessary to underline that the opinions of the French geographer are partly confirmed by the recent research of the German scientist, Dr. A. Herrmann.

Before I dedicate some pages to his conjectures and calculations I find it necessary to review certain statements of the ancient geographers.

The classical authors record that very long ago a river, called by the name of an ancient god Triton, discharged itself into the Mediterranean Sea on the northern African shore. A city dedicated to Poseidon stood on an island in the estuary of this river. Describing the researches of Borchard, we have already seen there were many Atlantean colonies in Tunisia and it is possible that the city in the above-mentioned estuary was one of them. According to the testimonies of the ancient authors, this city had a circular shape with a radius of 656 yards. The existence of a city of Poseidon on the North African shore has been for a long time considered a fiction, like Plato's story of Atlantis. But 1931 came and Herrmann found the vestiges of Poseidon's city in Tunis. The German scientist had worked already for a long time in Southern Tunis, in the land of the Kabils, on the archæological excavations in Shott el Djerid. His researches some years ago justified the old hypothesis concerning the large salt-marsh between Neftah and the Gulf of Gabesh, which is called now Shott el Djerid : this is proved to be nothing more than the dried bottom of an interior sea, the ' Triton's Sea,' which long years ago was connected with the Gulf of Gabesh.

This discovery of Herrmann accords with the hypothetical map of the Mediterranean depression, which depression later, after the formation of the Straits of Gibraltar, and the destruction of the European–African isthmus, was called by the name of the Mediterranean Sea. This map has been traced out by the Chilean scientist, Luis Thayer Ojeda, whose works are mentioned in detail in a later chapter of this book.

Once the location of this prehistoric interior sea had been determined, Herrmann began to seek also the Triton's river. In the course of these researches the German archæologist discovered west of the oasis Fauah, under the sandhills, the vestiges of a prehistoric city which corresponds in full to the ancient descriptions of Poseidon's city.

He found under one hill of sand and petrified slime clay vessels of hitherto unknown shape, household goods and pieces of ostrich eggshell with artistic carving. These ostrich eggs evidently served for ornamentation, as they do even now in Egypt, Palestine, Arabia, and Northern Africa. Dr. Herrmann hopes to make much more interesting finds and, when the mighty strata of sand and alluvium are removed, perhaps even to uncover the ruins of Poseidon's city itself.

The German archæologist is convinced that the priests of Sais had in view this particular African city when they told Solon about the Atlantean capital. Here Herrmann contradicts the French geographer Berlioux, who placed Plato's Atlantis more to the west, near the Atlas ridge.

Dr. Herrmann considers that Solon conversed with the priests of Sais through interpreters, who might erroneously translate the Egyptian measure of length, the *shoinos*, which corresponds to one foot, as the Greek stadium, which is 604 times longer. According to Herrmann's opinion, this mistake had the following consequence : Solon, as well as Critias and Plato, gave to the Atlantean capital colossal dimensions.

The German archæologist came upon this conclusion by chance : deeming the dimensions of the capital of Atlantis too improbable, he tried substituting feet for stadia and arrived at a diameter of 1750 yards, which corresponds perfectly, as it happens, with the diameter of the ruins in Shott el Djerid. By this method he found also that the canal, which united Poseidon's City of Atlantis with the sea, should be only 13 feet wide, which corresponds again with the width of the ancient canal excavated in Shott el Djerid.

Although Plato affirms that the island of Atlantis was in the middle of the ocean, Dr. Herrmann believes that the ocean, which according to Plato surrounded the island of Atlantis, was nothing more than an interior sea, the remainder of which is now Shott el Djerid. The German scientist found also the old bed of the above-mentioned Triton's river and the ruins are at its former estuary.

These discoveries of Herrmann seemed to close definitely the controversy between the atlantologists and their adversaries. All attempts to determine the geographical situation of Plato's continent, or island, would also be settled for ever, if the conclusions of the German scientist were not met by some very serious objections.

Firstly, Plato, writing about the magnificent Poseidonis, could not have had in view a comparatively insignificant settlement on the North African shore : he would not describe it in such a high-flown style and with such numerous details.

It also seems unlikely that the priests of Sais would describe an insignificant colony as a magnificent and mighty metropolis of a powerful prehistoric empire. Also the ancient authors who mentioned Poseidon's city in the estuary of the Triton's river, would inevitably retail also the legends concerning Atlantis. They evidently did not do so for the reason that these two cities had nothing in common.

Secondly, the disappearance of Atlantis was accompanied by phenomena quite different from those which were involved in the disappearance of the city at the estuary of Triton's river : while the capital of Atlantis sank into the ocean, in the case of the other town the sea receded from it and left it and the dry river-bed a prey to the desert sand.

Thirdly, I feel Herrmann's hypothesis ,concerning Solon's erroneous interpretation of the *shoinos* is rather far-fetched : Solon had lived in Egypt for such a long time that he could not have made such a mistake, nor would such a serious thinker and mathematician as Plato ever have been satisfied with careless information. As to the dimensions of Poseidonis given by Plato, I am inclined to think that they were not meant for the city alone, but for its whole province. And finally : where in Shott el Djerid are the three peaks which, according to Plato, crowned Poseidonis ? I am also inclined to believe that the astonishing results of Dr. Herrmann's calculations represent a simple, although wonderful, coincidence. This coincidence cannot serve as a criterion of the truth because it is very difficult to determine the diameter of a city in ruins, so much the more when it happens to be covered by desert sands.

* * *

My next point is to establish the ethnical connection between some Western European prehistoric nations and the Mayas, who

long ago inhabited a certain land in the ocean. This connection
existed in a very remote period and at a time when both sides had
already attained a certain level of cultural development. For this
purpose I cannot do better than refer to the recent discovery of
Professor Baudouin.

In the western part of the department of Vendée, in Brittany,
the estuary of the rivulet La Vie periodically suffers from very
low ebb-tides : they occur ordinarily at the time of the autumn-
equinox. One of these very low ebb-tides occurred in September,
1928, and Professor Baudouin profited by this occasion to explore
a certain rock near the beach. This rock of quartzite, called by
the local fishermen the ' Large Stone,' is usually very dangerous
to navigation because it is almost always under water. When
Professor Baudouin was young he had heard from natives that
the Large Stone was covered with mysterious signs and drawings :
this brought him to the conclusion that the rock was nothing
but an ancient menhir which at some time fell into the water,
or was inundated following some lowering of the shore.

On the day of the fall equinox Professor Baudouin went in a
boat to the Large Stone and began to clean it of slime and seaweeds. This work was difficult because the stone was covered
by a thick layer of various deposits but, when the operation of
cleaning had been concluded, Baudouin saw amazing bas-reliefs
on the surface of the stone. The clay-moulds which he made
showed the following images : a disc within which is carved a
human profile, a carved human footprint, a mysterious letter, or
symbol, and a carved horse-skeleton.

The disk, or medallion, has a diameter of eight inches and the
human profile represents a musician because his lips are stretched,
as those of a man playing the trumpet. The forehead of the
profile is very sloping (this type of forehead is called in French
fuyant), the skull is brachycephalic, the lips very thick and
protruding ; but the nose is exceedingly characteristic, being of
the perfect Mayan eagle-type. You can see this type of nose on
all the images of the Mayan gods and on the Mayan statues. The
figure on the Large Stone has no whiskers but possesses a pointed
artificial beard, as have all the ancient Mayan images, and on the
top of the skull is a tuft of hair, also very characteristic of
the Mayan images.

Some details of the carving enabled Baudouin to place the

approximate age of this prehistoric sculpture at about the end of the Neolithic Period, i.e. *circa* 9,000 years ago.

The French archæologist finds a complete analogy between the types of the profiles of the Mayan sculptures and that of the Large Stone : the two profiles on the bas-reliefs in the Palenque ruins, e.g., are a striking example. The same striking resemblance reappears in the images of Mexican deities in the Codices Cospi and Borgia, the noses of the gods of which are practically identical with the nose of the profile of the Large Stone.

The following still more interesting fact established by Professor Baudouin and other French anthropologists, is that the same noses as those of the profiles on the Large Stone and of the Mexican gods of various statues and images are possessed also by the modern inhabitants of the country in the neighbourhood of the Large Stone and particularly by the inhabitants of the village Marée de Mont. Many peasant families have inhabited this region for generations, sometimes since the remotest times, and minute investigations have failed to determine even approximately the epoch in which their ancestors settled in Brittany. Although it is true that similar researches among peasant families are in general quite inadequate because of the lack of genealogical data, they still can show the remoteness of their origin, which allows us to contemplate the influence of the Mayan civilization on the aboriginal population of La Vendée. At any rate, the frequency of Mayan eagle-noses in La Vendée and throughout Brittany is definitely established by the anthropologists.

Baudouin's discovery, and the results of his anthropological investigations, lend support to the hypothesis concerning the existence in a remote epoch of a traffic between Western European shores and a certain land beyond the ocean. This land may have been Yucatan, inhabited by the Mayas, but it is also probable that some of the ancestors of the Mayas came from Atlantis. The latter migrated eastwards and, coming into Brittany, intermarried with the aboriginal population. It is also probable, even, that the entire prehistoric population of Brittany was composed of Mayas, especially since the Breton language bears a resemblance only to Gælic, remaining isolated from the other European languages.

Now it is necessary to turn the reader's attention to that false beard which we see on the profile of the Large Stone. This imperial is so arranged that its point touches the upper part of the chin and is analogous with those of many American deities. While certain figures of the Palenque ruins do not possess such imperials Baudouin considers that the latter images represent priests and not gods.

The tuft of hair which we see on the profile carved on the Large Stone is identical with those on the heads of Mexican deities : e.g., we find such a tuft on the head of a warrior on p. 37 of the Codex Telleriana Remensis, on the heads of the 'Masters of the Night' in the Codex Cospi and on the head represented on a Peruvian vessel from the Chama ruins. One prehistoric monument found in Albacete (Spain) represents a mother with her child who also has such a tuft, and Professor Baudouin believes that such tufts were signs of divine descent. This scientist has no doubt that the bas-relief of the Large Stone represents a monument of Atlantean culture and the multiplicity of prehistoric effigies with such tufts of hair shows the spread of this culture. I can add that the modern Coreans are adorned up to the present time with similar tufts.

Professor Baudouin is certain that the profile on the Large Stone belongs to a representative of the Mayan race and not to a European of the Neolithic Epoch. The Large Stone itself served as an altar and its situation was evidently selected astronomically because one of the lines carved on its surface follows strictly that of the sun's movement during the spring-equinox.

The French archæologist cannot explain the meaning of the mysterious symbol, or letter, carved on the stone, but supposes that the design as a whole represents the sun-god fecundating the world with his mighty breath.

I have already mentioned the footprint carved on the Large Stone : this symbol of unknown significance is very common on prehistoric monuments, and the Brazilian scientist Gustavo Barroso (see his interesting work, *Aquem da Atlantida*) mentions that analogous footprints are found everywhere, frequently on the petroglyphs. I have seen such an image in Ceylon in the large ' Footprint of Bouddha ' in a Buddhist monastery and also in Russia, in the monastery of Pochaieff.

The carved parts of the skeleton of a horse on the Large

Stone point to the worship of Poseidon : horses were always offered to this deity whose cult was the foremost in Atlantis. Probably the Large Stone was an altar consecrated to this god on the very same spot where the Atlantean emigrants, or sea-farers, disembarked in Europe. Maybe the new-comers celebrated on this altar a thanksgiving to Poseidon, the terrifying master of the seas, for their safe arrival on the shores of savage Europe.

It is possible that not only the Bretons and Irish derived their origin from the Atlanteans, but also the Picts and Scots : all these tribes mixed with the barbarous autochthons of Europe and with the Gauls and German tribes who came from Asia. This hypothetical affinity between the Atlanteans and the ancient inhabitants of the British Isles is supported by the following find : some years ago in the Kelvin caverns near Glasgow was found a splendid female trunk made of red sandstone. This sculpture, believed to be 30,000 years old, is well preserved and shows a highly-artistic standard. Archæologists suppose that this statue represents the goddess of fertility, probably Cybele, or Kera, whose cult was widespread not only throughout prehistoric Europe, but, according to certain investigations, even as far as South America. On the other hand it is highly improbable that any cultured nation able to create such a refined statue as that found in the Kelvin caverns can have existed in Europe 30,000 years ago.

* * *

All the above conjectures, observations, finds, and discoveries represent a variegated collection of data taken from many branches of science : historic and prehistoric geography, topony-my, anthropology, archæology, ethnology, linguistics, the history of culture, mythology, folklore, etc., all these have contributed to create our picture. A good deal of the data is contestable and sometimes bears the mark of the personal opinions and con-victions of the investigators, i.e. of a certain preconceived point of view. But here I wish to cite the phrase of Immanuel Kant concerning sundry mysterious phenomena, such as justified predictions, apparitions, miracles, etc. The German philosopher said : ' I do not believe in the reality of each single phenomenon, or in the truthfulness of the narrators, but the multiplicity and the conjunction of such stories convince me that the so-called supernatural phenomena really exist.'

The same applies to the various proofs of the existence in a remote epoch of Atlantis and its cultured population : they are so numerous and came from such various sources that, although each single proof can be contested, their general validity seems to me more than satisfactory.

Among all these proofs we observe an intimate connection, although sometimes they belong to absolutely heterogeneous scientific disciplines. Other facts, conjectures, and proofs belong simultaneously to two or three scientific realms and the task of their classification offers sometimes serious difficulties. Such a category of proofs sometimes represents a complicated arabesque, but its general aspect is very convincing.

Therefore the work of the atlantologist is akin sometimes to the work of the archæologist who reconstructs an ancient vessel from its fragments, or of the paleontologist who reconstructs from a heap of bones and fragments the entire skeleton of a prehistoric animal. So, for instance, Dr. Barnum Brown in New York constructed out of some thousands of small bones and bone-fragments the complete skeleton of a very rare prehistoric lizard, the hoplitosaur, which inhabited the North American forests about 120,000,000 years ago.

The scientist who desires to reconstruct the picture of Atlantis has to do something of the same kind. He also is obliged to use for this purpose a multitude of little facts, insignificant, as it seems, archæological finds and various allusions scattered amongst the ancient monuments, manuscripts, and inscriptions. From time to time a hypothesis is necessary for the purpose of cementing various indications and information into one eloquent picture.

But the roles of the paleontologist and historian differ in one very important point : the first knows at the very beginning of his work the approximate aspect of an animal, the second knows almost nothing and works at random. In the best cases the outlines of the intended historical picture are dim and the historian has to be very careful not to let his imagination run away. As a result of such work the atlantologist will create a merely hypothetical picture which can be used only as a basis for the detailed researches to follow, but cannot claim to be a true reflection of the remote past.

But we also have at our disposal weighty proofs taken from the realm of the so-called 'exact' sciences, such as seismology, oceanography, astronomy, zoology, and botany. We will now examine them.

*　　*　　*

As we have seen, geology does not deny the existence in a very remote epoch of a continent between the Old and New Worlds. Moreover, the same science admits that various continents and islands were submerged in various epochs by the oceans, or emerged from their depths. We will cite some striking examples of such changes on the Earth's surface.

The Arctic Ocean of to-day, the Baltic and the North Seas, for instance, are of comparatively late formation, because they appeared only at the beginning of the contemporary Quaternary Period. During the preceding Tertiary Period the site of these seas was occupied by the so-called Pleistocene Continent, which stretched from the North Pole to the Sahara, which was then a sea. In the still more remote geological periods this area was the scene of alternating replacement of sea by dry land and vice-versa. It is known, for instance, that about 25,000,000 years ago the territory of the present Scandinavia, Finland, and Northern Russia was occupied by an ocean, dotted by numerous islands, one of the larger of which, perhaps, corresponded to the present-day Sweden.

According to Dr. H. Convenz (see his *Monographia der Baltischen Bernsteinbaeume*), the islands of this primeval ocean enjoyed the climate of contemporary Algeria and Tunis and boasted of rich flora. Twenty-five million years ago, instead of miserable polar moss and lichens, these Arctic islands were adorned with palms, cedars, cypresses, euphorbias, sequoyas and a special sort of tropical pine. These latter trees produced the aromatic resin which, after 25,000 millenniums, petrified into golden amber. Yes, however strange it may seem, the amber found in large quantities on the Baltic shores is the token of the days when the severe North of Sweden was a smiling region of the world, and are a witness of terrific geological upheavals of long ago. For this reason alone the story of amber deserves more than passing attention.

It seems that millions of years ago a gigantic catastrophe devastated the above-mentioned large island of the Mezozoic

Period. Violent cyclones uprooted the trees and laid waste tropical forests, destroying the abodes of billions of insects. When the hurricanes were over, the surviving giants of the forests attempted in vain to patch up their wounds by the secretion of resin, which flowed abundantly from broken trunks and branches. The virgin Mezozoic forests perished and later on the sea flooded the land, covered by the skeletons of sub-tropical trees, buried under a thin layer of their own golden resin. During the following hundreds of millenniums this resin hardened in the water and the sea currents dragged it to every corner of the newborn Baltic.

A legend relates how once an unknown fisherman of these shores, pulling in his net, noticed in it strange dark-yellow stones, entangled amongst the seaweeds. Thrown into the cooking fire, these strange light stones burned brightly, to the astonishment of the fisherman. Thus was discovered amber, or ' the burning stone ' (*Brennstein* in old German, later on—*Börnstein*, and at present—*Bernstein*).

It is not known precisely when and by what tribe amber was discovered. Perhaps it was first found by the semi-legendary Gutons, the ancestors of the Goths, or even by the ubiquitous Phœnicians, who in antiquity adventured as far as the Baltic shores. At any rate, H. Schliemann's excavations have shown that as early as 2,000 B.C. the Mycenian kings placed amber necklaces in the tombs of their favourite concubines. Chemical analysis has demonstrated the presence in the Mycenian amber of the so-called succinite acid, so characteristic for Baltic amber, and it is evident that the Mycenian Epoch was familiar with the Zamland amber beds, the richest in the Baltic. It is also established that, hundreds of years later, the blackhaired Roman matrons adorned themselves with ' German golden stones,' which they bought from the Syrian merchants in the Via Sacra. In the days of the Emperor Augustus amber was the most fashionable stone amongst the ladies of the Roman aristocracy.

Pliny dedicated much of his attention to Baltic amber and recorded the hypothesis concerning its origin which circulated in his days. The Greeks, for instance, supposed that amber, or ' elektron,' as they called it, originated from the hardened secretions of certain sea animals, or even was simply sea-foam, hardened by the action of the sun's rays. The Greek myth about Phæthon relates that, when the irate Zeus threw Phæthon's

chariot into the infernal river of Eridan, the sisters of the unfortunate competitor of Phœbus were transformed into poplars
and for a long time shed tears which became amber. The great
Aristotle in the fourth century B.C. was the first to suggest
the correct theory of the origin of amber: this remarkably
versatile scientist declared that, in his opinion, amber was nothing
else than the petrified resin of certain trees. Pliny adopted the
theory of Aristotle probably because, serving in Roman cavalry
stationed on the Baltic shores, he had an opportunity of making
observations on the spot, which corroborated the insight of the
great Greek. The sound deductions of Aristotle and Pliny were
soon forgotten and in the fifteenth to eighteenth centuries we
come upon erroneous hypotheses, advanced by George Bauer
(nicknamed by science 'Agricola'), Bombastus Paracelsus and
even by the great Buffon. All of them agreed that amber is of
mineral origin, something like the asphalt of the Dead Sea in
Palestine. The opponents of Aristotle attempted to contradict
his theory by asking why only insects are found in this petrified
resin and never fish and shells? The reply to this objection is very
simple: the sinking of the Mezozoic archipelago occurred at a
time when the resin was already so dense that the sea animals, or
fish, could no longer penetrate it. However, we know of several
incidents of amber having been found with small crabs inside it.
Amongst the 70,000 amber exhibits in the Koenigsberg Museum
not one piece contains seaweeds or fish, but one can see in many
of them the leaves of plants of the Mezozoic Period and about
2,000 species of now extinct insects, imprisoned in their transparent golden sarcophagi. Pliny expressed the conviction that
such plants and insects belonged to the flora and fauna of Scandinavia contemporary to his period. If the latter is really a part
of the above-mentioned Mezozoic island, we have to admire the
perspicacity of the famous naturalist.

In all, about 220 sorts of amber are recognized, but the best
is, as it was 3,000 years ago, that beautiful amber which, in the
metaphor of Pliny, resembles in its transparency and pale-gold
colour the precious Falerno wine.

The ancients considered amber the best remedy against kidney
calculi and this reputation lasted into the Middle Ages: we
know, for instance, that Martin Luther wore permanently a small
amber necklace in order to cure his kidney affliction.

Millions of years separate us from the times when the luxuriant islands of the Arctic displayed their gorgeous tropical vegetation and filled the air of the Mezozoic Epoch with the spicy aroma of fir giants of a species unknown to us. And that beauty of the twentieth century A.D., who proudly displays on her bosom an amber necklace, does not suspect that these golden stones are an irrefutable and a most poetical proof of the gigantic changes which took place at one time on the surface of our planet.

*   *   *

Among the submerged continents, the so-called Lemuria particularly is worthy of consideration, because the fate of the legends describing its disappearance, resembles the fate of the traditions concerning Atlantis. Moreover, it is very important for my subject that Lemuria, as it seems, disappeared simultaneously with Plato's continent. Therefore, the hypothesis that both cataclysms were due to the same cosmic phenomenon, seems to me at least plausible.

The ancient classic authors affirmed that some millenniums ago a vast continent with a highly cultured population existed in the Indian Ocean between Africa, Arabia, and Hindustan, and stretched much farther eastwards. In that remote epoch the Moon (*Selena* in Greek), according to the said authors, did not yet exist and so the inhabitants of the legendary continent were called by the Greeks ' Preselenites.' This continent enjoyed a fine climate and great fertility of soil, and the Preselenites were prosperous and happy. But suddenly the wrath of the gods beset the blessed country and it disappeared in the ocean's abyss.

We can find analogous traditions and myths concerning the existence of Lemuria also amongst the Arabs and Hindus. For a very long time these vague legends were taken by the scientists for popular tales : but in the nineteenth century the famous zoologist, Ernst Haeckel, advanced the hypothesis that this mysterious land really had existed many millions of years ago and had been the birthplace of certain species of mammalia called lumurians. Another scientist, Sclater, went still further and, supposing that this continent was the cradle of mankind, baptized it by the name of Lemuria. According to these and other scientists, Madagascar, the archipelagos in the Indian Ocean, South India, Sumatra, and some Pacific islands are merely the last remaining fragments of the sunken Lemuria. In the opinion of the English scientist, Blandford, both paleontology and physical geography unanimously confirm the existence of Lemuria from the beginning of the so-called Perm Epoch until the end of the Miocene Period, but other scientists suppose that Lemuria sank much later, probably in the fifteenth thousand year B.C., or even later. An earlier disappearance of Lemuria would make it unlikely for the ancient Greeks and Hindus to retain any legends concerning the catastrophe. Personally I think that these vague legends concerning Lemuria were inherited by the Greeks from the Pelasgi, or possibly the Phœnicians and Egyptians.

Some years ago Professor Stanley Gardiner organized an expedition in order to explore the ocean between Africa and India. After nine months it returned with a rich collection of data concerning Lemuria, rebaptized under the name Gondwana. The most important result of his investigations was the theory that the sunken continent still existed in the epochs of the giant lizards, but sank before the appearance of mankind. Further, the English scientists established that this enormous continent was very mountainous and some of its summits attained the height of more than 10,000 feet. At that period neither the Himalayas nor the Alps yet existed. Gondwana sank very deeply and even its highest summits are 1,500 feet below the waters of the ocean.

The opinion of Professor Gardiner concerning the date of the Gondwana cataclysm, although based on his investigations, places before us a dilemma. We must either conclude that the ancient legends concerning Gondwana came to the Greek authors as an inheritance from nations millions of years old, or else that the methods of scientific investigation have failed and the conclusion of Professor Gardiner is wrong : Gondwana disappeared not so very long ago. . . . Personally, I prefer to await the results of future, more detailed, investigations and not to form an opinion at the moment.

But one apparently small circumstance among the classical information concerning Gondwana perplexes me : as mentioned earlier, the legend affirms that the population of Gondwana did not know our Moon. Here, we are in the realm of astronomy : was our satellite always our fellow-traveller in space, or has it joined us comparatively recently ? If the latter theory is correct, when and why did the Moon join our planet? What cosmic perturbation brought the gloomy Selena into our neighbourhood? . . . My reader will note that many tribes have analogous legends concerning the Moon and its recent appearance in the heavens. Many legends mentioned in this book tell that there was a time when mankind was without the gentle moonlight.

Here is another example of an analogous character. The Polynesian myths tell us about a mysterious continent which existed a long time ago in the Pacific Ocean. Certain scientists have believed that this land really existed and that the present Rapa-Nui, or Easter Island, represents a remain of the sunken Pacific continent, although the recent expedition of Professor Lavachery has proved that Rapa-Nui never belonged to more or less extensive firm land. On the other hand, it is quite probable that a continent really has existed in the Pacific. Some years ago in Southern Australia were discovered prehistoric cavern-paintings: they belong to the cavern-men who inhabited that country many millenniums ago. In those paintings are seen artistic images of alligators, which never have existed in Australia, and Professor Montford concludes that the prehistoric painter could have found the subject of his creations only on the hypothetical continent which once connected Australia with South-Eastern Asia, or elsewhere in the vanished Pacific territories.

The South African Bushmen affirm that a long time ago a vast continent existed west from Africa, but was sunken by the wrath of gods. A curious circumstance connects this myth with the Greek one concerning the Preselenites: the Bushmen affirm that at the time of that continent's disappearance the Earth was lighted by two moons. Later on we will try to analyse this myth, but for the moment I would like only to attract the attention of the reader to this curious circumstance: the catastrophe legends of various tribes are often linked up with the Moon.

*   *   *

Among the hypotheses and theories concerning the processes of modification of the Earth's surface, special consideration may be given to the so-called 'hypothesis of floating continents' of the Austrian geologist, Dr. Alfred Wegener.

Before giving an exposition of this interesting hypothesis I would like to turn the reader's attention to a very curious circumstance : if we cut out of the map the outlines of certain continents and bring them together, we will immediately see that they fit perfectly. This is true, for instance, for the eastern shore of Brazil and the western shore of Africa, for the eastern shore of Greenland and the western shore of Scandinavia, for the eastern shore of Africa and the western shore of Arabia, and also for others.

Dr. A. Wegener dedicated some years to the study of this strange phenomenon and finally came to the conclusion that at one time all the firm land formed a single continent. According to Dr. Wegener, this single world-continent possessed 50,000,000 years ago approximately the following outline : Australia was the continuation of the eastern shores of Africa, Greenland connected Scandinavia and Newfoundland, South Africa and South America formed one territory and the mysterious Antarctic continent filled the space between South Africa and the present Patagonia. The continuity between Africa and America was destroyed during the Cretaceous Period and the continents began to drift apart like icebergs in the polar seas. During the Tertiary Period occurred the same process for Europe and North America, the Antarctic, Africa, Hindustan, and Australia.

So, in various moments of the Earth's history, there gradually occurred the splitting of the once single continent and its parts withdrew one from another, floating in various directions on the subterranean ocean of magma. We must remember that, under the comparatively thin earthcrust, there rages an ocean of incandescent liquid lava, or magma, and that the foundations of the firm lands are immersed in this ocean. Naturally, the mass of firm land is subjected to the centrifugal force of the Earth's rotation : this force split the primeval single continent and its parts began to glide apart with a velocity of about two miles per million years.

According to Wegener, the separation of South America and South Africa took place perhaps 30 or 40 million years ago, but the separation, for instance, of Ireland and Newfoundland occurred much later, about 3,000,000 years ago, and Greenland left Europe very recently : only 50–100 thousand years ago. If the latter event is correctly dated, it would have been witnessed by the primeval races which inhabited Europe and Greenland during that epoch. According to the opinion of Dr. Wegener, this movement of the firm land continues to-day with various velocities for different parts : Greenland possesses a maximum velocity of about six feet per year in a westerly direction.

At first sight this theory seems to deprive the atlantologists of one of their best arguments, but later on I will show that Wegener's hypothesis is not really contrary to their theory. Incidentally, this hypothesis is supported in the case of the separation of Greenland from Europe by the very curious phenomenon of the periodical migrations of the lemmings. In Northern Scandinavia these little rodents represent a real calamity for the farmers because, like all rodents, they are incredibly prolific. But when their number increases beyond the resources of a given region they gather together in millions and depart. They descend from the tablelands and run to the seashores, destroying everything on their way : no obstacles exist for the migrating lemmings and even mass-extermination by men, wolves, and foxes cannot stop their advance. They continue irresistibly on their way and upon arriving at the ocean leap into the water and swim directly ahead until, exhausted, they drown. Scientists have attempted many explanations of this strange mass-madness of the lemmings, but the hypothesis of Wegener has been recognized as the most plausible hypothesis. The Austrian geologist believes that in the millions of years during which Europe was nearly joined to Greenland the lemmings formed the habit of migrating across the narrow straits, tempted by the then splendid pasture-grounds of Greenland. And now, although the distance between Europe and Greenland has increased enormously, the lemmings continue to remain under the spell of their ancient instinct, expecting to land within a short distance from Scandinavia.

It is very interesting to note that the Norwegian legends affirm much the same : they report that the lemmings came to Norway from a certain sunken continent and that when they leap into the sea, they intend to swim to their birthplace in the West.

I agree with the explanation of Dr. Wegener, but I can hardly accept the genuineness of the Norwegian legend : the reader must remember that the Scandinavians, together with other German tribes, came to their present abodes only 6–8 thousand years ago, while the separation of Greenland from Europe must have taken place at least 100,000 years ago. . . . Therefore the Norwegians cannot possibly have any traditions concerning the epoch when Greenland was a part of Europe. It is possible, however, that they heard this legend from the ancient aboriginal inhabitants of North Europe. But, if the separation of Greenland from Europe really occurred in the period of the forefathers of the Norwegians, we are obliged to reckon the velocity of the move-men of Greenland westward at much more than 66 feet per year, because its present distance from Norway is about 2,000 miles.

Wegener mentions various legends concerning a certain land which existed in the Atlantic Ocean, and supposes that all of them tell the story of the separation of Greenland from Europe. As the inhabitants of Wales possess a legend of the land of Avalon, as the ancient Druids told about the same mysterious country, as the Greeks possessed the legend of Atlantis, the Egyptians that of Aaru, or Aalu, and the Babylonians that of Arallu, Wegener is inclined to ascribe the origin of all these dim myths to the memory of the separation of Greenland from Europe. The evident consonance of the names Aaru, Aalu, Arallu and Avalon, and the possible one of the term of Atlan, or Atztlan, permitted to Wegener this bold supposition.

But I cannot agree with it. The similarity of the names of that mysterious country which disappeared some millenniums ago is really obvious : but I think that this similarity can serve only as an argument in favour of Plato's account and can in no way lead us to suppose that Greenland was that legendary continent and its separation from Europe was considered by the ancients to be that terrific Atlantis catastrophe. The processes of the tearing apart of various portions of the mainland has been always very slow and lasted probably some millenniums, not possessing any catastrophical character. At first very narrow straits were formed and then slowly grew wider. Not even popular fancy with all the millenniums at its disposal could transform this slow process into a terrible cataclysm.

The appearance of Wegener's theory, in the opinion of many scientists, gave a death blow to the Atlantis hypothesis, because the new explanation of the origin of the Atlantic Ocean left no room for any large continent, or island, between the New and Old Worlds. But this conclusion was premature and short-sighted. One must remember that the 50,000,000 years which separate us from the splitting of the primeval conflict is a long enough period to allow for the appearance, or disappearance, of new continents in the Atlantis gap. We have already seen that the geologists do not deny the existence of Atlantis in the middle of the ocean some millions of years ago.

Wegener's hypothesis failed to solve the problem of Atlantis, and destructive criticism was poured upon it from all sides. The majority of the geologists sided against Wegener and sought to defeat his theory by serious scientific objections. The critics, for instance, do not admit that the dynamics of the floating continents is either clearly or convincingly explained. Some scientists explain the movement of the continents by radioactivity and some others, basing themselves on the results of Captain Williams' measurements, declare that Wegener has much exaggerated the velocity of the movement of Greenland.

Recently another Austrian geologist, Professor J. Keindl, added to the hypothesis of A. Wegener his own conjecture : he found that, owing to some unknown factors, the surface of the terrestrial globe continually is on the move. Apparently this is a consequence of the activity of the interior terrestrial gases, whose pressure enlarges the volume of the earth and sometimes produces crevices on its surface. Keindl agrees with Wegener concerning the formation of the oceans except for the Red Sea and the Persian Gulf, which were formed by the interior pressure of the gases.

CHAPTER III

I WILL now dedicate some words to the so-called ' seismo-logical' argument as it is presented by Moreux. Abbé Moreux says that the volcanoes are always surrounded by seismic zones. If a volcano is encircled by the sea, in its neigh-bourhood there is always a zone of submarine earthquakes. West from Portugal, for instance, there are many volcanoes; therefore Portugal, being situated in a seismic zone, suffers often from earthquakes and subterranean eruptions. The largest seismic zone of the Atlantic Ocean begins near the North Pole, where the volcanoes of Bird's Island and Jan Mayen are situated. Iceland, in the same zone, possesses many volcanoes and geysers, which are divided into seven groups. The largest volcano in Iceland is Hecla: its eruption in 1783 covered the Scapta valley with a layer of lava of 7 cubic miles in volume. The lava flowed out of 500 craters, situated along a 12-mile crack. The eruption of Hecla in 1845 lasted seven months and the clouds of volcanic ashes reached Europe. Going southwards, we find in the same zone the submarine table-land of the nine Azores islands situated on the 50° parallel of the North latitude. This table-land serves as a pedestal for five islands with active volcanoes and new little islands often arise and disappear around the Azores archipelago. The volcanic activity there is very energetic: in 1867, for instance, the island Terçeira was a theatre of seismic catastrophe which destroyed an entire village and produced near the island a new submarine crater, which soon sank again in the sea-abyss. South from the Azores is Madeira, an island of a volcanic character, and on the 30° North latitude—the Canaries group, which represents another seismic centre: in 1909 occurred a violent eruption of the Canarian volcano, Pico de Teyde. Following this seismic zone southwards, we meet under the 20° latitude the volcanic group of Cape Verde Islands: one of its islands, Fuego, possesses a volcano which is always in eruption. All the neighbouring shore of the Gulf of Guinea is strewn with

volcanoes: there are the volcanoes of Cameroun, Mongoma
Loba, Fernando Po, St. Thomas, Annobom, Ascension, and St.
Helena. Under the 40° of the South latitude we find the
volcanic group of Tristan d'Acunha, Diego Alvarez and Gow.
More to the south are situated the volcanoes of the Orkney
Islands, South Sandwich Islands, and Shetland Islands, where
the depth of the ocean attains three miles. Finally, near the
South Pole, there are two terrific volcanoes, Ereb and Terror.
West of this seismic zone, which traverses the whole ocean
following the line of the meridian, we see the volcanoes Mont
Pelèe on the island of Martinique, Santa Lucia and others.

So, according to Moreux, the geological picture of the Atlantic
region is definitely clear: it is a very agitated and relatively
young part of the Earth's surface.

If it is so restless now, it would have been much more agitated
some millenniums ago, at the end of the Tertiary Period, when
the volcanic processes were in the heat of their activity. Therefore, the appearance or disappearance of more or less extensive
parts of firm land is quite feasible, and the Atlantis catastrophe
does not represent anything miraculous. Even now, analogous
events are registered in the Atlantic Ocean just along the described
seismic zone: in 1931, near the Fernando Noronha group of
islands appeared two new islands. Their appearance caused a
certain effervescence in the diplomatic offices of various countries:
some powers immediately sent their battleships there in order to
take possession of the new-born sea-stations, and an argument
seemed inevitable. But, fortunately, those two islands disappeared again in the sea and simultaneously there disappeared the
cause of a possible quarrel.

An analogous event occurred in the eighties of the last century,
in the Mediterranean Sea: suddenly from the depths there arose
a little volcanic island, which existed only a few hours: however, an English ship had time to plant on it the Union Jack.
This little island was baptized Sabrina.

Lewis Spence, contrary to the opinion of the geologists,
supposes that Atlantis sank not a great time ago, but disagrees
with Plato concerning the date of the catastrophe. Spence
holds that the lava blocks extracted from the ocean's depth near
the Azores were older than 9000 B.C. and supposes that the
catastrophe must have occurred 13,000 years B.C. As the reader

can see from the next chapters of this book, Spence's date corresponds to that of the catastrophe which destroyed the Tihuanaco culture in Bolivia. The latter date was calculated by R. Mueller and A. Poznansky.

Further, Spence is of the opinion that not very long ago two large island groups existed in the Atlantic Ocean : one of them included Plato's Atlantis and farther west were situated numerous islands. This last group was called by the ancients Antillia. The present Caribbean Islands, or Antilles represent the remainder of this archipelago. Some South American archæologists suppose that 'Antillia' is derived from 'Atlantillas,' i.e. 'little Atlantis.'

* * *

Here is a brief exposition of the so-called 'bathymetrical' argument in favour of the existence of Atlantis taken from the work of Abbé Moreux. It is based on the somewhat eloquent results of investigations of the ocean's depths in the region of the Azores and neighbouring parts of the Atlantic.

Examining the bathymetrical map of this ocean, i.e. the map of its depths and bottom, we see that east from the Caribbean Islands extends a vast submarine table-land. The average height of this raised platform, called the Dolphin's Ridge, is 9,000 feet. It extends along all the central and eastern parts of the Atlantic, from Ireland through the Azores and Tristan d'Acunha as far as the South Polar Circle. This table-land is divided into three segments : the first is nearer to Europe, the second one to Africa, and the third to South America. So all the islands of the Atlantic, save probably certain parts of the Caribbean group, are nothing else than the summits of the ridges of the above-mentioned submarine table-land. Its eastern and western slopes either disappear into the deepest submarine valleys, or, as for instance near the European shores, merge with the slopes of the ridges actually existing on the Earth's surface.

About 1860 a Swedish expedition attempted the first investigation of the depths of the Atlantic. Then Wyvill Tompson and Carpenter began methodically to investigate the bottom of the ocean. Their old steamer *Lightning* was nearly lost, but the results of their work attracted the attention of the British Government and they received a better ship, the *Porcupine*. In 1872 the five months' expedition of the famous *Challenger* covered 80,000 miles, making 370 soundings, 255 measurements of the submarine temperature and 129 dredgings. These investigations showed that the bottom of the ocean is not flat but presents a relief like any firm land. Occasionally depths over 7,000 feet were discovered. The bottom of the Atlantic possesses two parallel depressions stretching meridionally and separated by a ridge, which occasionally comes out the water to the height of 6,000 feet. The western depression is 4 miles deep and the eastern one, called Ross's Valley, is only 3 miles.

Many oceanographic expeditions measured the depth of those regions and a detailed survey resulted. The best-known work in this field, apart from the trips of the *Challenger* and *Porcupine*, belongs to the expeditions of the British ship *Hydra*, the U.S.A. *Dolphin* and *Gettysburg*, and the German *Meteor* and *Gazelle*. The *Meteor*, for instance, performed more than 10,000 soundings. In 1922 two expeditions simultaneously discovered a long submarine ridge extending from Cape Cod on the North American shore to Gibraltar.

The famous French geologist, P. Termier, in 1912 read a paper at the Oceanographic Institute of Paris, reporting the very important results of his investigations in 1898 near the Azores. During the laying of a cable between Cape Cod and Brest the cable parted. This occurred at a point under 47° of North latitude and 29° 40' of West longitude from Paris, i.e. about 500 miles north of the Azores.

It was necessary to pull the cable up from a depth of about 2 miles. During the work it was established that the sea-bottom consists of rocky valleys and mountains and the dredge often brought up solid materials, which consisted exclusively of specimens of glassy basaltic lava, or tachylite. Its amorphous structure proved that it had been cooled under normal atmospheric pressure : had it been cooled under the pressure of a water-layer 2 miles thick, it would have been crystalline. On the other hand it is well known that lava takes about 15,000 years to disintegrate under water. Therefore it is clear that the lava taken up by Termier came not long ago from a dry-land volcano.

Further, Termier tells us that the region of the sea-bottom where the cable snapped consists of rocks and mountains with very sharp edges, which shows that they were submerged soon after the eruption. Were it otherwise, the erosive and abrasive processes and the action of the breakers would have polished away the sharp edges of the rocks.

P. Termier affirms categorically that the investigated region sank during the current Quaternary Period and that mankind must have witnessed this event. Moreover, according to the same scientist, the catastrophe occurred suddenly: this opinion of the famous French geologist justifies Plato's account.

The following fact proves the organic union in the past between the Old Continent and this submarine table-land: the western shores of Africa gradually and insensibly are falling in a westerly direction until eventually they will tend to merge completely with the submarine table-land.

An examination of the bathymetrical argument allows us to conclude that the Azores are the surviving parts of a large island, or, perhaps, of a true continent, which existed in the middle of the Quaternary Period. In the next page the reader will find a description of the discovery of K. Bilau and his conjectures concerning the exact situation of Poseidonis.

Scientists suppose that the Atlas Mountains in Africa and the Alps in Europe are a continuation of the Dolphin's Ridge and were also submerged comparatively recently. This hypothesis seems plausible: apparently both folds represent a mutual geological continuation and the Azores are the last link in this chain of mountains and eminences, most of which is submerged.

The German scientist, Major K. Bilau, basing his work on the newest maps and the exact data of the Geographical Institute of Berlin, drew a magnificent map of the bottom of the Atlantic in the region of the Azores. This map indicates also the submarine depression of Cape Breton, which has been formed as a result of a long erosive process. This submarine valley is $1\frac{1}{2}$ miles below the surface, and Major Bilau has established that all the river-beds which run from the Pyrenees and the northern shore of Spain rush into this depression. According to Bilau, this depression has all the signs of being the result of a continuous washing out of soil, made by some river, which opened its way through the mountains. It is evident that no river is possible under the sea. According to Bilau, the erosive action of any river stops when the river reaches the ocean, because the fresh water is lighter than the salt and remains on the surface. It is easy to verify this assertion by observing, for instance, the Nile in its delta : the brown water of the Nile brings along much slime which only gradually sinks in the sea-water. For hours and hours the departing steamer travels in the brown stream of the Nile, sharply separated from the turquoise waters of the Mediterranean Sea. It is clear that the depression of Cape Breton was formed by a river, which flowed there when this region was a part of the firm land, and disappeared not very long ago, when this region sank under the ocean.

All the river-valleys of the Spanish and the Portuguese shores as well as those of the Atlas mountains upon reaching the ocean's shores descend to $1\frac{1}{2}$ miles below sea-level. Therefore, Bilau contends that at one time the sea-level was $1\frac{1}{2}$ miles lower than at present. This is absolutely the opposite to what we can observe in the Western hemisphere, in the region of Titicaca : it has been unquestionably established that the sea-level there was once 2 miles higher than at present.

Both phenomena prove that there was a time when tremendous catastrophes of ocean positions and modification of the sea-level occurred on our planet. I say 'tremendous,' but this term is adequate only from the human point of view. If we reason from the planetary aspect, we immediately realize that the elevation, or the lowering, of the sea-level for 2 miles is no cataclysm at all. ' Imagine,' says Bilau, ' a terrestrial globe with a diameter of 14 yards. If we desire to show on it proportionally the depth of the oceans along the Equator, we should draw a line 0.1 inch thick. But it is impossible to draw such a line with the chalk and we would be obliged to use the compass. Were the diameter of our globe only 39 inches, the proportional depth of the oceans could be well represented by that thin layer of varnish, which is always used for the covering of terrestrial globes.' Therefore it is clear that the slightest alteration in the rotation of the Earth is quite sufficient to cause more or less important modifications of the sea-level and for us, micro-organisms on the planet's surface, these really insignificant events would spell tremendous catastrophes.

Basing his argument on the above-mentioned facts, Major Bilau establishes the truth of Plato's account in the following words :

' Deep under the ocean's waters Atlantis is now reposing and only its highest summits are still visible in the shape of the

ANOTHER CLAY IDOL

CLAY IDOL OF THE PRE-
HISTORIC INHABITANTS OF
SAN SALVADOR

THE PYRAMID OF THE SUN IN TEOTIHUACAN
(MEXICO)
Note the stepped formation.

THE SO-CALLED AZTEC THEATRE' IN TEOTIHUACAN
(MEXICO)

Azores. Its cold and hot springs, described by the ancient authors, are still flowing there as they flowed many millenniums ago. The mountain-lakes of Atlantis have been transformed now into submerged ones. If we follow exactly Plato's indications and seek the site of Poseidonis among the half-submerged summits of the Azores, we will find it to the south of the island of Dollabarata. There, upon an eminence, in the middle of a large and comparatively straight valley, which was well-protected from the winds, stood the capital, the magnificent Poseidonis. But we cannot see that mighty centre of an unknown prehistoric culture: between us and the City of the Golden Gate is a layer of water 2 miles deep. It is strange that the scientists have sought Atlantis everywhere, but have given the least attention to this spot, which after all, was clearly indicated by Plato.'

I share entirely the astonishment of this honoured German scientist, and wonder at the inertia which still prevents many archæologists from seeing in the legends of Atlantis anything more than a poetical myth.

*   *   *

Now I will dedicate a few words to the so-called ' biological ' argument in favour of the atlantologists.

We see, for instance, that the animal species of the Azores, Canaries, and Madeira do not present any peculiarity, when compared with the species of the continents of Europe and America. The dew-worms of the species *Oligochetes* of the Canaries are analogous to the South European species, the shell-fish of the Atlantic archipelagos resembled the Mediterranean species, and the butterfly, *Setomorpha discipunctei*, is to be found in Africa and America, besides the Canaries. The island of St. Thomas, in the Gulf of Guinea, possesses six distinct species of corals: four of them are to be found also in the Bermudas, and one on the shores of Florida. On the shores of Senegal live fifteen species of shell-fish, which we can find nowhere save on the shores of the Caribbean islands. The mollusc, *Oleacinida*, is a very typical example for our subject: it can be found only on the shores of Portugal and in the Azores, Canaries, and Caribbean islands. This fact clearly shows that at one time a continent-bridge extended from Portugal to the shores of Mexico and Yucatan. Shell-fish attach their shells to the rocks on the shore and multiply and expand only in determined zones of the ocean, each species requiring a certain definite average temperature of water necessary for its existence. Therefore, it is easy to imagine that at one time the shore-rocks of that ancient continent-bridge were strewn with the shells of *Oleacinida*, but that when that bridge was destroyed, the shell-fish remained only on the shores of the surviving parts.

The structure of the Quaternary layers of the Canaries is analogous to that of the Quaternary layers of Mauretania. The sweet-broom, *Adianthum reniforme*, which lives now only in the Azores and Canaries, has disappeared in Europe, but we can find its fossil remains in the Portuguese Pliocene layer.

It is very interesting to note that there was a time when lions, tigers, camels, horses, and elephants lived in America : paleontologists and archæologists have found many fossil remains of these animals, so characteristic of the Old World. The archæologist, Dr. Requena, for instance, discovered in the ancient tombs of Venezuela the tusks of the forefathers of modern tigers, the so-called sabre-toothed primeval tiger. In the surroundings of the town of Natchez, in U.S.A., were found the remains of *Felis spelæa*, the giant cavern-lion of the Quaternary Period. Earlier scientists were of the opinion that the horse was introduced into America by the Spaniards, but recently fossil remains of the primeval horse were discovered in the New World. The famous German aurocks, *Bos priscus*, was numerous in Europe at the time of the Roman emperor Augustus, but later on became almost completely exterminated : some hundreds of this primeval ox, which is identical with the American bison, were preserved in the famous forest of Belovej, which belonged to the Russian Emperors, but their almost complete extermination was one of the first actions of the liberated Russian people during the Revolution of 1917. The few examples of the American bison which were spared by the hunters (among them the first and most famous was the late President of U.S.A., Colonel Theodore Roosevelt), are now preserved in special reservations.

The fossil remains of the camel were found in Kanzas and recently, in 1934, the expedition of the Carnegie Institute discovered them also in New Mexico. The reader will probably remember the above-mentioned myth of the Chibchas in Colombia concerning Bochica: the latter and his wife came to Colombia mounted on camels, which proves that camels disappeared from South America not long ago and that the primeval races of the New World witnessed the presence of camels there. Petrified camels' bones, which are to be found in Bosa, a Colombian locality, are worshipped by the natives.

New Mexico is situated on a desert table-land at an altitude of 6000 feet, and the fossil remains of camels have been discovered in one of its solitary valleys. Scientists consider that camels never belonged to the autochthonous fauna of America: this supposition is based on the scarcity of such finds. Although the atlantologists explain the presence of camels in America by the fact that in some remote epoch they were able to reach it through Atlantis, this hypothesis seems to be erroneous: on the primitive paintings of the oldest Egyptian monuments all kinds of animals are represented save the camel, which apparently was not known to the first Egyptians. It appears only on the comparatively younger monuments, dating from much later, after the disappearance of Atlantis. If camels penetrated into America through Atlantis, the Egyptians' forefathers, who, according to Plato, were contemporaries of Atlanteans, should have shown these animals on their paintings.

If we do not agree with Wegener's hypothesis, we can conclude that the camels came to America through the isthmus which once connected Alaska with Asia. The vestiges of this isthmus, the Aleutian and Kurile islands, were recently investigated by Dr. Collins, a member of the Smithsonian Institute, who discovered on these islands the traces of some plants which are to be found on both sides of the straits, in Asia and America. This proves that many millenniums ago the migration of plants and very likely of animals through this isthmus was possible: perhaps the camels also used this way coming into America from the Gobi desert.

As regards the elephant family, their fossil remains in America are represented by numerous skeletons of mastodons found in Florida, Mexico, Ecuador, and Colombia. This fossil species is called *Mastodonto Humboldtii*, because the famous German naturalist was the first to find their remains. Near Bogotà in

Colombia, about 7000 feet above sea-level, exists a vast field covered by innumerable mastodons' skeletons entirely petrified. Being under the impression that these bones belong to some prehistoric giants, the natives call this site ' The Giants' Field.' The existence of such a cemetery of mastodons makes us wonder : what calamity killed so many of those antediluvian monsters ? and how did they manage to reach such an altitude ? were they not caught and destroyed by the sudden rising of their pasture-ground ?

Some years ago in Marion (Florida) many skeletons of elephants, mammoths, and mastodons were extracted from the bottom of the Silver Springs. They were mixed with the remains of a primeval race of hunters, evidently contemporary to those giant pachyderms. The noted archæologist, Edgar Howard of Philadelphia, says that this race existed 20,000 years ago.

Although until now the fossil remains of elephants have not been found north of Florida, scientists believe that the oldest inhabitants of North America were aware of their existence. Some examples justify this hypothesis. There are, for instance, in Wisconsin, numerous mounds, or funeral tumuli, one of which possesses a profile resembling an elephant's head. It is necessary to mention that the mysterious prehistoric tribe of ' Mound Builders ' always gave their tumuli the shape of some animal ; this custom shows that they had totemistic beliefs.

The archæologist John Short, on page 530 of his work concerning the ancient Americans, mentions the find in the excavations in Iowa of an artistically carved prehistoric smoking pipe, representing an elephant's head. The scientist Donnelly affirms that elephants, or, perhaps, mammoths, appear very often on the ancient American monuments. In fact, there is no doubt concerning the acquaintance of primeval American races with the elephant. It is enough to mention the images of elephants on the old Mexican manuscripts. Unless these paintings reveal intercourse between the Toltecs and the Hindus, which supposition is at least plausible, they indicate that the old races of Central America have seen elephants. Later on, in the chapter dedicated to the Mayas, we will give more details concerning the affinity between Toltec and Hindu mythologies, but for the moment we will mention only the famous bas-relief at Palenque :

it represents the figure of a priest, adorned by a mask, which reproduces faithfully an elephant's head.

If we take for granted, as we should, that there was a time when camels, elephants, and horses existed in the New World, we are confronted by two problems : why did they disappear ? and why did the ancient inhabitants of America not domesticate these useful animals and thus preserve them ? We cannot explain their disappearance by the unfavourable climate, because horses, for instance, introduced by the Spaniards, were very soon acclimatized, and multiplied. The Texas mustangs and the wild horses of the Argentinian *pampas* also multiplied very rapidly from a few heads brought by Spaniards from Europe.

*   *   *

Now I would like to draw the reader's attention to the very curious phenomenon of the multiplication of eels, which clearly proves that some millenniums ago there was in existence a continent between Europe and America. Aristotle was the first naturalist interested in the multiplication of eels, but, not being able to discover anywhere the spawn of eels, he passed on this problem to the following generations of scientists, who, during the next 2000 years, did nothing important towards its solution. They could only establish that the eel, a fresh-water fish, yearly leaves its abode in the European rivers and goes in millions to the sea. If their river does not flow into the sea, the eels wriggle across the land to another river which does. Once in the sea-water, the shoals of eels disappear somewhere in the ocean until they return to their rivers some months later. It was understood long ago that they go into the sea for spawning, but as to how and where they performed this process remained a mystery, particularly since only the adults were observed during those migrations and no one had ever seen their young.

The Danish scientist, Dr. T. Schmidt, especially studied the lives of eels and gave in 1922 the solution of the problem first advanced twenty-two centuries ago. It turned out that only female eels live in the European rivers and their residence there is limited to two years. During this period eels often change their abodes, crawling from one river, or pond, into another. After two years the female eels begin to swim towards the mouths of the rivers, where the males are already waiting for them. Then the separate shoals of eels merge into a large one and start their long journey westwards across the ocean.

They swim at a very great depth and, making 18 miles a day, after 140 days of swimming across the Atlantic reach the so-called Sargasso Sea, near the Bermudas. This migratory movement is comparatively easy to observe, because it is closely followed by dolphins, various rapacious fish, and flights of sea-gulls. Reaching the Sargasso Sea the eels disappear in its submarine forests.

It is necessary to remind the reader that this sea is six times larger than the territory of European France, and is covered by a thick tangle of sea-weed, which often even impedes the navigation of small ships. Our reader will, perhaps, remember what was said about the Sargasso Sea by the cunning Phœnician seafarers to the pharaoh Nechao : the same conditions exist in the Sargasso Sea to-day. Incidentally the scientific expedition of the American zoologist, Dr. Beebe, investigated this sea in 1927 and discovered there many new species of deep-water fauna.

The spawning of eels takes place in the Sargasso Sea at a depth of about 1000 feet, and after this the females die. The new-born eels soon start their trip to the European shores, forming one enormous shoal 260 feet wide and 70 feet deep. At the beginning, the tiny eels are transparent, but at the end of their journey, which lasts about three years, they become green, and finally brown. Then, near the mouths of the European rivers, the shoal of grown-up eels divides into two : the males remain in the sea, and the females enter the rivers and begin their two-year sojourn in Europe. Thus the eel represents really two species : the male, a sea-fish, and the female, which spends one-half of its life in fresh water.

The phenomenon of the multiplication of eels is a very important fact for our subject. It proves that at some time a continent with a great river existed between Europe and the Bermudas. Perhaps the Sargasso Sea is the survival of the swampy delta of this giant prehistoric river and the eels, accustomed during millions of years to spawn there in safety from their enemies, have preserved this habit until to-day, when not only that river, but the continent itself have disappeared.

There is another curious phenomenon from the same range of biological proofs of the existence of a continent between America

and Europe. It consists of a peculiarity in the behaviour of
European birds during their yearly migrations to South America.

We possess accounts from many observers to the effect that
the birds, reaching the parallel of the Azores, invariably begin
to turn round and round above the sea. These pointless movements of the tired birds can be explained only by their instinctive
recollection of the land which once existed in these regions.
The hereditary instinct of the birds prevails over their senses
and they look for this land in order to rest even if they cannot
find it. After an unsuccessful search the flights of birds continue
their long trip to the warm countries of South America, but next
year, passing over the region, where many millenniums ago
were situated the mountains of Atlantis, they will again search
for land.

Certain atlantologists of the past century have thought that the
fact of the world-wide distribution of some species of useful
plants and their non-existence in a wild state, leads us to the
following conclusion: all these plants were cultivated by the
Atlanteans, their primitive wild species disappeared, and it is
from the sunken continent that these useful plants have been
distributed throughout the world. The best-known plants in
this category are: wheat, maize, tobacco, the banana, and the
pine-apple.

The Hindu legend concerning wheat and the ' wonderful
kandali,' i.e. the banana-bush, says that the highest spirits, the
protectors of mankind (the so-called *Manu*), brought them to
our planet from another celestial body more advanced on the
path of evolution than our Earth. It is necessary to explain
that the banana-' tree ' does not exist at all : it is an annual plant,
a bush, which multiplies not by seeds, which it does not possess,
but by off-shoots. As a matter of fact the banana-problem is very
interesting: when, where, and how did mankind learn to
obtain from a wild banana-bush (*Musa paradisiaca*, or *Musa
sapientum*) this magnificent cultivated plant, which furnishes
food to millions of inhabitants in all parts of the world ? You
can find the cultivated banana even on the solitary islands of the
Pacific, as well as in Central Africa, India, etc. The banana-bush
is a true benefactor of mankind : its fruits contain everything
necessary for man's nutrition and are even used for the distilla-
tion of alcoholic beverages, its leaves and stems furnish fuel and

materials for roofs and its fibres are employed for the weaving of primitive tissues.

The scientist Kuntze thought that the domestic species of banana was created by the Atlanteans at the beginning of the Quaternary Period, and that many millenniums of cultivation were necessary in order to bring this useful plant to its present perfection. But recently there was found in Brazil the so-called *pacoba*, a wild species of banana which multiplies by seeds. Its fruits are edible, but not so palatable as those of the cultivated variety. So the hypothesis of Kuntze failed in its part concerning the exclusive role of the Atlanteans in banana-culture. Certainly it is not impossible that they contributed much patience and labour to the production of the best species of banana-bush, but we cannot now suppose that Atlantis at one time represented that centre of banana expansion wherefrom this plant was diffused everywhere.

The same fate was reserved for the hypothesis of the preponderant role of the Atlanteans in the expansion of the cultivated species of wheat : recently a Russian scientific expedition found in the Himalayas a wild species of this precious plant (*Triticum*).

Certain scientists had supposed that the fatherland of wheat was Palestine, but some years ago the famous egyptologist, Sir Flinders Petrie, attempted to prove the Caucasian origin of wheat. This scientist relates a legend concerning Osiris, which is contained in the famous Book of the Dead : this legend tells that Osiris taught the first Egyptians to cultivate wheat. But this god came to Egypt from the Caucasus and therefore Flinders Petrie thought that the seeds of the wheat must have been imported from that country. Moreover, Flinders Petrie found in the layers of the so-called Badrian culture (the oldest Egyptian culture), wheat-seeds, which resemble very much the Caucasian species. At the same time it was proved that neither Babylonia, nor any other neighbouring land, possessed such a species of wheat. Only much later was the Badrian type of this plant substituted by the Babylonian one.

It is interesting to mention here the account of a find made by a group of Bombay students in 1933. This group visited the ruins of the oldest city of Mohenjo-Daro in the province of Sind (Northern India). This city is so ancient that the Brahmin chronicles mention it for the last time in 3000 B.C.

Wandering among the ruins of the prehistoric capital, one student found a broken ancient clay-brick and within it a spike of some unknown gramineous plant resembling rye. The brick was dated 5000 years B.C. Evidently it had fallen by chance in the clay during the making of the bricks and had remained there ever since. This discovery of the Bombay students has proved that many millenniums ago there existed some *Graminœa*, which produced later on by the way of evolution, or through man's labour, our modern species. Perhaps, the Mohenjo-Daro plant is one of the intermediate species of our rye, which was diffused on some vanished continent, e.g. on the earlier-mentioned Gondwana.

The wild species of maize has not yet been found, but certain scientists suppose that its fatherland is somewhere among the Andean valleys : we find there numerous species of maize, one of them with very large seeds. I have personally seen seeds of maize larger than one inch.

According to Professor G. G. Bondar, a noted Russian naturalist, now working in Brazil, the wild species of tobacco has now been discovered in America.

The origin of the pine-apple is as mysterious as that of the banana : it is found in Asia only as a cultivated plant and is known there from antiquity : we can see, for instance, images of the pine-apple on Assyrian and Babylonian monuments, but it is amazing enough that those images represent the American variety of the pine-apple. In America for a long time, also, the wild species of the pineapple was unknown, but recently it was discovered in the Brazilian virgin forests.

It is well known that certain plants are restricted to definite regions and are not found in others. So, for instance, with the so-called ' dragon-tree' : it is to be found only in the Canaries, whose flora, in general, is very peculiar. This circumstance is, it seems, another proof in favour of the Atlantis hypothesis.

In 1934 Professor Mangin read a paper at the Academy of Sciences in Paris concerning the works of Professor Chevalier. This paper provoked some polemics among the scientists because Chevalier affirms that the aboriginal flora of the Cape Verde archipelago has nothing to do with that of the Black Continent, and that the African plants found on those islands derive their origin from the seeds brought there occasionally by winds, sea-currents, and birds. Therefore, these islands never were a part of Africa : they are of volcanic formation and, according to Chevalier, never belonged to Atlantis either. The French scientist has reached the conclusion that the Cape Verde archipelago originated from the Tertiary Period. However, these islands were at one time inhabited by some advanced race, because Professor Chevalier found on the rocks of Cape Verde, at São Antão, some mysterious inscriptions.

The statements of Chevalier and Mangin provoked an energetic answer from P. Le Cour, President of the French Society of Atlantologists : he declared that Professor Chevalier was wrong in thinking that the atlantologists ever affirmed an organic union between the Cape Verde Islands and the sunken continent. According to P. Le Cour, only Madeira, the Azores, and Canaries can be considered to be remains of Atlantis. As to the Cape Verde archipelago, it appears to be merely the continuation of a submerged part of Africa, or it may have originated after some seismic phenomenon.

As far as the value of the biological argument is concerned I must say that although it is not so striking as the seismological and bathymetrical, nevertheless it gives some indications in favour of the Atlantis hypothesis.

CHAPTER IV

SCIENTISTS like Cuvier and Buffon admitted in the beginning of the last century the so-called 'cataclysmic theory,' which affirmed that many modifications on our planet occurred following great catastrophes, but later on science abandoned this theory. The fresh hypothesis insisted on the slow graduation of all processes on the Earth and on the unimportance of the great cataclysms for the process of life. In our times science is returning again to the forgotten theory of Cuvier concerning the immense role of various cataclysms.

The priests of Sais told Solon how, after long periods, perturbations occur in the movement of celestial bodies and great catastrophes on our planet follow these perturbations. The famous astronomer, the Abbé Moreux, affirms that the ancients were inclined to confound the astronomical perturbations with telluric and even meteorological effects : thus he cannot attach to the words of the priests of Sais any great importance. Moreux says that a collision, for instance, of the Earth with any celestial body like a comet, cannot be periodical, and perturbations in interplanetary space have nothing to do with our 'home-cataclysms.'

I cannot agree with this opinion of the French scientist concerning the meaning of the words of the priest. It seems to me they had in mind definitely events of an interplanetary character which influence the life of our own abode because the priests mentioned the story of Phæthon, who, according to the legend, was guilty of a great calamity which befell the Earth : as I related before, Phæthon burnt one-half of the Earth's surface. We can easily see in this myth a poetical description of some terrific cosmic catastrophe reflected on the Earth, but having its source in some enormous astronomical perturbation.

Further, Moreux combats the opinion of the scientist, R. M. Gattefossé, who in his book, *The Truth concerning Atlantis*, ascribes the priest's words to the phenomenon of the so-called 'precession of the equinoxes' and its consequences. These consequences, according to Gattefossé, consist of alterations in the position of the poles of the Earth, which occur every 25,796 years. Certainly, the explanations of Moreux are sufficient to establish that the Earth's axis never can be almost perpendicular to the plane of the ecliptic, as affirmed by Gattefossé, and oscillations of that axis never could provoke such a terrific earthquake as that which destroyed Atlantis; however, the mistake of Gattefossé consists only in the above-mentioned hypothesis. But his fundamental idea, namely, the possibility of phenomena in Space causing terrestrial catastrophes, seems to me perfectly feasible.

Moreux declares that even an exceptional accumulation in some regions of the Earth of water (rain, snow, or ice), or the movements of the magma within our planet, can provoke yearly a shifting of the poles for only a few metres. Such slight alterations in the position of the poles could not provoke any cataclysm. A serious disturbance would require movements of giant masses, such as, for instance, the transposition of the whole tableland of Tibet to the Polar regions.

I quite agree with Moreux in his statement to the effect that the catastrophes which occur in interplanetary space are sporadic and not subjected to any definite periodicity. However, I am inclined to think that the word 'periodically,' as employed by the priests of Sais, was not intended to indicate any definite recurring period, but was simply meant to state that these phenomena occur again and again. Thus, not 'periodically,' but 'occasionally' 'terrible conflagrations occur in Space,' was what the priests may have intended to convey. Certainly those conflagrations have their fatal influence on the life of the Earth. Moreover, I doubt whether the traditional memory of mankind is long enough to retain even two such similar events. . . . Even the Egyptians with their long history, enriched by the Atlantean traditions, could probably remember only one of these terrific alterations in the arrangement of the Cosmos, that very one, in fact, which the priest had in view.

Presently we shall see that there is enough material at any rate for an attempt to determine the possible character of that particular catastrophe.

*   *   *

Although all the various celestial bodies in their everlasting movements follow strictly determined orbits, sometimes sundry collisions occur between them or their parts. To this category of phenomena belong : the appearance of so-called ' Novæ,' or ' new-born stars ' ; the fall of comparatively large pieces of planets and comets on the surface of other celestial bodies ; the crossing by planets of the comet's orbits near their heads, and perturbations in solar systems ; shooting-stars and the common aeroliths. Here a short survey of all the enumerated phenomena would not be out of place.

From the epoch of the Greek astronomer Hypparch (second century B.C.) until nowadays hundreds of cases of the appearance of Novæ have been recorded. The best known are : the Nova of Hypparch (134 B.C.), the Nova of Tycho Brahe in the constellation of Cassiopea (1572), the Nova of 1848 in the constellation of the Serpent, the Nova of 1876 in the Swan, the Nova of 1891 in the Charioteer, the Nova of 1910 in the Perseus, the Nova of 1918 in the Eagle, the Nova of 1920 in the Swan, and the last Nova of 1925 in the constellation of Pluteum Pictoris. Ordinarily the ' biography ' of each Nova is as follows : the first few days following its appearance the new-born star possesses considerable brightness, which grows continuously, sometimes to equal the brightness of Sirius. Later on it begins to diminish rapidly, and finally the Nova either becomes almost invisible, or disappears altogether. But the last one, that of 1925, has proved to be most unusual : according to the observations of the astronomer Finsen, it is a double star. The probability of the appearance of such Novæ seems to be very small : only once during billions of years. . . . Thus our generation can be proud of having seen a rare celestial phenomenon.

The appearance of Novæ signifies always some giant and remote catastrophe, a cosmic conflagration : two or more dark celestial bodies collide and the energy of their movement is transformed into heat, which instantaneously converts their masses into an accumulation of incandescent gases. However, although some scientists suppose that similar catastrophes are due sometimes also to the explosions of interior gases, in the case of Nova Pluteum Pictoris is very likely that it appeared as a consequence of a collision of two dark bodies. Since both happened to be similar in volume and mass, they began to withdraw mutually with an enormous velocity like two billiard balls. Their distance from each other in 1928 was a hundred times greater than the distance of the Earth from the Sun and their velocity was 124 miles per second.

The distance of Nova Pictoris from us is 540 light-years: thus this great conflagration occurred in 1385, one century before the ' discovery ' of America, but the rays of light, which travel 186,000 miles per second, brought us the news about this catastrophe only in 1925. . . .

The Russian astronomer W. Vorontzoff-Veliaminof discovered in 1937 a Nova which is exceedingly interesting because it does not belong to our own galaxy, but forms part of the neighbouring one, and is seen by us as a faint nebulosity. The distance from us of this Nova is over 19,000,000 light-years, and this circumstance shows the enormous quantity of light irradiated by this newly-discovered celestial body. In fact, having traversed such a distance as 19,000,000 light-years, its light is still strong enough to influence our retina.

The above-mentioned Russian scientist calculated that the brightness of this Nova must be some billions times greater than that of our Sun and a hundred times greater than that of the nebulosity in which it exists, although the latter is composed of billions of stars !

Evidently many quadrillions of years ago, somewhere in the depths of the Space, occurred a gigantic catastrophe which resulted in the birth of this Nova, but the news about it reached us only in A.D. 1937. The quantity of energy liberated during that cataclysm cannot be calculated. . . . Incidentally one should remember that the source of the newly-discovered cosmic irradiations is still enigmatical : it is not improbable that these mysterious irradiations come to the Earth from such enormous conflagrations as those which give birth to Novæ.

When a smaller body collides with a much larger one there occurs a fall of the first upon the surface of the second. The falling body becomes heated to such a degree that an explosion may occur and break it into numerous small pieces. Sometimes the falling body does not explode, but enters unbroken into the larger one, forming one body which remains intact.

The telescope has permitted us to see the effects of a falling body on one of the solar planets. The astronomer, W. Hay, during the night of 3 August 1933, observed a large white spot on the equator of Saturn, and informed the astronomer, Dr. W. H. Stevenson, of his discovery. The latter immediately made a detailed study of Saturn and concluded that this white spot was probably due to the fall upon Saturn of a giant meteorite. The high temperature of the latter had caused an instantaneous transformation of the surrounding medium into an accumulation of incandescent gases. The fall of this meteorite produced a large breach in the famous ring of Saturn, which could be distinctly seen through powerful telescopes. This gap was 20,000 miles long and 12,000 miles wide.

Catastrophes identical to those above-mentioned are possible also here, in our own abode, the old Earth : they have occurred in the past ; our generation has witnessed some similar ones and our descendants undoubtedly will also see such cataclysms.

Apart from such catastrophes, our planet, like any other celestial body, is always subject to the influences of our neighbours in Space. These influences are various : they range from the influence of our satellite the Moon, to those which reach us from remote constellations, producing innumerable phenomena in our home. The attraction of the Moon is the most evident and ordinary example of such influence : it produces the notorious phenomenon of the tides and the less-known phenomena of similar tides occurring in our atmosphere and in the subterranean magma. The air-tides are responsible for many meteorological phenomena and the magma-tides for earthquakes and volcanic eruptions. Undoubtedly the law of universal gravitation takes a large part in many phenomena on the Earth : it is, for instance, responsible for the uncommonly high tides occurring during the so-called ' conjunction of the planets,' which takes place whenever the centres of gravity of two or more planets are situated on the continuation in Space of any terrestrial radius. It is evident that for the point of the Earth's surface which is situated on the extremity of that radius the force of attraction reaches its maximum, because it is equal to the sum of attractions of the planets in conjunction. Thus such points (' nadirs ') are always the centre of a zone of considerable storms, tides, earthquakes, and volcanic eruptions. Analogous phenomena, sometimes of a catastrophical character, occur also on the Earth when a large comet, possessing a considerable mass, approaches our planet. The subterranean magma follows the great force of attraction and rushes to the points of the earth-crust which are nearest to the new arrival. Therefore, in such events, various cataclysms are always possible: destructive earthquakes and volcanic eruptions, the sinking of more or less vast pieces of land, the heightening of mountains and the appearance of new islands in the ocean. Recently, scientists discovered the striking connection between many geophysical and even biological phenomena and the appearance of sun-spots. This connection permits us to consider that certain social events, such as wars, revolutions, famines, etc., may also obey the mysterious influences of the Sun. From this point of view it seems that the astrologers of old were not completely in the wrong when they affirmed that the fate of every earthly being depends largely upon the influence and position of the celestial bodies. . . .

Let us return from these general speculations to the (most important for our subject) cases of collisions between various celestial bodies and their parts. These phenomena are called, according to their scale, by various names: we know, for instance, of ' the rains of stones,' the phenomenon of the falling of meteoric dust, aeroliths, shooting-stars, bolis, and we suppose the likelihood of there falling on our planet of very large cosmic masses, perhaps, small satellites of the Earth, or independent minute planets, attracted by the comparatively enormous mass of the Earth.

We have to realize that the earth-crust, in comparison with the Earth's volume, is only a thin envelope: it is but 36 miles thick, i.e. only 1 per cent of the terrestrial radius. Thus this envelope is less solid even than an egg-shell, which represents about one-sixtieth part of the shortest radius of the egg. And we, mankind, with all our culture, progress, history, etc., are nothing more than the mould, which sometimes covers the surface of ponds. . . .

Thus even a comparatively light blow on the Earth's surface could cause fatal consequences for mankind. I have not in view the possible collision between our planet and any celestial body approximately equal to it in volume and mass—such a collision would simply destroy not only the life on our planet, but also the planet itself: both bodies would immediately be transformed into an accumulation of incandescent gases and thus a new star would be born in Space. I have in view only collisions of the Earth with comparatively small masses, such as, for instance, more or less large meteorites and our unknown satellites. The fall of such a body could provoke local cataclysms and possibly some alterations in the mechanics of the Earth's rotation and revolution.

Falls of aeroliths of considerable size are well known and almost every Natural History museum possesses specimens of such visitors from Space, but sometimes the meteorites are so large that it is impossible to bring them into a museum, or to find a place for them. As a rule, these large stones remain on the spot where they fell. Such, for instance, are the famous Pallas's Iron in Siberia, the large meteorites of Greenland, of Brazil, and some others. The celebrated black stone of the Kaaba, in Mecca, the most important holy relic of the Mohammedans, is nothing else than a large meteorite, fallen millenniums ago in the Arabian desert.

Strange to say, the fall of meteorites played an immensely important role in the history of culture : as a matter of fact they almost always consist of iron and iron-oxides mixed with nickel and some other metals, and scientists suppose that mankind made first acquaintance with iron through meteorites. Professor Quiring affirms that almost all the earliest iron implements were made from meteor-iron.

A chemical analysis of two iron ornaments of the fifth millennium, found during excavations in Egypt, demonstrated a high percentage of nickel, which proves the meteoric origin of the material. The word ' iron ' in the old Egyptian language signifies ' the heavenly ore.' It seems that the smelting of iron ore began only in the second millennium and iron metallurgy began in ancient Armenia : we possess some old Armenian monuments which mention metallurgy in 1490 B.C. On the other hand, in the pyramid of Cheops were found iron works much older than the Armenian ones, and we can only conclude that they were of meteoric origin. As to steel, we find the first mention of it in the letter of the king Tushratta, accompanying his gift to the pharaoh Amenophis III : this gift consisted of 318 concubines, and of a still more precious commodity, some steel daggers and adornments.

The ' rain of stones ' is a well-known phenomenon. It is

explained by the crossing, by our planet, of 'clouds of the meteorites,' which revolve around the Sun. These clouds are nothing else than the remains of certain destroyed bodies, planets, or comets, which still continue their revolution along their ancient orbits as accumulations of more or less large pieces of stones. The Jewish Bible (see the Book of Joshua, x, 11) tells that such an event took place during a battle between Jews and Amorites. When the latter ran away from the Jews, Jehovah threw at them large stones from heaven, killing them in great numbers.

The mediæval chronicles have numerous records concerning such 'rains,' which were considered to be a manifestation of the God's wrath. Recently Professor Lacroix read in the French Academy of Sciences a paper concerning geological investigations in the French Sahara. There is a region called Tanesruft, which is known among the natives under the name of 'The Valley of Thirst.' It is covered with innumerable little white stones and thus the surface of the desert is very brilliant. Professor Lacroix and the French geologists who worked in Tanesruft for several weeks discovered that all these stones were meteorites. Their weight varies from a few grains to 10 lbs., and chemical analysis demonstrated that they consist of iron, nickel, and quartz. This rain of stones occurred in the Sahara probably during the last century.

It has been established that a thin meteoric dust continually falls from Space on the whole surface of the Earth. This dust is composed of minute iron particles. It is easy to demonstrate this phenomenon in the middle of the ocean, where any other dust is impossible. In order to obtain this meteoric dust you should place a sheet of white paper in any part of the ship, protected from wind and the soot of the funnel. After a while you will find on the paper numerous black dots : the microscope and chemical analysis will demonstrate that these dots are nothing else than the minutest iron particles of meteoric origin. The same phenomenon can be observed on the snowy summits of high mountains. This dust has been settling down everywhere since the birth of our Earth and will continue to do so for ever. The weight of our planet is at present 6000 trillions of tons ; Professor Baur has calculated that the average yearly increase of its weight, due to the fall of meteoric dust and meteorites, is equal to 650 tons.

Thus, in one million years the weight of this increase will reach 650,000,000 tons. It means that every 500,000 years a hill 650 feet high, with a base of 150,000 square yards, is falling from Space on to our planet. These figures seem to be unimportant in comparison with the weight of the Earth, but we have to remember that this increase has been going on for many hundreds of millions of years. . . . Therefore this mass of meteoric dust has contributed considerably to the increase in the thickness of the earth-crust and to the formation of the soil.

But the consequences of this phenomenon are still more important in the realms of geophysics and even of celestial mechanics: the increase in the weight of the Earth reflects on its rotation and revolution. Moreover, the permanent increase in that weight augments the intensity of the force of gravitation of our planet and thus the probabilities of falls on its surface of larger and larger cosmic masses. Therefore it is easy to predict that in the future such occurrences will become slightly more frequent.

Apart from the occasional falls of various meteorites, our planet receives also periodical falls: twice every year numerous meteorites fall upon the Earth. These rains of aeroliths, occurring always in August and November, are known to the science as Perseides and Leonides, because their ' radiants ' (their visible centres of irradiation) seem to be situated in the constellations of Perseus and the Lion. The public calls them shooting stars. The Perseides represent the remains of Tattle's comet, which, owing to unknown causes, exploded some years ago: its fragments continue to move along the orbit of Tattle's comet, which is yearly crossed by ours. Up to now our meeting with this accumulation of the comet's remains has represented only a magnificent show of celestial fireworks, but it is not impossible that in the future a large piece of stone might fall upon the Earth and destroy a more or less extensive part of its surface. The small meteorites, penetrating into the terrestrial atmosphere with the velocity of 36 miles per second, burst into flames at the height of 72 miles and burn like a firework. Sometimes they leave a fire-trace of bright white or green light.

Fortunately, cases of the falling of large meteorites are comparatively rare, although such phenomena have occurred sometimes in the past. Perhaps some of the existing islands and rocks which stand sometimes solitarily in the middle of plains, are nothing else than meteorites. A similar suspicion exists, for instance, concerning the island of Elba in the Mediterranean Sea : its geological structure permits one to suppose that Elba fell from Space as a giant meteorite.

Sometimes it is possible to detect the presence of a large meteorite within the earth-crust, thanks to the so-called magnetic anomalies : the visible manifestation of its presence is unrest of the compass. Near the place where such an anomaly is observed, the compass oscillates and loses its faculty to show the direction of the north. Such behaviour of the compass is due to the presence somewhere in the vicinity of a large subterranean iron mass the origin of which can be determined as only meteoric. The best-known magnetic anomaly is at Kursk in European Russia.

Some miles from Natchez in U.S.A., in the vicinity of the Mississippi, exists a large cavity in the soil, resembling the crater of some extinct volcano. The natives call this cavity ' The Devil's Cup.' The compasses of steamers on the Mississippi begin to be agitated even at a distance of several miles from the Devil's Cup. This large and deep cavity undoubtedly was created by an enormous iron meteorite, which fell there very long ago and since that day has remained deeply buried in the earth-crust.

Another giant meteorite fell in the remote past in Arizona. American engineers discovered there in 1891, in the middle of a desert plain, a giant crater, and ascribed its origin to an unknown prehistoric volcano, extinct since time immemorial. The diameter of it is 1 mile. Only in 1933 this alleged crater was investigated again and the scientists discovered that it is not of volcanic origin, but that its formation was due to the fall of an enormous meteorite. In its vicinity were found many fragments of meteoric iron, and chemical analysis proved something absolutely new : the iron of that meteorite is mixed with . . . platinum ! By means of a very sensitive apparatus the geologists discovered that a mass of 500,000 tons is buried there at the depth of 735 feet. Moreover, the approximate date of its fall was calculated : it occurred 50,000 years ago. The American newspapers, commenting on this discovery in Arizona, state that a commercial company will exploit this platina-ore by means of a new metallurgical method.

*   *   *

But all hitherto-known cases of the falls of meteorites are nothing in comparison with the catastrophe of a similar character, which occurred in 1908 in Siberia (to be exact, in the northern part of the Yenisseysk forests, 800 miles from the city of Turukhansk), in the wilderness of the Siberian virgin forests. This meteorite was probably either a hitherto-unknown satellite of the Earth, or one of the numerous asteroids. Here is the description of this remarkable event written by the Russian astronomer, Professor Kulik.

'At 7 o'clock in the morning of June 30th, 1908, in the vicinity of the river Podkamennaya Tunguska (61° North latitude and 102° East longitude from Pulkovo) there was precipitated on the Earth such a mass of cosmic matter, that the effect of its fall surpassed everything that ever was seen before. Although it was a bright sunny day, the radius of visibility of the flaming bolis in the sky was more than 360 miles. Thunderlike sounds were audible within a radius of 900 miles and the sound of the explosion within a 420-mile radius. This meteorite had travelled through the terrestrial atmosphere along a curve for not less than 300 miles. The pressure of the air-wave was so great that it threw down men and horses at a distance of 400 miles from the spot of the fall. Apart from this air-wave there appeared a mighty seismic one which spread around the Earth with the velocity of 347 yards per second and was noted by all observatories as a catastrophical earthquake in Siberia. This wave, according to the records of the Potsdam observatory, encircled our planet in only 30 hours and was repeated. This meteorite brought into the atmosphere colossal masses of meteoric dust, which created the so-called "silvery clouds" in the sky. These clouds everywhere in Western Siberia and Europe transformed day into a lingering red twilight, because they spread immediately over the whole surface of the northern part of the Old Continent. They were observed everywhere in Europe and their light was so intense that the scientist Max Wolff in

Heidelberg was prevented from making photographs of the stars that night; around the Black Sea it was easy to read a newspaper at midnight on the 30th June.'

Professor L. A. Kulik and the British astronomer Kirkpatrick have calculated that were this meteorite to have fallen 4 hours 47 minutes earlier, it would have precipitated itself upon St. Petersburg and completely destroyed the Russian capital. From the spot where the meteorite fell there instantaneously arose a fire column 12 miles high, because all the energy of the movement of the bolis had been instantly transformed into heat. Simultaneously with the Siberian meteorite there fell near Kiev another small one. Professor Kulik, who visited the place of the Siberian cataclysm in 1927, found pieces of the meteorite which weigh 150 tons. Therefore the total weight of the Siberian meteorite should be estimated at not less than one million tons and probably much more. The Russian scientific expedition of Professor Kulik stated that a wooded area within a radius of about 60 miles has been mowed down as if shaved off: the giant Siberian larch-trees and pines are lying with their tops outwards and all the soil within a 12 miles radius is burnt. To-day the numerous craters which appeared as a result of the fall of the portions of the meteorite have been filled. As to the main part of this cosmic mass, it is impossible to see it because it entered deeply into the earth-crust. The natives still tell various stories concerning this cataclysm of 1908 and describe the colossal fire-brand in the sky.

Although the phenomenon of silvery clouds remains unexplained, some scientists suppose that this meteorite was the head of a comet whose tail consisted of a thin dust and therefore the silvery clouds were nothing else than this dust floating in the highest strata of the Earth's atmosphere. But it is also possible that the Siberian meteorite was a hitherto unknown satellite of our Earth, or an independent asteroid, which approached too near to our planet and was attracted by its force of gravitation. The hypothesis of Professor Hoerbiger favours, as it happens, the first supposition: Hoerbiger proved that all celestial bodies follow orbits which are not elliptic, as it was thought before, but represent the shape of elliptical volutes. Thus the distance between a rotating body and its centre of revolution constantly decreases. When this distance reaches a certain minimum the rotating body, obedient to the force of gravitation, rushes towards the central one. According to Hoerbiger's theory, this fate is reserved for every celestial body, planet, comet, or satellite : sooner or later they will join their central bodies, around which they have rotated for millions of years. The Moon, for instance, approaches the Earth more and more and its fall is only a question of time, but, naturally, many millions of years separate us from this tragic catastrophe. Were it to occur now the consequences would be immense : the earth-crust would sink over the area of an entire continent and on the periphery of this depression would arise many volcanoes, or a volcanic ring like the present Pacific one. But were the Moon to fall into an ocean, a new continent would appear and the waters dislodged by it would inundate the whole surface of the Earth. The aspect of our planet would be totally altered, entire races would disappear together with their cultures, and the possibility of establishing the origin of the spared tribes would be completely nil. Before the historians and ethnologists of future mankind a range of difficult problems would arise. . . .

To-day the Belgian astronomer, Professor Delporte, is known as an authority on asteroids. This name, by the way, is given to the small planets which rotate around the Sun between Mars and Jupiter. Their orbits are mostly concentric with the orbits of these two planets, but often are placed on different planes. The first asteroid, Ceres, was discovered in 1801 by the Italian astronomer Piazzi, and during the last 135 years many other small planets were found : the astronomical catalogue of 1936 records 1301 asteroids. Their diameters vary from 480 miles to only 1 mile. Professor Delporte discovered many of them and recently found two small ones, Adonis and Anteros. Adonis possesses a peculiar orbit, which is elliptical, reaches almost the orbit of Mercury, the nearest planet to the Sun, and passes close to the orbit of the Earth. This character of the orbit of Adonis offers some danger to our planet, because there is a possibility of the small asteroid being attracted to the Earth and falling on its surface.

In the beginning of February 1936 Delporte observed on one of his night-sky photographs the presence of a short line. Such lines always betray the existence of a planet, because they displace themselves in relation to the fixed stars. Hitherto no such line had appeared on the photographs of this particular region of the sky. Thus Delporte realized he was in the presence of a new asteroid, and he baptized it by the name of Anteros and calculated its orbit. It transpired that Anteros passed in the beginning of February 1936 only at a distance of 1,200,000 miles from the Earth. This discovery was highly sensational, because our nearest neighbour in Space, the planet Mars, rotates at a distance of 48,000,000 miles from the Earth and the nearest asteroid, Amor, never has approached us nearer than 9,600,000 miles.

Further, Delporte calculated that a difference of 1 ° 30' in the inclination of the orbit of Anteros would be sufficient to place it within the sphere of the attraction of the Earth. According to the opinion of the Belgian astronomer, such a catastrophe is likely. Anteros makes its way around the Sun within two terrestrial years and in February 1940 will again be very near our planet: the gravitational force of any planet it approaches on its way can compel this small celestial body (the diameter of Anteros is only 1·2 miles) to modify the angle of depression of the plane of its revolution and thus compel it to penetrate into the sphere of Earth's attraction. Then the fall of Anteros upon the Earth would be unavoidable.

Certainly, were Anteros to fall upon the Earth, the catastrophe would not be universal, but only local. Although the weight of this asteroid reaches one billion tons and its velocity is equal to 18 miles per second, its fall would provoke only comparatively unimportant calamities such as, for instance, earthquake or inundation in some neighbouring region to the spot of the cataclysm. The probability of this fall is one against 50,000 and thus seems to be insignificant. But the reader should remember the probability, for instance, of gaining the first prize in the French State Lottery: it is one against 1,200,000, i.e. much smaller than the above; all the same each owner of a ticket in the French Lottery hopes to win the first prize. . . .

*   *   *

Many times I have turned the reader's attention to various legends of different tribes concerning the Moon. The most interesting for our subject are the following myths: the legend of the Greeks concerning the Preselenites, who inhabited Gondwana before the appearance of the Moon, the myth of the Chibchas in Columbia concerning Bochica, who created the Moon after a great inundation of the Funza valley, the myth of the Bushmen, who affirm that a large continent west from Africa disappeared at an epoch when there existed TWO moons, the Mayan myth concerning a great calamity, during which the Great Serpent, i.e. a certain celestial body, was ravished from the heavens, and the myth of the Tupis, who affirm that the Moon falls periodically upon the Earth and a new Moon takes the place of the old one in the heavens. The Aravacs of Guiana affirm that the Great Spirit sent a double calamity to the world: at first it was struck by fire and next a great flood covered the Earth. We can add to this accumulation of legends the words of the priests of Sais concerning certain modifications in the arrangement of the celestial bodies, which are always followed by great catastrophes on Earth. These priests told Solon of great conflagrations in Space, which occur from time to time when the wrath of the Gods overtakes mankind. The Greeks possessed a myth concerning Phæthon, who burnt one half of the surface of the Earth, and the Egyptians another myth concerning Typhon, who elevated the sea-level by 600 elbows, divided the firm land, burnt one half of the Earth and inundated the other half. The Codex Popul-Vuh relates that the god Huracan flooded the Earth and a great conflagration was observed at that time in the heavens. This myth and that of the Aravacs resemble much the Greek and Egyptian traditions concerning Phæthon and Typhon. St. Austin, in his book *De Civitate Dei*, cites two authors, Adrast and Dion, at present unknown: these writers described a great calamity, a universal deluge, which overtook our planet at the epoch of Phoroneus, the king of the Pelasgi. During this catastrophe there appeared in the heavens a terrible flaming phenomenon, which was so mighty that it changed the orbit of Hesperus, i.e. of the planet Venus. Undoubtedly some great prehistoric cataclysm occurred, accompanied by an exceptional cosmic phenomenon, although we cannot determine its nature.

We will try to classify all these vague allusions into two categories: certain of them affirm that a cataclysm took place at a time when the present Moon did not exist at all, and the others, contrarily to the first, affirm that this cataclysm occurred when, besides the well-known Moon, there existed in the heavens another, or some celestial body apparently resembling our present satellite.

There arises first the problem of the date of that mysterious catastrophe, related and described by various ancient sources from different aspects. According to some, it was an inundation on an immense scale ; according to others, a sinking of a continent or large island, according to yet others, the fall of a certain celestial body, or its disappearance from the heavens, and finally certain sources tell of a world conflagration which devastated the Earth.

Plato indicated 9500 B.C. as the date of the catastrophe of Atlantis. The legends of the Bushmen, of the Chibchas and Tupis, are so vague that it is impossible to obtain from them any more or less precise date for their catastrophes. The Mayan legend (see the Book of Chilam Balam from Chumayel) does not give any date for the destruction of their ancient fatherland in the ocean, but permits to conclude that the catastrophe in question occurred some thousands of years before the creation by the Mayas of an organized state of Yucatan.

According to the opinion of Professor Gardiner, the disappearance of Gondwana occurred during the epoch when giant lizards inhabited the world : at present most geologists and paleontologists accept the theory that these colossal reptiles began to disappear at the end of the Jurassic Period, i.e. some millions of years ago, before mankind, let alone cultured mankind, existed. If we accept the hypothesis of Professor Gardiner, we must place the disappearance of Gondwana also millions of years ago, but in that case how could we explain that the Hindus and ancient Greeks retained traditions of that old continent ? If Professor Gardiner bases his hypothesis on some remains of giant lizards found on the site of Gondwana, but these finds could be easily explained by the survival of some isolated example of these prehistoric reptiles up to the date of the catastrophe and their presence does not necessarily imply a distant epoch for the disappearance of Gondwana. I mention in one of the following chapters some facts indicating the survival of giant lizards until times comparatively near our own. Moreover, recently there were found the last living representatives of this once numerous class of reptiles on the solitary island of Komodo in the Indonesian archipelago and almost all natives preserve various myths and legends concerning the struggles of their ancestors against giant dragons and large serpents. Thus we are inclined to date the Gondwana catastrophe much later than the end of the Jurassic Period : it occurred probably ten to fifteen thousands of years ago and the Greek myth concerning the Preselenites represents evidently a tradition concerning a certain nation which really inhabited Gondwana before the appearance of the present Moon. It is even probable that this mentioning of the Moon in Greek tradition is not without significance : perhaps the appearance of the Moon may have coincided with the destruction of Gondwana. . . .

The account of the priests of Sais, mentioning great ' conflagrations ' in the heavens, seems to be connected with their tradition concerning Atlantis : perhaps that connection was described in detail in the lost part of the Dialogue of *Critias*. I doubt whether the Egyptian priests would have mentioned conflagrations unless they considered that they might be connected with the cause of the cataclysm of Atlantis. Therefore we must hypothetically conclude that the last of such conflagrations occurred during the cataclysm.

The identity of the Greek and Egyptian legends concerning Phaethon and Typhon is evident : they treat the same event from two different mythological points of view. Therefore we can also hypothetically conclude that the catastrophes in question occurred simultaneously. Perhaps the action of Typhon, who, according to the Egyptian version, divided the firm land into continents, can be connected also with the activity of the Hindu deity and hero Priawata, whose chariot dug up the oceans and thus divided the continents.

Now we come to the account of St. Austine in his work *De Civitata Dei* concerning the flaming apparition in the heavens during the universal deluge at the time of King Phoroneus. This great inundation is known in mythology under the name of ' the Deluge of Ogyges ' and we will later on treat this event in detail in connection with the cycle of the myths concerning the deluge, or deluges.

As a matter of fact Phoroneus, according to some indications, was contemporary to Hercules, and the epoch of the latter has been always determined as the last century before the fall of Troy, i.e. at the end of the second millennium B.C. But one should remember that the legends of the ancients mention many heroes with the name of Hercules : the classical historian Varron found among prehistoric nations of the Mediterranean basin forty-three different personalities who bore this famous name (see the chapter of this book concerning the ' Pillars of Hercules '). We have some reasons to believe that the true Hercules, who visited the kingdom of Atlas and ' created the Straits of Gibraltar,' lived at the end of the fifth millennium B.C. Thus, his contemporary, the Pelasgian king Phoroneus, should be considered as living at the end of the fifth millennium B.C. also, and the mysterious catastrophe called the Deluge of Ogyges should be dated at about 4000 B.C.

It is interesting to determine the nature of the dreadful phenomenon in the heavens, which occurred during the reign of Phoroneus. Taking into consideration the superstitions of that epoch we can only suppose that it must have been a giant comet, whose enormous, flaming tail produced the impression of a conflagration in the heavens. Its mass must have been considerable, because, according to St. Austine, the mysterious phenomenon influenced the arrangement of the solar system and modified the aspect and movements of the Evening Star, the solar planet Venus, known to the ancients under the name of Hesper, the god of twilight. This giant comet, appearing in the middle of the family of the solar planets, could easily influence by its enormous mass the neighbouring celestial bodies and compel some of them to approach the Sun, or to withdraw from it.

Undoubtedly the Earth, as one of the nearest planets to Venus, also had to suffer the fatal consequences of the comet's proximity, and various cataclysms on the surface of our planet must have taken place during that remarkable period. The hemisphere of the Earth, facing the comet in the moment of its least distance from us suffered, perhaps, the fatal effect of a very high temperature, while the other hemisphere was probably tormented by terrific earthquakes and giant inundations due to the exceptionally high tides of the sea-waters and unrest of the subterranean magma. As the Egyptian tradition concerning the activity of Typhon tells us that at its time the sea-level was augmented by

600 elbows, i.e. about 327 yards, it seems to be very possible : such exceptionally high sea-tides are not really miraculous or fabulous.

Thus, uniting the Deluge of Ogyges with the exploits of Phæthon and Typhon, we come to the hypothetical conclusion that at about 4000 B.C. a giant comet produced a series of modifications in the Solar system, followed by cataclysms on the surface of our planet. Perhaps the widespread superstition that the appearance of a comet is always a sign of impending calamities, takes its origin from that distant epoch in the history of mankind.

I would like to incorporate in this combination of myths also the story of Plato concerning the catastrophe, but I am prevented by the exact date given by the Greek philosopher. The difference between 9500 B.C. and 4000 B.C. is too great, unless the date given by the priests of Sais is absolutely erroneous.

As the corresponding legends of the Bushmen, Tupis, Chibchas, and Mayas do not possess any chronological indication, we are allowed a considerable latitude in conjectures concerning their dates. I can say the same concerning the Gondwana catastrophe : it might have occurred in the tenth, as well as in the fifth, or even the fourth millennium B.C.

Moreover, I could incorporate in the same series of remarkable events the world-wide legends concerning the Great Deluge : the deluge described in the Jewish Bible, for instance, is dated 3852 B.C., i.e. approximately contemporaneous (hypothetically . . .) with the Deluge of Ogyges. But I prefer to examine the problem of the world-deluges later on, in a separate chapter of this book.

For the moment I would like only to mention the catastrophe which destroyed the famous Tihuanaco culture in Bolivia. My reader will find later on a detailed description of the archæological finds in the Tihuanaco region, but here it is only necessary to mention the discoveries of R. Mueller, A. Poznansky, and K. Bilau. The first two have established that the ruins of Tihuanaco are 11,500 years old : a great unknown cataclysm suddenly heightened the ridge of the Andes and the shores of the Pacific in the regions of the present Colombia and Peru and simultaneously raised Tihuanaco by 2.1 miles. The work on the construction of Tihuanaco city was interrupted, the builders perished or fled, and the new-born capital was completely abandoned.   K. Bilau, by means of a very ingenious method, confirmed the calculations of both scientists.   Thus we have another indication of some cosmic catastrophe which occurred in the Western hemisphere *circa* 9500 B.C.   This date is the same as the one mentioned by the priests of Sais.

Therefore we are in the presence of at least two groups of indications : the first refers to a series of catastrophes at about 4000 B.C. and the second has in view events which occurred about 9000–10,000 B.C.   Of course, it is possible that these indications refer to two distinct cataclysms, which occurred at two different epochs.

This contradiction in the chronology of the series of prehistoric cataclysms is very puzzling for the researcher.   However, I hope that the complete deciphering of the Mayan manuscripts in the future will elucidate this very important chronological problem. Later on the reader will see that some collateral facts and con-jectures incline me to accept Plato's dating in preference to any other.

But we have to overcome another discrepancy.   Some of the enumerated sources tell of the appearance of our present Moon in the heavens during the cataclysm (the Chibchan version), one of them (the Mayan version), of the disappearance from the heavens of a certain celestial body and one, the Bushmen's legend, of the presence before the catastrophe of two moons in the heavens.   How can we reconcile these three versions ?

It is comparatively easy to admit that, at a certain period BEFORE the catastrophe, our planet possessed a small satellite. Owing to its small dimensions and great distance from the Earth, this satellite must have been seen only as a luminous point, or, at the most, a very small disk, similar to Venus or Jupiter.   On the other hand, the present Moon existed then as an independent solar planet and its orbit passed somewhere between the orbits of Venus and ours.

The irruption of the said giant comet into the solar system produced the following modifications : Venus came nearer to the sun and therefore became less visible to us than before, the Moon was thrown aside, and, entering into the Earth's gravitational field, became an earthly satellite, and our old, small satellite, thrown still nearer to our planet, fell upon its surface.

Thus, this hypothesis gives an explanation capable of satisfying all questions concerning the contradictions in the legends of the Greeks, Mayas, Tupis, and Bushmen. The Greeks, telling of the Preselenites, had in view the present Moon, which was not in existence at the epoch of the unknown cataclysm ; the Bushmen, affirming that the cataclysm took place at the epoch when two moons illuminated the sky, have in view the old small satellite and the newly-appeared present Moon, the Tupis are right when they affirm that the moon periodically falls upon the Earth, and the Mayan Codex Chilam Balam, telling of the ravishment of the Great Serpent from the heavens, has in view the fallen small satellite.

Parallel to all these vague legends and allusions I wish to mention a very curious observation : some cultured, or semi-cultured, nations of the Old and New Worlds at a certain epoch felt the necessity to change their primitive and natural solar calendar either into a lunar one, or into a mixed solar-lunar one. Such a modification of the calendars was introduced, for instance, by the Babylonians at an undetermined epoch and by the Mayas at the epoch of the Nahoan invasion. Although the date of the latter has not yet been established, some researchers consider that the Nahoan race came into Yucatan about 4,000 years B.C. The codex Chilam Balam from Chumayel affirms that at the epoch of the ruin of the Itza culture the race of Nahoa, which occupied the former Itza territories, introduced some religious and astronomical reforms, and the solar cult, which up to that time had dominated, began to give way little by little to lunar rituals. What was the reason for such a modification ? Perhaps it was the appearance of a new luminary in the heavens, the present Moon, which compelled prehistoric nations to modify their religious-astronomical conceptions.

An ancient historian, the priest Manethon, affirms that the Egyptians possessed a chronology from 11542 B.C. Probably this year was chosen by the pre-Egyptians as an era following some unknown important event which took place in 11542 B.C. Some indications show that this Primeval pre-Egyptian calendar was a lunar one. Later on, in 4241 B.C., this ancient system of chronology was changed for a solar calendar with twelve months and five supplementary days, instead of thirteen months and one supplementary day. Thus, the process of calendar reform in

Egypt seems to be just the opposite of the Babylonian and Mayan, although the Jews, who seemed in a position to adopt the Egyptian system of chronology, or, perhaps, the Babylonian one, remained faithful to the lunar calendar.

Scientists consider that the great inclination of the Earth's axis in relation to the plane of the ecliptic is due to the fact that at some time our planet suffered a strong blow from a giant meteorite and thus its axis became inclined. Let us see if there are any objective proofs for the possibility of such an event in the past.

The well-established phenomenon of the nutation of the poles consists of the following. The extremities of the Earth's axis, i.e. the poles, are not immobile but are constantly oscillating. Thus this axis deviates from the theoretical one, maintaining always an angle with the latter equal to $3° 30'$. In reality this movement of the poles is much more complex, but it would be out of place here to enter into the details of this interesting, but intricate, phenomenon. It is, however, necessary to point out that the amplitude of the nutation has gradually diminished : thus, everything occurs in such a way, as if our planet at some time suffered a strong blow which altered the previous angle of its axis with the perpendicular to the plane of the ecliptic, bringing it to the present roughly calculated $23° 30'$.

Scientists affirm that while this angle was never equal to $0°$, at some time it must have been much less than now. The inclination of the Earth's axis caused the alternation of the seasons and therefore reflected on the life of plants, animals, and men. Before this hypothetical event the whole surface of the Earth was divided into zones, each with its own perpetual average temperature : thus, like some other planets of the solar system, our Earth had zones of eternal winter, summer, and spring.

The same or some other blow provoked the phenomenon of the nutation of the poles : the axis of our planet cannot re-stabilize now, and continues to oscillate like a disturbed pendulum. The fact of the lessening of the amplitude of the nutation perfectly proves this conjecture.

That popular toy, the spinning-top, gives a beautiful illustration to this hypothesis : if during the rotation of the spinning-top you strike it slightly, the axis of the toy will become inclined towards the floor and, although the spinning-top

CARVED MONOLITH OF COPAN (HONDURAS)
Note the Mongolian style.

ANOTHER MONOLITH OF COPAN (HONDURAS)

TWO FURTHER EXAMPLES FROM COPAN
(HONDURAS)

will continue its rotation and revolution, its poles will slightly
oscillate with a constantly diminishing amplitude.

Although the famous French astronomer, the Abbé Moreux,
affirms that any sudden modification of the angle of the Earth's
axis could not provoke an instantaneous modification in climate,
nevertheless the instantaneous mass-death of the Siberian mammoths constitutes a very convincing proof of the possibility of
such a catastrophical change. 1 will examine here in detail this
interesting phenomenon.

*   *   *

According to the oldest Chinese chronicles, the first mammoth
tusks were brought to China from the distant north-eastern
regions of Siberia in the fourth century A.D. From that epoch
until now, i.e. during 1600 years, many thousands of tons of
these tusks have been sold by the Siberian natives to the Chinese.

Even now North-Eastern Siberia and the Novosibirsk archipelago furnish two thirds of the entire world-output of ivory.
During the last 150 years an average amount of 250 mammoths
has been exhumed yearly in the zone of the everlasting frozen
strata of Polar Siberia. Therefore, Russia, where elephants can
be found only in menageries and zoological gardens, is the leading
supplier of ivory for the whole world.

The carcasses and skeletons of the mammoths are found not
very deeply buried under the ice and frozen soil of the Arctic
zone : the low temperature has been responsible for the preservation of those giant corpses in a state of perfect freshness. Pallas,
who visited these regions in the eighteenth century, tells us that
he ate a steak of mammoth flesh and found it very palatable.
Arctic foxes eat the carcasses of the mammoths and the natives are
always eager to feast themselves upon flesh many thousands of
years old, and feed their dogs with it. The age of the strata
where the mammoths' remains are found is approximately
12,000 years.

Some years before the Great War the carcass of a mammoth's
cub was brought to St. Petersburg; it was well preserved and
was brought within the enormous block of ice in which it was
found. The trip of about 7,800 miles from the Novosibirsk
archipelago to the Russian capital, which lasted several months,
did not cause any deterioration in the 12,000 year old carcass,

which remained as fresh as any piece of meat in the butchery. The Russian scientists profited by this occasion in order to make some histological investigations, and the flesh of the mammoth was then used for gastronomical purposes : the cook of the Geological Museum made some magnificent steaks out of it and the members of the Academy of Sciences were delighted with this prehistoric meal.

But the finds of entire well-preserved carcasses are now comparatively rare : during the last 150 years only 84 such remains have been found and the others were only more or less well-preserved skeletons. An analysis of the undigested food in the stomachs of the mammoths showed that those giant pachyderms fed almost exclusively on the needles of pines, larch-trees and firs, which formed at that epoch enormous forests in the Arctic zone of Siberia. At present all this rich flora has disappeared and in its place there grow only dwarf-birches, lichens, and polar mosses.

Apparently the destruction of the innumerable herds of mammoths in North-Eastern Siberia occurred suddenly and even instantaneously, because their stomachs contain much undigested food. If this mysterious destruction had been of a gradual character, the wise pachyderms could have migrated southwards in time to escape death and save their cubs. A flora analogous to that which existed in their time on the Novosibirsk archipelago can be found at present not nearer than the Baikal Lake, i.e. about 3,600 miles south.

The carcasses are also sometimes found in standing position. This circumstance particularly proves that death overtook the mammoths suddenly, while they grazed peacefully on the prehistoric pasture-grounds, and they perished instantaneously like the mastodons near Bogotà in Colombia (see a preceding chapter concerning the elephants in America and ' The Field of Giants ').

Certain researchers believe that some of the mammoths were suffocated by a colossal deluge of slime, which at one time suddenly inundated North-Eastern Siberia, while others were killed by the sudden freezing of this deluge. In any case, it was anatomically proved that many of them died from asphyxia. Probably the same causes exterminated also the Alaskan mammoths, but the said causes could hardly have been responsible for the disappearance of the European mammoths, which were very numerous. The mammoth and the long-haired rhinoceros, which lived everywhere in the Old World from the Pacific shores to Gibraltar, disappeared doubtless gradually: the primeval inhabitants of the Old Continent hunted those valuable animals energetically and must have almost exterminated them in Europe by the time the Asiatic races began to settle there. It is quite possible also that the modification of the European and Asiatic climates played a considerable role in the extermination of our pachyderms.

Some scientists explain their disappearance by the hypothesis of 'gigantism': they affirm that the giant organisms were defective in virtue of their own exaggerated dimensions, and, so to speak, not practical from the point of view of Nature. Thus, little by little, they had to give way to smaller and more 'practical' forms. One would say that Nature experimented with various kinds of animals and gradually dropped the species which turned out unsuccessful attempts.

This point of view represents a striking example of modern 'scientific metaphysics': doubtless the causes of the disappearance of the mammoths, as well as of the giant lizards in the epochs preceding, were more simple, but we still cannot determine them. I cannot believe that Nature is able to make errors in creating new species, but I think that each species possesses a certain amount of vitality: when this is exhausted, new species take the place of the extinct forms. This quality is, perhaps, that imperceptible substance which by Maeterlinck is called 'l'ésprit colléctif de l'éspèce'; however, this term is also a metaphysical one. . . .

Let us return from these conjectures to the problem of the disappearance of the mammoths in the North-Eastern Siberia, where even to-day real 'ivory mines' still exist. The apparently simultaneous and instantaneous destruction of the mammoths in the Novosibirsk archipelago and in Alaska represent a very interesting scientific problem. The natives of North-Eastern Siberia affirm that these mammoths perished from the Great Flood: our forefather Noah was unable to procure a place for a couple of these giant animals in his ark, which was terribly crowded, and it was thus impossible to provide for their future multiplication. Another version of the same legend tells that Noah did take a couple of mammoths into his ark, but that at the disembarkment of all passengers on the mountains of Ararat the giant pachyderms stumbled, fell into a slime-swamp, and perished. All the other mammoths had died during the Flood.

It will not be out of place to examine the circumstances of the natural death of modern elephants. It is known that Africa is very rich in elephants and that they are there energetically hunted on account of their precious tusks. But it is very strange that never a hunter, either European or Negro, ever found the corpse of an elephant dead from natural causes. If an elephant's corpse is found, it is always the corpse of an animal which has died from the wounds of some hunter, or following some misfortune. The *English Hunters' Annals*, which represent the best literature of that kind in the world, mentions during the last 25 years only one case of the finding of an elephant's carcass which belonged apparently to an animal that died from natural causes.

This strange fact was responsible for the creation of a belief that elephants are accustomed to withdraw to secret places, so-called ' elephants' cemeteries,' in the jungle, whenever they sense the approach of death. This opinion seems to be quite gratuitous and the finds of accumulations of elephants' skeletons can be explained by the elephant's love of water. They spend many hours in rivers and swamps and it has been established, for instance, that even wounded elephants make straightway for water, which apparently acts upon them in a soothing manner. Therefore, an old or a sick elephant almost invariably dies in water, where its corpse little by little becomes buried under the slime, or swallowed by the marshes. Thus, thousands of elephants' corpses are probably lying at the bottom of the Nile and in those vast swamps which encircle the Albert Lake. Perhaps at some time it happened that one of these swamps dried and the natives found on its bottom many elephants' skeletons : thus was born the legend concerning elephant cemeteries.

This explanation is plausible in relation to the fate of African and, perhaps, modern Asiatic elephants, but absolutely inadequate for explaining the fate of the Siberian mammoths and much more so of those mastodons whose remains cover the ' Field of Giants ' in Colombia.

I offer my own hypothetical explanation of these two phenomena. The strong blow, suffered by the Earth 12,000 years ago, disturbed the equilibrium of the Earth's axis. It became inclined instantaneously to the plane of the ecliptic, forming an angle with the perpendicular to the latter equal to 23°30' and began to oscillate (the phenomenon of nutation of the poles). The climate of North-Eastern Siberia and Alaska became instantaneously modified, and the lowering of the temperature and the enormous slime masses brought by the inundation from the sea-bottom killed the mammoths.

As to the destruction of the Colombian mastodons, it occurred following the rapid heightening of their pasture-ground by 2·1 miles. It is very probable that this phenomenon also was in consequence of the fall of a large meteorite upon the Earth's surface. Thus, both phenomena, the Siberian and the South American, occurred simultaneously.

Certainly the meteorite must have been of exceptionally large dimensions in order so to disturb the equilibrium of the Earth. Therefore a very natural question arises : where is this meteorite now? Among all the known meteorites not a single one could claim dimensions sufficient to cause such important consequences for the whole planet.

*   *   *

Some scientists supposed that this meteorite was our former satellite, which approached too near to the Earth and thus was pulled down by our planet. It fell upon the Earth and formed the Continent of Australia while the innumerable splinters broken off by the fall became the island groups of the Pacific. They tried to prove this bold hypothesis by pointing out the comparative newness of the alluvial strata in Australia which, according to some investigators, are only 12,000 years old. But I have had an opportunity to hear from some geologists an absolutely opposite opinion : the Australian alluvium is very old and geologically the continent itself is the continuation of certain islands of Indonesia, particularly of New Guinea. Other scientists affirm that Australia and some neighbouring islands represent the surviving parts of a continent which existed in the past between Africa and the South-Eastern Asia. Perhaps Australia is a remainder of Gondwana, or of the mysterious land which figures in the Polynesian myths. In any case, the peculiar fauna of Australia possesses some affinities with those of Madagascar.

The German anthropologist, Professor Klaatch of Leipzig

University, considers that there are serious proofs of the existence of Australia during the earliest Tertiary Period. This expert even affirms that at that epoch Australia was already populated by a prehistoric human race and goes so far as to consider the island-continent to be the cradle of humanity in general. This hypothesis is certainly nothing more than one of the countless analogical suppositions relating to various sections of our planet : the modern, so-called 'ologenetic,' theory does not admit any special 'cradle' for mankind, which, it seems, appeared almost simultaneously everywhere on the surface of the Earth. . . . But as to the existence of Australia many millions of years ago the finds at Raglan Parade, Warrnambool, Australia, represent a strong enough proof in favour of Dr. Klaatch's opinion.

There were found at a depth of ten feet several human foot-prints in sandstone which, according to a moderate estimate, was apparently a sand-dune close to an ancient sea beach from 20,000 to 30,000 years ago. This find naturally proves the existence of Australia much before the catastrophe of Atlantis and the hypothetical fall of a giant meteorite.

At the same time the phenomenon of nutation and the sudden death of the mammoths in Siberia and Canada show that such a cosmic catastrophe occurred about 11,000 years ago. . . . I think that if an enormous meteorite fell at this epoch on the surface of the Earth, the fall took place somewhere in the Pacific Ocean : in this case the disappearance of a large continent in this ocean would be explained, and also the presence of innumerable islands and archipelagos between Asia, Australia, and America.

The adherents of the above-mentioned hypothesis affirm that the fall of our former satellite provoked a series of extensive changes on our planet. This terrific blow wiped out Gondwana, or Lemuria, the hypothetical Pacific continent, and Atlantis. The giant stresses caused in the earth-crust ruptured the ancient isthmus between Asia and America and, perhaps, the isthmus between Europe and Africa also, producing the Behring Straits and the Straits of Gibraltar. The latter rupture caused the inundation of the former Mediterranean depression and its transformation into a sea. A number of new islands were formed in the Pacific and, as the disturbance reached even the subter-ranean magma itself, a series of volcanoes appeared forming the Pacific volcanic ring around the site of the catastrophe and awakening general plutonic activity throughout that ocean. One of the most important results of this activity was an increase in the height of the Andean ridge to its present level and the ruin of the Tihuanaco culture. Finally, the consequences of this upheaval were the nutation of the poles and the periodicity of the seasons for every given region of the globe. The very fact of the decrease in the amplitude of the nutation is a proof that the latter was caused by a blow. This hypothesis would be adequate for the explanation of all the above events were it not for the problem of chronology. We do not admit the possibility of reconciling these chronological contradictions by any conjecture save on the supposition that at least some of the sources of our information are in the wrong concerning the date of the catastrophe.

In any case it seems to me probable that the adoption of a lunar calendar instead of a solar one by certain prehistoric nations followed the appearance in the sky of the present Moon. The tremendous catastrophes accompanying this appearance of a new large and bright luminary excited the religious feelings of the primeval races and generated a series of myths and superstitions.

Among the various hypotheses concerning the causes of the Atlantis catastrophe I wish to note here those which are likely to connect that cataclysm with some cosmic phenomenon, although the Abbé Moreux, while admitting that our planet in its inter-planetary voyage might meet with an accumulation of the remains of a comet, or a giant asteroid, does not see any proof in favour of the assertion that the Atlantis catastrophe was due to a cosmic perturbation. At the same time the French scientist admits that some unknown oscillation of the Earth's axis could provoke a strong earthquake. In his book concerning the problem of Atlantis the Abbé Moreux cites the hypothesis of the astronomers Saintignon and Carli. They first considered that at the moment of the catastrophe there occurred in the zenith of Atlantis a conjunction of certain planets, which conjunction provoked an extraordinarily strong flood-tide of the subterranean magma and therefore a series of terrific earthquakes. Other scientists affirm that the sudden heightening of the Andean ridge, Alps, and Caucasus was responsible for a series of corresponding depressions in other regions of the Earth's surface and one of them caused the sinking of Atlantis. The last explanation leaves in the dark the causes of the heightening itself, which doubtless may have been considered to be due to some abnormal subterranean activity. P. Lima was of the opinion that the sinking of Atlantis was due to a sudden inclination of the plane of the ecliptic, followed by an instantaneous translation of the magma. Count Carli, on the ground of the hypothesis of Whyston, offered in 1778 the following hypothesis : some millenniums ago our planet met a comet and this meeting changed our orbit, transforming its former circular shape into an elliptic one and augmenting the period of the Earth's revolution by 10 days 1 hour and 30 minutes. The attraction of the comet's mass provoked an eight-miles-high flood-tide of the oceans and this circumstance, together with the immediately impending condensation of an enormous quantity of the water-vapours in the Earth's atmosphere, produced a great inundation. The astronomer de Lalande, examining the hypothesis of Carli, asserted that the approach of the head of the comet within a distance of 3,000 miles from the Earth would be sufficient to drain the oceans and to assemble the waters on the firm land, holding it there in a layer 12,000 feet thick and naturally drowning the summits of most of the mountains. Carli affirmed that the movements of comets are subjected to many sudden and unexpected perturbations : therefore it is almost impossible to calculate exactly the complete ephemerides of a given comet. These assertions of Carli were brilliantly justified by the sudden appearance of the comet of 1759 and by the visit of the famous Halley's comet on 25 May 1910. The diameter of this comet had been calculated during its previous appearance in 1835 at 348,000 miles (the Earth's diameter is only about 7,200 miles) : therefore it is easy to imagine the extent of the perturbations that might be created in the mechanism of the solar system by this enormous guest from Space if it should approach near Venus and the Earth !

Was Halley's comet really responsible for the series of catastrophes, which, rightly or wrongly, are considered as simultaneous to that of Atlantis ? Was this dreaded wanderer the heavenly sign recorded by St. Austin in his work ? And finally, was Halley's comet that malicious Typhon or Phæthon which, according to the myths, inundated one half of the Earth and burnt the other half ?

*   *   *

Let us describe the approximate aspect of some regions of our globe as it was 15–20,000 years ago. At that epoch the sea which we call the Mediterranean probably did not yet exist and its place was occupied by a vast depression. This depression, except occasional swamps traversed by many water-courses and canals, was firm land. Thus the European peninsula formed a solid block with the Asiatic and African continents. The Atlas ridge branched off into Spain and the Straits of Gibraltar did not yet exist. Western France, Northern Spain, and Portugal were not maritime countries and the firm land stretched much farther west up to the shores of Yucatan and Cuba comprising, perhaps, the present Azores and Bahama islands. Thus this vast region was indissolubly united to the present Old World. It was indented all over by numerous gulfs, bays, and straits and, perhaps, was even not a solid block, but simply a vast archipelago of islands separated by narrow water-courses and canals. The present Azores, Canaries and Madeira were not islands, but table-lands and summits of a great ridge, which stretched almost meridionally, dividing that prehistoric continent, or archipelago, into two parts. It represented only the remains of a vaster firm land, which millions of years ago occupied almost the whole surface of the present Atlantic Ocean from Iceland to the South Pole.

Thus we can assume that some 15-20,000 years ago one could travel on land from Cuba to Babylon and farther. If we take into consideration the fact that at that time the isthmus between Asia and America still existed, it will be clear that practically the entire surface of the globe was encircled at that epoch by an almost continuous band of firm land. Such a geographical situation facilitated the migrations of the prehistoric races, as well as of animals and plants, in ever direction. Later on I will try to demonstrate that many tribes in Europe and America came through that prehistoric bridge to their present abodes. At the moment I will mention only the migrations of some American Indian tribes, the Polynesians, the Gauls, the so-called Celts, the Phœnicians, the Egyptians, and mysterious peoples such as the Ligurians, Tyrrhenians (Etruscans), and Pelasgi.

Nowadays it is regarded as proven that some tribes of Indians came to America from the Asiatic continent : the anthropological affinities between the Mongols and those Indian races are indisputable. One stream of migrants from Asia was directed westwards, and the other eastwards : the first contributed to the peopling of Europe, and the second, of Polynesia and North America. Later on a considerable proportion of the Asiatic newcomers penetrated into South America and contributed to the formation of some of the native states. On the other hand, certain American autochthonous races, as, for instance, the forefathers of the Gauls, of the so-called Celts, and of some others, emigrated eastwards and occupied the territories of France, Spain, Italy, and Egypt. After the catastrophe of Atlantis, or even, perhaps, before it, some ethnic waves from this continent migrated into Europe and Northern Africa : they formed a series of Atlantean colonies which later on became known as Etruria, the country of the Pelasgi, Phœnicia, etc. These emigrants from Atlantis were the kernels of various enigmatical tribes in the Africa of present times, such as the Berbers, Tuaregs, Lybians, etc. One of the largest and richest Atlantean colonies established itself on the Iberian peninsula and gave rise to Portugal. Other Atlanteans contributed to the peopling of the present Spain : Ibers, Celt-Ibers, Basques, and Gerions represent, perhaps, nothing else than the descendants of the oldest migrants from Atlantis. The westward migrations of Atlanteans probably contributed to the formation of several American civilized states. Finally, it is not improbable that the forefathers of the Japanese and Koreans issued also from the Plato's continent and after thousands of years of wandering through Polynesia settled in Eastern Asia.

Another great process of Europe's colonization originated from Asia : millions of men left from time to time their primeval abodes in the heart of Asia and rushed westwards to the warm shores of the ocean, but this great swarming of wild races in the heart of the immense Asiatic continent was only beginning at the time of the Atlantis cataclysm. . . .

The western and eastern new-comers in Europe had to sustain a cruel struggle with the European aboriginal tribes, the descendants of the Neanderthal race, which populated the European virgin forests. . . .

CHAPTER V

THE French scientist, Adhemar, in 1842 created his famous theory of the Glacial Periods and the phenomena of universal floods connected with them. Here is this theory briefly explained.

Our planet in its revolution describes an ellipse, in one of the focuses of which is the Sun. This point is traversed also by the so-called ' line of the equinoxes,' which divides the elliptical orbit of the Earth into two unequal parts. The line of the equinoxes is immobile but, owing to an optical illusion, it seems to us that every year it is slightly late in meeting the Earth at the equinoxes. During a cycle of roughly 25,800 years (exactly 25,796 years), as a result of these delays, the line of the equinoxes appears to describe a complete ellipse, returning gradually to its original position. Thus it seems to us that this line is moving in a direction opposite to that of the Earth's movement. This phenomenon was first observed by the Greek astronomer Hypparch, about 2,000 years ago and received the name of ' the precession of the equinoxes.' In accordance with the teachings of the old astronomy, Hypparch believed that this line really moved westwards. The phenomenon of the precession can be explained now by certain peculiarities of the Earth's rotation, combined with the perturbations caused by the influences of the Sun and the Moon on the equatorial earth-crust layers. These layers are a swelling of the earth-crust due to centrifugal force : their presence gives to our planet its present shape of an oblate spheroid. Were it not for their existence, the Earth would have been much more like a true sphere.

The precession influences the duration of the seasons : the summer period in one of the hemispheres is slowly growing, and in the other, correspondingly diminishing. Adhemar calculated the period of the precession as equal not to 25,800 years, but to 21,000 years : thus he supposed that every 10,500 years, or about half of the total period of precession, summer is transformed into winter in one hemisphere, while in the other the opposite phenomenon is observed.

During the period of 21,000 years occur two moments when the difference between the duration of summer at the opposite poles reaches its maximum : at one time this difference is in favour of the Arctic region and at another time of the Antarctic. During these moments the pole which possesses the longer summer receives from the total quantity of hours in a year (8,760 for a simple and 8,784 for a leap year) only 4,296 night-hours and 4,464 day-hours, and the opposite pole : 4,464 night-hours and 4,296 day ones. Thus, the first pole receives at the moments of maximum 168 day-hours more.

The average quantity of warmth which the poles receive during the long polar day is gradually lost during the long polar night, thanks to the radiation of the warmth into Space. But the temperature at a given point of the Earth's surface depends always only upon the difference between the warmth received and the warmth irradiated, or lost. Therefore it is clear that the other pole in our example will have more ice than the first. This increase in the quantity of ice will remain at the second pole during the whole period of 10,500 years, until the first pole slowly approximates itself to the moment of the maximal difference in the durations of each polar summer. Thus the second pole accumulates every year more and more ice until finally this accumulation, according to Adhemar, provokes a displacement of the centre of gravity of the Earth. As a matter of fact, as long as the icebergs are floating in the polar seas, their weight does not affect the position of the Earth's centre of gravity, because, according to the law of Archimedes, they displace a quantity of water equal to their own weight. But, when the icebergs, increased in their volume, begin to touch the sea-bottom, the situation totally changes : from this moment the centre of gravity of the planet begins to move towards the region of the ice conglomeration. Then the waters of the oceans, obeying the force of gravity, gradually move in that direction. At the same time the ice on the opposite pole begins to melt and the resulting waters rush towards the other already overloaded pole. If this happens a violent inundation of one hemisphere will be unavoidable. The stretch of some thousands of years, previous to such a cataclysm, is a Glacial Period, because the ice of the alleviated pole will also begin to creep slowly in the wake of that already melted. Thus, according to Adhemar's theory, the Glacial Periods, followed by universal floods, occur every 10-11,000 years and last at least 2-3,000 years.

The existence everywhere on the Earth's surface of so-called ' erratic stones ' and ' moraines ' is an excellent proof in favour of this theory of Glacial Periods. During such periods the ice-masses, or glaciers, moving towards one of the poles, dragged with them stones and sometimes great rocks. As the glaciers were moving along they pounded these rocks into pieces of various size and polished their surfaces by rubbing them against the soil. Later on, when the glaciers melted under the hot rays of the sun, these rocks and stones remained in the very places where the ice had been melted. Thus these erratic stones are to-day mute witnesses of the tremendous processes which once operated on our planet. If the stones had been encrusted in the base of the glacier, they formed after its disappearance a sort of border, which is called a ' moraine.' The geologist Elie de Beaumont thinks that the presence of these serrated stones and moraines is a proof that not long ago giant glaciers were moving southwards on our planet.

At present we are witnessing the approach of a new Glacial Period, but this time the glaciers will move northwards : since 1248 the northern hemisphere has been growing steadily colder. The culminant year will be 11748, but the scientists (Professor L. von Post) affirm that the new Glacial Period in Europe will begin after three to six millenniums. The culminant year for the preceding Glacial Period was 9252 B.C. This date is very near to Plato's for the Atlantis catastrophe and to that calculated by R. Mueller and A. Poznansky for the ruin of Tihuanaco.

It is likely that the preceding Glacial Periods destroyed several prehistoric cultures. We should always remember the scantiness of our historic science : recently many proofs have been found that mankind is much older than had been previously believed. . . .

About a century passed after Adhemar first propounded his theory and it suffered much criticism and underwent many modifications. I can even say that the problem of the Glacial Periods is still far from being solved. Are the modifications in the Earth's revolution responsible for the decrease in the heat received by our planet from the Sun and the resulting Glacial Periods ? Or are they caused by changes in the intensity of the solar irradiations themselves ? Or are there some unknown cosmic, or geophysical, factors, which introduce periodical modifications in the state of our atmosphere ? Or, finally, should we admit that Adhemar was right and the Glacial Periods are really due to some perturbations in the revolution of the Earth ?

In the middle of last century the scientist J. Kroll created his own theory of the Glacial Periods. He thought that the fluctuations in the duration of the seasons were due to a combined effect of the phenomena of precession and the periodical increase in the eccentricity of the Earth's orbit. This last phenomenon, according to him, is caused by the periodical increase in the perturbations of other planets. The result of this is a considerable increase in the differences of the duration of summer and winter alternately on both hemispheres. Robert Ball completed Kroll's theory, and in its definite shape it affirms the following : 67 per cent of the whole quantity of warmth received from the Sun comes always in the summer, and 33 per cent in the winter. The differences in the quantities of the warmth, received alternately by both hemispheres, contribute little by little to the accumulation of ice-masses. The remaining part of the Kroll-Ball theory is in agreement with Adhemar.

During a certain period the Kroll-Ball theory was admitted by almost all scientists : even Wallace and Lyell confirmed its adequacy. The calculations proved that the maxima of the eccentricity of the Earth's orbit took place twice, about 800,000 and 160,000 years ago. Lyell thought that, during the first maximum, or about a million years ago, occurred the Pleistocene Glacial Period.

But later on Kroll's theory was found inadequate : scientists have proved that the Glacial Periods do not alternate on each hemisphere but occur simultaneously on both. Now the Kroll-Ball theory has been resurrected again, but considerably modified : during the last fifty years the geologists and astronomers have introduced into it many rectifications, based on modern investigations and discoveries. Geologists have established, for instance, that during the present Quaternary Epoch there have occurred at least four Glacial Periods with more or less long intervals between them. These Periods, together with the intervals, took about 600,000 years in all and astronomical calculations have brilliantly justified this assertion.

Recently the same calculations have been employed in order to establish the chronology of the Quaternary Epoch in relation to the process of the evolution of animals and mankind. It has resulted that the so-called Man of Heidelberg lived 500,000 years ago and the Neanderthal man about 110,000. The Paleolithic Period ended about 40,000 years ago and the Siberian mammoths perished 15,000 years ago. Contrarily to the above-mentioned calculation of the chronology of the Paleolithic Period, other scientists have established that it ended in France only 15,000 years ago: moreover, the finds in Perigord have proved that at that time France was still covered by ice and large herds of reindeer existed there. Therefore this epoch is called the Epoch of the Reindeer. The paleolithic man of that day possessed remarkable artistic talent: the paintings of the so-called Magdalenian culture, produced as it seems by these men, prove their comparatively high standard.

* * *

The scientist Moreux, who at the same time is also a representative of the Roman Catholic Church, considers that the Greeks received the legend of the Great Flood from the Egyptians, Jews, and Chaldeans, who in their turn adopted it from much more ancient sources. As to Biblical chronology, Moreux considers it very erroneous: according to the French astronomer, its errors are due to the incompleteness of the list of the patriarchs. Later on I will have an opportunity to give an account of the interesting hypothesis of the Chilean archæologist, L. Thayer Ojeda, concerning the real meaning of the term 'patriarch.'

For a long time scientists did not recognize the truthfulness of the Biblical legend concerning the Universal Flood: except for the orthodox commentators of the Scriptures, who take the Hebraic myths literally, all scientists took this legend only to be intended as an illustration to the morals of the author of the Pentateuch. But now the numerous analogous legends of other tribes and the archæological finds in Mesopotamia compel the science to accept the Biblical myth as a somewhat naïve description of real events. Further on I will relate some traditions of various ancient and modern nations concerning this interesting epoch of the world's history.

The assyriologist George Smith, studying in 1872 the ancient cuneiform texts from the library of the king Assurbanipal IV, found in the ruins of Nineveh, became interested in the myth of Gilgamesh. This hero of the Chaldeans plays in the Sumero-Babylonian epoch approximately the same role as Hercules in the Greek myth. The texts found by Smith contain a description of the world flood that is almost identical with the Biblical account. Later on archæologists, investigating the ruins of Nippur, found a more ancient Sumerian version of the world-creation and the Universal Flood : it also resembles the Biblical text. In addition, we have a version by Beroz, the Babylonian priest of the god Mardook. This priest, who lived in the thirteenth century B.C., wrote a Babylonian history, but we know only some quotations from it made by other ancient authors.

Here is the gist of the Nippur text. At the beginning of Time the universe was nothing but a chaos and the Supreme Being arranged everything in order. This Being created the animals and then, using clay, man. The first pair of men inhabited Paradise, a splendid garden, but later on, when men disobeyed the will of God, they were banished out of Paradise. The descendants of this first pair possessed remarkable longevity, but, when mankind sank into sin, God sent a Great Flood. Everybody perished, save the blessed Ut-Napishtim : the god Enkee, loving him, warned Ut-Napishtim beforehand of the coming calamity and advised him to build a large ship and to embark on it with all his family, taking along a pair of each animal species and supplies sufficient to begin a new life after the calamity. The Enkee's prediction was faithfully fulfilled : a flood began and lasted six days and six nights. During the inundation occurred such tremendous storms and such a deep darkness reigned that the gods themselves were afraid. Finally the elements calmed down and the sun appeared. When Ut-Napishtim looked out of his ark, he saw that everything on the Earth's surface had been transformed into mud. The ship of Ut-Napishtim stopped at the mountain of Nizir (another version spells it Nistir) and the blessed man began to let loose the birds, in order to know if there were already pieces of dry land. At first he let loose a pigeon and a swallow, but both returned to the ark. When Ut-Napishtim let loose a raven, the latter did not return and thus the blessed man realized that the flood was over.

The Nineveh version is almost identical with the Nippur: the most important difference is that, while the first version asserts that the animals were created after man, the Nippur story claims the contrary. The myth of Gilgamesh in the Nineveh version tells the story of the Flood in this way:

The Universal Flood was sent by the gods as a punishment for the sins of mankind. The god Ea warned Ut-Napishtim, or Sit-Napishtim, beforehand about the coming flood, and advised him to build an ark. Further the text describes the terrific consequences of the Flood and the panic which overcame even the gods. The goddess Ishtar, for instance, repented that she had given her consent to such a calamity. Another Babylonian deity whose activity was also connected with the Flood was the god of storms, thunder, lightning, and rain, Adad, or Ramman, called in the Bible ' Rimmon.' He announced the Flood by a sinister darkness throughout the world and by a waterspout so tall that it reached the sky. According to the Nineveh version the Flood lasted seven days and seven nights. At the end of the inundation Ut-Napishtim and his wife were transformed into gods and inhabited the ' Mouth of the Rivers.' This term probably signifies the actual region of Shat-el-Arab.

The priest Beroz tells us that the Flood occurred during the reign of Xisuthros, the tenth king of Babylon. As to the rest of the account of Beroz it resembles both preceding ones except for one important detail: Beroz says that the Ark stopped on the mountains of Kardiray, which word signifies ' The Barrier of the Mountains of Paradise.' This term, if applied to the Gurneh region, where the Mesopotamian paradise was supposed to have been located, is senseless, because not a single mountain exists there. To give sense to the term ' Kardiray ' we must seek the origin of the legend somewhere else.

The words of the myths concerning the transformation of everything into mud are also worthy of attention. As a matter of fact the Flood left very much slime in Mesopotamia. The Oxford expedition working among the ruins of Ur discovered under several cultural layers of the Sumerian epoch mighty clay layers with numerous remains of freshwater fish, but without a trace of human activity. Under these layers appeared again a cultural one and the archæologists realized that this last culture had absolutely nothing to do with the late Sumerian and gave it the name of pre-Sumerian. Thus the excavations demonstrated that in the epoch of pre-Sumers the Great Flood occurred and the expression of the myth ' everything has been transformed into mud ' corresponds perfectly to a reality of those times. This Flood occurred about 7500 B.C. and thus the date given in the Bible, 3852 B.C., must be considered erroneous. The thickness of the clay layers proves that the Flood lasted probably several centuries.

The similarity of the story told in the Sumerian texts concerning the Great Flood to the Biblical story is evident : moreover, the recent discoveries in Ras-Shamra (ancient Phœnicia) have furnished us with the Phœnician version of the same legend which is also similar to the Hebraic. Certainly at the time of Noah, Gilgamesh, and other heroes, the waters did not cover the entire surface of the globe and it would be impossible for them to have reached the summits of the highest mountains in accordance with the Book of Genesis. One scientist has calculated that in such an event the earth-crust could not support the weight of a water-layer 6 miles thick and, moreover, it would be impossible for such a quantity of water to disappear after the Flood. As a matter of fact, where could this water-layer have run after the appeasing of Jehovah's wrath ?

The opinion of geologists is that universal floods never occurred and such events always had only a local character. Generally speaking there are numerous hypotheses concerning the causes of the famous Mesopotamian cataclysm, but it is interesting to note that the scientist Frazer, for instance, is of the opinion that it occurred as a consequence of some cosmic phenomenon and was not of earthly origin. I think that the main question before us is that of the contemporaneity of several floods concerning which mankind has retained a more or less vivid recollection. If we demonstrate that the great floods of the Celtic, Asiatic, and American tribes occurred at the same time as the Biblical Flood, the flood of Phoroneus and Deucalion, the calamity caused by Phæthon and Typhon and the cataclysm mentioned by the Codex Popul-Vuh, i.e. about 7000–9000 B.C., we prepare a ground for the hypothesis that all these catastrophes were connected with that of Atlantis. We are led to this con-

THE SHADOW OF ATLANTIS

clusion also by some particularities in various analogous
descriptions : different traditions mention the darkness which
reigned upon the Earth during the Flood, others indicate the
volcanic and seismic activity which was developed by subterranean
forces during the Universal Deluge, still others affirm that one
half of the Earth's surface was burnt and that some terrific signs
appeared in the sky. I dedicate the next chapter of my work to a
brief résumé of these traditions.

But it is also possible that vague recollections of the so-called
Pluvial (post-Glacial) Period are at the bottom of all these
flood-legends. If this hypothesis is true we must deduce that
before the last Glacial Period mankind was cultured enough to
preserve, at least in a mythical shape, a record of such an extended
and terrible calamity. The Book of Genesis, e.g., tells (ch. ii, 6)
that after the creation of the world, but before the creation of
men, water vapours rose from the surface of the Earth and
moistened it. Is not this an allusion to the Pluvial, or post-
Glacial, Period ?

*   *   *

It is a remarkable fact that almost all ancient tribes possess
more or less similar traditions concerning the Great Flood. The
ancient Greek legend tells us about the terrible inundation which
occurred during the reign of Phoroneus, the king of the Pelasgi
of Argos, and about Deucalion and his wife Pyrrha. The Celtic
legend concerning the Flood mentions the hero Dwifah, the
Persian, Yima, the Hindu, Waiwasata, etc. We find allusions
to the Flood in the Scandinavian *Edda*, in the Hindu poems of
the Rig-Veda, the Mahabharata, in the books of Hari-Purana, and
in the Part III of the Book of Manu. The French writer, Fabre
d'Olivet, believed that the yearly so-called ' Feast of the Lanterns '
in Japan represents nothing else than a recollection of that
gigantic catastrophe. Only some of the African and Polynesian
tribes do not preserve any memory of the Great Flood.

The American Indians possess numerous and various legends
concerning this prehistoric calamity, and the heroes who played
a preponderant role during that time. Thus, for instance, the
Mayas tell about the epoch of the inundation of forests, when
millions of men perished, and about an unknown calamity. This
is described in the Book of Chilam Balam from Chumayel.

The Paraguayan and Brazilian Guaranys possess a cycle of legends concerning their national hero Tamanduare who, with his family, were the only survivors spared by the catastrophe which destroyed ' The City of Shining Roofs.' The Mexicans assert that only the hero Nala and his wife Nena survived the Great Flood, the Patagonians tell a similar story about their hero Zeu-Kha, the Canadian Indians about Manibosho, the Delawares about Powako, the Columbian Chibchas possess a very interesting myth concerning Bochica (see the preceding chapters of this book), the Tarasks concerning the blessed Tespi, etc. We find similar traditions among the Caribs, the Seminols of Florida, the Iroquois, Haitians, and even the Esquimaux. The Orinoco Indians call that enigmatical period of the Earth's history ' The Time of Catena-Ma-Noa,' the legendary cycles of Cox-Cox in Mexico and the famous Codex Chimal-Popoca in Guatemala, which mention the name of the hero Nata, also tell about a tremendous prehistoric inundation.

The Vth chapter of the Mayan Codex, the Book of Chilam Balam from Chumayel, relates the history of a tremendous cataclysm through which the forefathers of the Mayas lived. Later on I will dedicate to this remarkable book a special chapter, but at present I will limit myself to some details of it which resemble the corresponding fragments of the account handed down by Moses. It is not a case of ' analogies,' but rather of ' parallelisms.'

The Mayan Codex tells in this chapter of a certain terrific cataclysm which occurred at the epoch when the forefathers of their nation inhabited, evidently, some unknown maritime country. The book affirms, in somewhat esoteric language, that this calamity was sent by the gods and especially by a certain god who, according to the Mayan mythology, rules the eastern part of the subterranean world. I consider this an indication of the seismic character of the catastrophe, and also an indication of the location of the fatherland of the Mayas : it was situated, evidently, somewhere east from the present abode of this nation. The book describes the calamity which overtook the forefathers of the Mayas in language which sometimes resembles by its epic simplicity and solemnity the style of the Book of Genesis.

Only an insignificant fraction of the former population of that unknown country could have been spared, emigrating westwards, probably to Yucatan. The catastrophe, as far as we can recognize and decipher the esoteric language of the codex, consisted of earthquakes, inundations, volcanic eruptions, and the sinking of the firm land. The great waters submerged the country during the catastrophe, but when it was over, a rainbow shone in the sky ' as a sign of the destruction below.' This fragment of the codex reminds one of the words of the Book of Genesis, where it is stated that the rainbow shone at the end of the Flood as a sign that Jehovah promised not to send any more such calamities.

Then, at the end of a series of calamities, there arose out the waters three trees : black, white, and yellow, and a bird sat on each tree. The colour of each bird corresponded to the colour of the tree it occupied. The ' Great Mother Seiba,' a Mayan symbol for mankind, addressed a prayer to the Almighty, asking Him not, in future, to inflict such terrific catastrophes upon her children, i.e. men.

Such, in brief, is the Mayan myth. Comparing it with the corresponding fragments of the Hebraic and Sumero-Babylonian legends concerning the Great Flood, we perceive immediately some resemblances. The rainbow shone at the end of both cataclysms, but in the Hebraic version it was a symbolical sign of the end of Jehovah's wrath, while in the Mayan version it shone as a ' sign of the destruction below.' But both versions ascribe to the rainbow a symbolical significance.

Noah and Ut-Napishtim at the end of the Flood released a white bird, a pigeon, and a black one, a raven : at the end of the Mayan catastrophe white, black, and yellow birds appeared from nowhere and sat on trees of corresponding colours.

Jehovah promised to Noah that such a calamity would never be repeated : in the Mayan myth mankind begged for the same promise from the Supreme Being.

Such parallelisms in the versions of such widely separated nations concerning the same calamity lead us to deduce a common source for at least three of these legends. Further, we will see that the Flood myths of other American tribes than the Mayas also possess analogies with the Babylonian and Hebraic versions. On the whole there are a great many salient analogies between the Book of Genesis and the folklore of the American tribes concerning world-creation, Paradise, the first men, etc., but I shall leave a detailed study of them for a later chapter.

At the moment I must limit myself to myths which are of immediate interest to our present inquiry. Among these myths the legend of the Tarasks about the Great Flood is particularly interesting.

This Central American tribe of Indians believes that God is Unique: not only are there no other deities, but their very existence is an impossibility. God created the first pair of humans out of clay. But very soon, when men multiplied and sank into sin, God punished them by the Universal Flood. Everybody, save the blessed priest Tespi and his family, perished in the great waters which submerged the Earth. Tespi and his family were saved because he built beforehand a large boat. He placed therein all his family, a pair of each kind of animal and the seeds of all plants. When the Flood began to decrease, Tespi sent a raven (*urubu*) in order to find out if there was yet any dry land. But the *urubu* was attracted by the numberless corpses floating upon the waters, and his greed prevented his return to the boat of Tespi. Then the blessed priest of the Unique God tried other birds one after another, but none of them returned, save the little humming-bird, which brought back to the boat a small green leaf, and Tespi understood then that the Flood was over.

This remarkable legend of the Tarasks is taken from the book of the writer Herrera, *Décadas*, Part II, chapter 10, and is almost identical with the Hebraic version.

Lewis Spence considers that the dim remembrances of the catastrophe of Atlantis inspired the native American legends concerning the Great Flood. All such traditions always centre around a hero or a saviour, whose name often resembles the name of the Biblical Noah. It is enough to mention the Mexican Nala and the Guatemalan Nata. The presence of this legendary hero in almost every myth gives us ground for the supposition that at some time during certain difficult circumstances, a remarkable man arose among prehistoric mankind and by his activities contributed to the saving of many of his fellow-men. Later on, legend and myth surrounded the name of this unknown hero with a poetic aureole and his deeds formed a cycle of epic traditions. I will cite some other legends of the American and Asiatic tribes.

The legends of the North American Atapasks tell about a certain divine raven, Ietl, who saved their forefathers from the Flood and brought them the precious gift of fire from Heaven.

The story of the Algonquins is different. Their god and hero Manibosho plunged into a lake, causing it to overflow its shores and to inundate the Earth. Then Manibosho sent a raven in order to seek the dry land, but the bird returned without success. Manibosho sent another raven with the same results, and finally —a muskrat. The latter returned and brought to Manibosho something, out of which the god created the world again. Manibosho is considered to be a symbol of the Sun.

The Californian Ascochimi Indians affirm that the Flood inundated the whole Earth and everybody perished. But the god Coyot sowed birds' feathers and a new mankind appeared from the offshoots.

The Aztecs affirmed that there were three epochs, each of which was terminated by a terrible cataclysm : therefore these epochs were called ' The Epochs of Sudden Death.' The third one was ended by a great inundation called ' Hun Esil ' (' The Drowning of Trees '). During this time all the forests disappeared under the waters. This myth resembles the Mayan story related in the Book of Chilam Balam. The Mexican giant Shelua saved himself from the Flood by climbing the mountain of the water-god, Tlaloc (the Mexican Poseidon). After the Great Flood, Shelua built the famous pyramid of Cholula.

The Quiché Indians believe that before the Flood there were in existence only artificial wooden men, a kind of manikin, which were created by the gods for their amusement. They were destroyed by the Flood and later on the gods created mankind.

The Indians of Costa Rica tell us that the god Noncomala created the Earth and the waters, but forgot to create the luminaries and darkness reigned throughout the world until the Spirit of water, named Rutbi, gave birth to the Sun and Moon. Then men were created, but their behaviour provoked the anger of Noncomala and he sent a Flood. Everything was to be destroyed, but the good god Noubou kept the ' seeds of men.' When the Flood was over, Noubou sowed these seeds : from their mature offshoots originated men, and from the unripe ones, monkeys !

The Indians of the Caribbean Islands, now extinct, had a myth concerning the Great Flood which resembles that of the Arowaks. The hero of the Carib legend measured the depths of the waters by throwing into them the seeds of a certain tree. Another version of the myth tells us that an ibis created by its beak a series of mounds and mankind saved itself from the inundation by climbing on these mounds. The Caribs asserted that the Great Flood was caused by torrential rains.

The Tupis affirm that the Moon falls periodically upon the Earth and thus provokes floods. After the last Flood the god Tupan was the only survivor.

The Arowaks of the Guianas, Northern Brazil, and Colombia, possess a myth concerning a certain god named Sigoo. When the Great Flood occurred, Sigoo took all the animals and birds up a high mountain. A dreadful period of darkness and storm began and all the Earth's surface was inundated. Finally, Sigoo began to throw the seeds of a certain plant into the water, measuring its depth by the sound of their fall. When he heard that the seeds touched bottom, he knew that the flood was at its end. One tribe of the Arowaks, the Makusi Indians, affirm that after the deluge there remained only one man, but he transformed stones into men and populated the Earth once more. This myth resembles the Greek one concerning Deucalion and Pyrrha. The Arowaks of Guiana affirm that the Great Spirit destroyed the world by fire : thus everybody perished save those men who in good time hid themselves in subterranean caverns. After the fire-catastrophe came the Universal Flood : this time everyone perished, except the hero Marerevana and the few men he was able to take in his boat. This Arowak myth resembles a little the Greek one concerning Phæthon and the Egyptian one concerning Typhon.

The ancient Egyptians had their own legend concerning the Great Flood. The god Tem (otherwise Temou, Atem, or Atmou) drew the waters out of the abyss and inundated the Earth in order to destroy mankind. Everybody perished, save those who were in the boat of Tem.

The Persian myth concerning the hero Yima tells that Ormuzd ordered this hero to teach the divine law to mankind, but Yima refused to do so and consented only to protect mankind. When Yima knew that a terrible winter menaced the Earth (is not this an allusion to the Glacial Period ?) and that after it would occur a Great Flood, he built a large edifice. There he accumulated the best examples of animals and plants and lived there during 1000 years in full happiness together with the portion of mankind devoted to him.

The Scandinavians possess a myth concerning Imir, a giant, who was killed by the sons of the god Borra, Odin, Vili, and Ve. Imir's blood inundated the whole Earth and all the Ice-Giants, that enigmatical race who, according to Scandinavian mythology, inhabited our planet before the Flood, perished except for the giant Bergelmir. He embarked in a boat with his wife and thus was saved. This mention of the race of Ice-Giants is of great interest : does it not hide a suggestion of fact concerning a certain race which inhabited our globe before and during the last Glacial Period?

One of the Hindu myths greatly resembles the Babylonian story of the god Ea. It tells us that the god Vishnu underwent many transformations, or avatars. The first avatar is connected with the Great Flood. At that time Vishnu took on the aspect of the fish Matsia and was imprisoned in a pond. Waiwaswata, the Great Manou of Kali-Yuga (the Seventh, or modern Epoch), happened to see Vishnu in that pond, thinking, of course, that he was just a little fish. The fish, however, spoke to him, begging him to save it, promising future protection as a recompense. Waiwaswata rescued the fish from the pond, and the grateful Vishnu warned him about the coming Flood. Following the instructions of Vishnu, Manou built an ark. In the meantime the fish grew ever larger and larger, and finally reached such a size that only the ocean could contain it. When the Flood began, Waiwaswata tied his ark to a horn on the head of the fish and it quickly brought the ark to a large tree, where Manou finally moored his boat. Thus, Waiwaswata was the only survivor from the Flood.

Another Hindu myth, concerning the god Krishna, slightly resembles that of the first chapters of the Book of Genesis. The child Krishna was very frolicsome and once even stole a sacred tree from the garden of the god Indra. During his adolescence Krishna was very much loved by mankind, and the jealous Indra, out of revenge, sent a torrential rain which lasted seven days and seven nights. But Krishna raised the mountain Govardhana and sustained it in the air on his little finger. All mankind climbed on this mountain and thus were saved from the inundation.

I have cited only a few of the legends concerning the Great Flood, although there are many more in existence. My reader will have already noticed that all of them have several features in common. Everywhere the Flood was considered a punishment or vengeance inflicted by the gods; everywhere there was a man, or a demi-god, who enjoyed the confidence of the gods and was warned in time concerning the coming catastrophe; all the myths relate that this hero took care to preserve certain animals and plants, and almost every myth mentions that the only survivors after the Flood were this hero and his family, or a group of chosen friends.

Such analogies could certainly be explained by the theory of collective creative genius as being possessed by every primeval nation in the period of the creation of this myth : as the psychology of various races is, generally speaking, the same everywhere, the process of the creation of myths should be also the same everywhere. But it seems clear that some real event, known almost to all nations of the prehistoric world, gave birth to all these myths.

The similarity of the Flood legends gives us the right to suppose that if not all, at least the majority of them relate an event which occurred simultaneously in various parts of the world and was due to some cosmic cause. I even think that the kernel of all these traditions must have been bequeathed to prehistoric mankind by some race which produced the hero of the Flood, and in this connection the idea of the Atlanteans involuntarily haunts my mind. . . .

*   *   *

The Geological investigations show that the Iberian peninsula was under the waters of the ocean not long ago and emerged later than the other parts of Europe. This process first began in the northern part of the peninsula simultaneously with the appearance of the Pyrenean mountains, and slowly extended southwards. After Northern Spain appeared the present Galicia, then Northern Castilia, Catalonia, and Aragon, and finally the other parts of Spain and Portugal. The scientist Dumas affirms that during the Secondary Period Africa formed one continent with Europe and the Straits of Gibraltar did not yet exist. This union lasted, probably, not only throughout the Tertiary, but even until the middle of the actual Quaternary Period ; this hypothesis does not exclude the possibility of frequent ruptures of that union and of the formation of the Straits. Moreover, it is not entirely impossible that the ancient union of Europe with Africa may be re-established in the future.

Although we cannot produce historical testimony of the non-existence of the Straits of Gibraltar in those days, nevertheless, according to some legends and archæological monuments of which I will speak later on, we can consider that the rupture of the Iberian-African isthmus was witnessed by a mankind already cultured.

In fact there can be no doubt that the Straits of Gibraltar continue to widen even to-day. We possess a whole series of records of the width of these Straits, left by ancient and mediæval writers of various centuries. At the beginning of the fifth century B.C. the width was only half a mile, but the writer Euton, in 400 B.C., estimated it at 4 miles ; Turiano Greslio, in 300 B.C., at 5 miles ; and Titus Livius, at the beginning of the Christian Era, at 7 miles. Victor Vitensa, in A.D. 400, gives the width of the Straits as equal to 12 miles, and at present it is 15 miles wide. Therefore the width has increased during the last 2400 years by 14½ miles, or by an average of 0.6 mile per century. Certainly, according to Wegener's hypothesis, one could say that the floating continents must be drifting apart, but we have seen already that this hypothesis can be subjected to many criticisms and is far from being universally accepted. . . . I feel that it is more plausible to seek the causes of the enlargement of the Straits in some seismic activity.

Probably some millenniums ago the ancient isthmus between Spain and Africa suddenly split : this was due certainly to some cataclysm and since then the slow separation of the two continents has continued uninterruptedly. The dim details of the Mediterranean myths favour this hypothesis. At present the Straits almost throughout are safe for navigation, but in olden times they must have been very dangerous : the historian Avien, describing the fairway of Gibraltar, declares that it was full of submarine rocks and very dangerous for seafarers, and Pliny the Junior mentions the sand-banks abounding in the Straits. This indicates that simultaneously with the enlargement of the

Straits their depth has been slowly increasing, which can only be considered to be a result of continuing seismic activity. The Arab historian, Sherif el-Edrissi, relating the early history of Morocco, mentions some cataclysm which occurred in a very remote epoch. Evidently at the time of this writer certain traditions concerning this catastrophe still circulated among the population, because the statements of Sherif el-Edrissi have an air of precision : he relates, for instance, that at the period of the cataclysm the level of the sea rose by eleven stadia, and many cities along the shores were submerged, causing the destruction of thousands of lives. We can reasonably suppose that these legends concern the rupture of the isthmus at Gibraltar, when the waters of the Atlantic rushed through the breach into the low Mediterranean depression and inundated the countries east of the Straits. The existence of some union between the territories of Spain and Morocco in the past is undoubted : it is enough to say, that the geological structure of the Cadiz province in Spain and that of the ancient Tingitania (the present Morocco) on the opposite side of the Straits, are absolutely identical. But my task is to prove that this separation occurred within the memory of the ancient Mediterranean races.

I consider that the famous picture at Tarragona in Spain is a proof of this hypothesis. This picture was found during the last century on the walls of a very ancient mausoleum, and was studied by the archæologist Buenaventura Hernandez. It represents the zodiacal constellation of Cancer at the moment of the summer solstice, and under the sign of the Cancer, the king Hercules. By a mighty movement of his arms Hercules separates the rocks of the isthmus : near the European rock Calpe are depicted a cock and rabbit, which are characteristic for Spain, and near the opposite rock Abila, the figures of the ibis and the scorpion, typical for Morocco.

But it would be interesting to determine which Hercules is painted on the walls of the Tarragona mausoleum, because the ancients knew many heroes with this name : the historian Varron mentions forty-three heroes called Hercules. The Spanish writer, Rafael Urbano, who studied the Tarragona find, believes that it depicts the famous hero and demi-god, who received the commission of the king Euristheus to bring him the golden apples from the gardens of the nymphs Hesperides, daughters of Hesper, the god of evening-twilight. Hercules undertook a voyage to the remote West, and met, near the Straits, the giant Atlas, who supported the Universe on his mighty shoulders. Atlas agreed to help Hercules to get the golden apples and, during the absence of the giant, Hercules himself supported the Universe. Rafael Urbano mentions the old Iberian legends, according to which Hercules enlightened Spain and accomplished two more exploits: he separated Europe from Africa and held up for a while the course of the chariot of the shining Phœbus, i.e. stopped the Sun itself.

It seems quite evident that a description of some important real events is hidden behind the poetical veil of this myth. I consider that the legend of the stopping of the Sun by Hercules was born from the fact that the rupture of the isthmus occurred at the moment of the summer solstice, which is confirmed by the Tarragona picture. But in the course of millenniums the expression 'it occurred during the solstice' (i.e. when the Sun appears to be immobile), was transformed into 'Hercules stopped the Sun's movement and tore the isthmus.' Further, it is evident also that some exploits of Hercules were accomplished in a country where, according to the beliefs of that epoch, eternal evening reigned, i.e. the god Hesper. Such a country might be the present Morocco, which was thought by the ancients to be the end of the world, or Atlantis, the kingdom of the mighty Atlas, or even America, the land of the legendary 'Merops.'

As to the golden apples of the nymphs Hesperides, I think they were nothing else than the oranges, or tangerines, which are so common in Morocco: even the term 'tangerine' indicates the production of the first fruits of this kind by the Moroccan port Tangier.

Another explanation is possible. We know that the ancient emperors of the Inca dynasty possessed beautiful gardens with metal trees and golden fruits. It is quite possible that the Atlantean emperors also had such gardens and the custom of having artificial plants was inherited by the Peruvians from the Atlanteans: studying the prehistoric American cultures we are coming involuntarily to the hypothesis that some cultural connection existed between them and that of the Atlanteans. In such an event the myth concerning the golden apples of Hesperides, whose garden was situated near the great Atlas

Mountains, could be explained by the fact that Hercules visited Atlantis and the magnificent gardens of Poseidonis. However, the first explanation seems to me more plausible : according to some historical accounts Hercules arrived at Gibraltar through Lybia, i.e. by land. Therefore he should have visited Morocco, bringing from this remote country the first 'golden apples,' hitherto unseen by his countrymen, but very common in Morocco and Algeria.

The actual existence of Hercules seems to be an established fact, because his wanderings in the remote West are described not only by legends, but also by certain historians. In order to explain the name given by the ancients to the Straits of Gibraltar, ' The Pillars of Hercules,' I can advance two hypotheses : either the rupture of the isthmus coincided in time with the visit of such a famous personality as was the king Hercules, or else he was the first known man who ventured to pass through the Straits into the mysterious and terrifying Atlantic.

Later on Hercules was deified as a protector of the Iberian nations. Strabo and the historian Pomponius Mela, relate that the natives of the Iberian peninsula venerated Hercules greatly long before the coming of the Romans, and had a temple dedicated to him in Cadiz. No such temples existed in any other part of the peninsula, his cult being limited to a simple dragging of twelve big stones from one place to another, which symbolized his twelve exploits. The Straits themselves were venerated as a holy site : Avien relates that the ships had no right to remain in the Straits beyond a certain limited time. An offence against this law was considered to be blasphemy and the sea itself in such cases turned stormy. The Romans called the Straits *Frætum*, and considered them sacred. The writer Artemidor went as far as to affirm that the sun seems to be thirty times larger when viewed from the rock Calpe, the highest point of Gibraltar. . . .

The Hercules cycle is not Greek in origin : it was probably introduced into Greece and later on into Rome by the Phœnicians, but it is possible that it was the Greeks who gave these very ancient traditions a poetical form. Among the exploits of Hercules there are three which give much food to thought, namely, the victories of this demi-god over the lion of Nemea, the Stymphalides (birds with copper beaks), and the

monster Hydra. Lions did not exist in Attica at the epoch of
the forefathers of the Greeks, and as to the two other exploits,
their victims suggest giant prehistoric birds and large oceanic
octopi. Perhaps the whole Herculean epos is nothing else than a
personification of that struggle which the emigrants from Atlantis
had to sustain against the last representatives of the antediluvian
fauna in Europe. The cavern lion and giant birds could have
existed among these last survivors of the Tertiary Period.
Generally speaking, we feel throughout the cycle of the Hercules'
legends a reflection of some titanic struggle of primeval man
against various enemies, whether animals or elements.

Rafael Urbano mentions the oldest Iberian traditions relating
the arrival on the peninsula of unknown peoples. This invasion
probably occurred either simultaneously with the rupture of the
isthmus, or immediately afterwards. Perhaps the present Basques
derive from the Asil-Tardenos race which, according to the
supposition of Lewis Spence, came to Europe from Atlantis
about 10,000 years ago.

What was the character of the Mediterranean depression
before the collapse of the Iberian-African isthmus? Did it
contain more or less extensive water basins? Was it populated
and, if so, by what tribes?

I am of the opinion that the formation of the Mediterranean
Sea caused the so-called ' Deluge of Ogyges,' which I discussed
in preceding chapters. The sudden increase of the water-area
in the neighbourhood of the Balkan peninsula and Asia Minor
provoked unusual evaporation and accumulated in the atmosphere
a colossal quantity of water-vapour. Thus the torrential rains
could be explained. The seismic blow which tore apart the
ancient isthmus might have been caused by an extraordinarily
high tide of the subterranean magma, which in its turn resulted
from some perturbation in the solar system. I have already
advanced the hypothesis that such a perturbation could be
caused by the approach of the Halley's comet, and this latter
could be the ' heavenly sign ' of St. Austin's *De Civitate
Dei.*

Some authors believe that the Deluge of Ogyges occurred
at the end of the fifth millennium B.C., i.e. about the time of the
Biblical Great Flood (3852 B.C., according to Moses). But we
have already seen that the latest discoveries of Langdon and

Woolley have proved that the Flood of the Bible, or the Babylonian one, took place in the seventh millennium B.C.

Calculation shows that Halley's comet approached the Earth on 7 June 4015 B.C.: thus the difference with Moses' date is only sixty-three years. The Tarragona picture represents the rupture of the ancient isthmus as occurring on the day of the summer solstice, i.e. 23 June. Thus the difference between that day of the closest approach of the Halley's comet and the day of the collapse of the isthmus, is only sixteen days. But, taking into consideration on the one hand various deviations and irregularities in the movements of the comets in general and the imperfection of our chronology on the other, we can consider that this comet approached the Earth sixteen days later, i.e. on the day of the summer solstice, or on 23 June. The irregularities of our calendar could easily accumulate during 6000 years sixteen days of difference. Perhaps the Deluge of Ogyges and the formation of the Mediterranean Sea occurred simultaneously with Plato's catastrophe of Atlantis.

When in Valparaiso (Chile), I had an opportunity to meet the Chilean archæologist Luis Thayer Ojeda. A very interesting man and an independent thinker, a stranger to any form of routine, L. T. Ojeda has been working for a long time on Mediterranean toponymy, investigating the origin of various historical and geographical terms. Besides this, L. T. Ojeda has investigated the origin of Biblical and mythological names. This work requires a great patience and a profound knowledge of the ancient and modern tongues and their philology. Among the conclusions of Ojeda, I find it necessary to mention those which are connected with our subject.

Comparing the myths of various Mediterranean nations, the Chilean scientist has found many important analogies and has concluded that the classical mythology is nothing more than the poetized history of the nations who lived in the Mediterranean depression before its inundation by the waters of the ocean. The myths concerning the gods and heroes of the Greeks and Egyptians and the Biblical traditions of the Book of Genesis are, according to Ojeda, nothing else than short histories concerning various prehistoric tribes. The majority of the names of various gods, heroes, kings, and patriarchs, represents the names of tribes themselves and the names of their queens,

SIDE AND BACK VIEWS OF CARVED MONOLITHS FROM
COPAN (HONDURAS)

CARVED ALTARS OF COPAN (HONDURAS)

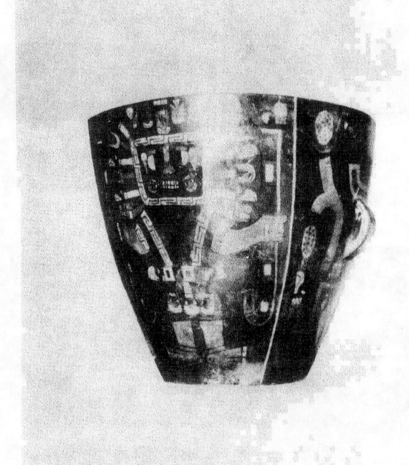

A PREHISTORIC VESSEL FOUND IN PERU
(Museum of Lima.)
The face is identical with the main figure on the temple of Tihuanaco.

goddesses, etc.—the names of prehistoric states, countries, and provinces.

The mythical language is a very symbolical one : if, for instance, the legend relates, that the king Amphytrion married the beautiful Alkmena, it very likely signifies that the tribe of Amphytrions conquered a country called Alkmena which was remarkable by its fertility, or prosperity. If Genesis told us that Israel possessed twelve sons, it means that the Hebraic nation was composed of twelve tribes, or clans. The name of a leader, or of the founder of any nation, is a collective one and applies to the whole nation : thus, for instance, the expression in the Book of Genesis : ' Abraham emigrated to the city of Sigor,' signifies that the Ibri nation (Jews) removed its camp to Sigor, etc. The duration of the patriarch's life is nothing else than the period of the independence of the corresponding tribe : if, for instance, the Book of Genesis affirms that Methuselah lived for 969 years, it means, that the tribe Methuselah was conquered, or destroyed by some conqueror, after almost a thousand years of comparatively prosperous existence.

Luis Thayer Ojeda thinks that many European tribes, which were hitherto supposed to have arrived in Europe from Asia, came on the contrary from certain western countries. They gradually populated the regions of Europe, Western Asia, and Northern Africa and gave to these regions the names of the remote lands of their origin in Atlantis, or in America. Thus the Chilean scientist supposes that many historical and geographical terms of the Mediterranean basin were taken from western countries. Those emigrants, who came to Europe after the catastrophe in Atlantis, gave to their new abodes the names of their old ones. This custom exists to-day : thus we see that the emigrants from Europe have given the names of their ancient European cities and provinces to the American ones. Hence, New Spain, New Castile, New Granada, New England, New York, New Brunswick, New Orleans, and other similar names in America.

By means of a very careful philological analysis Ojeda has proved the existence of an Egypt, a Lybia, an Ethiopia, a Persia, an India, etc., in the Mediterranean depression before its inundation. Later on, after the disappearance of them all, these names were inherited by the present Egypt, Lybia, Ethiopia, Persia, India, etc.

In the line of his discoveries, Ojeda worked out a hypothetical map of the Mediterranean depression before the rupture of the isthmus. It is a very interesting work and I am giving below some of its details.

It shows, for instance, a large lake between the present Balearic islands, Corsica, and the southern French coast. This lake was called ' The Triton's Sea,' and its southern boundary touched the African shores. Some years ago the German archæologist, Dr. A. Herrmann, found in Shott el Djerid in Tunis, the vestiges of the Triton's Sea. Sicily was the continuation of the Apennine peninsula and was united with Africa by a wide band of firm land. In the middle of this band existed also a lake called ' Charon's Sea.' The Balkan peninsula, Morea, and the islands of Cyprus and Crete were one with Asia Minor, and on the site of the present Archipelago extended a low and swampy country, which was a little hilly in its eastern part.

All the toponymic conjectures of L. T. Ojeda are more or less plausible and some of them were justified by direct investigations and soundings of the Mediterranean Sea. Such, for instance, was the conjecture of the Chilean scientist concerning the subterranean kingdom of Pluto, or Tartarus. The Greek traditions tell us that this gloomy kingdom possessed three infernal rivers with parallel courses, but with the following peculiarity: the river in the middle ran in a direction opposite to the directions of the other two. According to the opinion of the scientists, the region of Tartarus is the present region of the volcano Etna in Sicily, but Ojeda added to this region also the surroundings of Etna, which were submerged at the time of the Mediterranean catastrophe. The Chilean scientist asserts that the three infernal rivers should be somewhere in the now submerged territory. The recent hydrographic soundings brilliantly justified the Greek legend and the hypothesis of Ojeda : near Etna, on the seabottom, were discovered three parallel and extended cavities, the central one of which has an inclination opposite to the two others.

The wide band of firm land which united Sicily with Africa and was called Charon, was inhabited by a tribe with the same name : since the inundation of the depression and of that band, the name ' Charon ' has been applied to the infernal ferry-man, who transported in his boat the souls of the dead into Tartarus, i.e. into Sicily.

I recommend every student of mythology to the books of L. T. Ojeda : *La Geografía Premediterranea*, Valparaiso, 1927, and *Ensaio de Cronología Mitologica*, Valparaiso, 1928. Unfortunately these two books have not yet been translated into English ; but the work of this Chilean scientist is worthy of close attention.

I have had an opportunity to talk about Ojeda's hypothesis with that well-known specialist of prehistoric archæology, Professor Obermeyer of Madrid. This scientist cannot agree with it because, according to him, in the Mediterranean basin there have been found petrified shells of the Pliocene Epoch, which proves the existence of the Mediterranean Sea many millions of years ago. I do not think that this argument of Professor Obermeyer's destroys Ojeda's hypothesis, because from the Pliocene till the present geological epoch have occurred many transformations of sea and firm land ; but Ojeda's hypothesis has in view only the last transformation, witnessed by the ancient population of Europe. . . .

But, and this is important for our subject, this transgression was witnessed also by that famous and enigmatical hero of prehistoric mankind, the king Hercules. Perhaps the mausoleum of Tarragona at one time contained his remains ?

The ancient empires and large prehistoric cities are sleeping now under the turquoise waves of the Mediterranean Sea, but perhaps one day will emerge again from the waters, following some new seismical convulsion of the earth-crust.

*   *   *

CHAPTER VI

I AM of the opinion that our culture was inherited by the European tribes from some western race which came into the Mediterranean basin from the countries beyond Gibraltar. This race arrived during the Neolithic Period and was of the dolichocephalic type. Almost all mysterious nations of the Mediterranean basin were remarkable for the reddish colour of their skin and the scantiness of the beard save the Jews and Arabs. The pre-Egyptians, Pelasgi, Lycians, Crete-Egeans, Phœnicians, Philistines, the Biblical ' Kaftorim,' i.e. the inhabitants of Kaftor (Crete), the enigmatical ' Masinti ' of the old Egyptian frescoes, and on the other side of the ocean, the Toltecs, Mayas, etc., were reddish. The Aryan peoples, on the contrary, are rich in facial hair and are white-skinned and brachicephalic.

The usual history of the nations who play at present a more or less important role does not stretch beyond a thousand years B.C. Only the excavations and the deciphering of old inscriptions permit us sometimes to look a little deeper into the Egyptian and Mesopotamian past. Meanwhile the recent archæological discoveries have shown that, before the appearance in the Mediterranean basin of the oldest nations, such as, for instance, the Egyptians and Semites, cultured states already existed there. Moreover, we come involuntarily to the conclusion that all those nations were influenced by a common and mighty culture, whose focus remains for us entirely inexplicable. Thus the culture of the late nations appeared as the result of two factors at least, of the influence of that unknown civilization and of the activity of mighty cultural currents coming forth from Asia.

The primeval races which inhabited the territories of the present France, England, and Spain, created a culture remarkable for numerous megalithic buildings, the remains of which we see in Stonehenge in England and Carnac in Brittany. Similar megalithic buildings we see also in Spain and Portugal, where dolmens and menhirs are frequent. The Celtic priests, or Druids, were believed to have been the builders of these prehistoric structures, but now experts have come to believe that the epoch of their building should be removed to earlier periods of the culture, perhaps to the end of the Neolithic Age. These dolmens and menhirs, as well as the cromlechs, were erected, according to some investigators, for the purpose of immortalizing the memory of the dead ; others think that they were altars and still others that these prehistoric monuments have some relation to primeval astronomy. In any case all these buildings prove the existence at one time of a culture common to Western Europe. The nature of this culture still escapes our historic analysis. The earlier-mentioned discovery of Professor Baudouin permits us to suppose that the source of that unknown culture existed somewhere west from the European shores of the Atlantic, and I am inclined to think that it was the continent of Atlantis which played the role of its cradle.

The influences of Asiatic culture on the development of primeval European culture are beyond question : not only is it established that the ancient Sumerian culture was irradiated westwards, but even its route can be traced into the heart of Europe. This route was via the Danube, along which river penetrated into Europe ideas, customs, and goods. The recent finds in the village of Vincha, near Belgrade, prove incontestably this assertion, as they consist of adornments made of the shells of a certain mollusc, which were used for the same purpose by the inhabitants of ancient Ur. The same adornments have been discovered also as a result of excavations in South Germany and Bohemia.

* * *

The Phœnicians called themselves the ' people of Carou,' and the name of ' Phœnicians ' was given to them by the Greeks apparently after some event in the history of the Phœnicians. Concerning the origin of this name there exist two suppositions : the first derives the name from the Greek word *phoinix* (red), and the second, from the name of the legendary bird Phœnix which, according to the belief of the ancients, is resurrected every 500 years from its own ashes. This legend very likely originated from the Egyptian myth about the bird Bennu dedicated to Osiris. Bennu flew singing out of a burning tree and symbolized resurrection.

Both etymologies are interesting : the first would imply the hypothesis that the Phœnicians belonged to a certain red-skinned race, and the second explanation would easily lead us to suppose that this nation at some time suffered a destructive catastrophe, after which it not only recovered, but even created a mighty colonial empire. The Phœnician legend, repeated by the Hebrews, affirms that the first man was called Adam (made of red clay), and this circumstance favours the first explanation.

Phœnicia was situated along the shores of the Mediterranean Sea extending from the Cape Karmel to the Taurus mountains. Its capital was Toor, or Tzor, hellenized in Tyre.

The legends of Mediterranean tribes contain dim indications that the people of Carou were from time immemorial closely related to the Atlanteans from whom they inherited its remarkable culture. Probably the Phœnicians, being the most advanced of the Semites who possibly inhabited Atlantis, were spared after the collapse of their ancient centre. The rupture in the Gibraltar isthmus and the inundation of the Mediterranean depression that followed destroyed the last ties between the Atlanteans and Phœnicians, and the centuries wiped out even the recollection of the origin of the ' people of Carou.' Among all the nations which once populated the depression only the Phœnicians recovered and flourished again. Thus the new-comers to the Mediterranean shores, the ancient Greeks, viewing a nation which after two destructive catastrophes still found enough energy to re-establish its prosperity, could easily compare it with the legendary bird, the Phœnix. In fact, how could we explain the comparatively high level of the Phœnician civilization and the knowledge by Phœnicians of remote countries in the Atlantic Ocean, unless we assume that they inherited their culture from the Atlanteans ?

Sir Arthur Evans affirms that the Iliad and Odyssey were of Cretan origin, and that about 800 B.C. Homer translated and adapted to the Greek history the oldest traditions of the Cretans. This supposition finds support in the fact that the Achæans of the epoch of the Trojan war had little contact with Phœnician trade, while the Cretans had already for many centuries maintained a brisk intercourse with the Phœnicians. And yet there are in the Odyssey some passages which show that the author of this poem was acquainted with the activities of Phœnicia :

at any rate Homer's peaceful seafarers, the Pheakians, resemble much the Phœnicians, who possessed agencies and factories everywhere in the Mediterranean basin. Apparently some ethnical connections existed between the people of Carou and the Cretans because the Greeks called both nations ' phoinix,' i.e. ' red-skinned.' The old Egyptians, who called the Cretans ' Keftiu,' portrayed on their frescoes both the Phœnicians and the Keftiu with a red skin and minus a beard.

Crete in antiquity was called ' Kaftor ': hence the name ' Kaftorim ' given by the Bible to the Cretans and hence perhaps also the Egyptian ' Keftiu.' Homer records that many tongues were spoken in Crete and that there were there ninety cities (see Canto XIX of the *Odyssey*). Among the nations populating this island Ulysses names the Achæans, Kidons, three Dorian tribes and the ' Divine Pelasgi.' He specifies that the Kidons lived along the Cretan river Jardan, which name sounds very much like the Jordan, or Yordan, of Palestine. Perhaps the Biblical Philistines, with their religious cult resembling so much the Phœnicians, were of Cretan origin. They may have been the descendants of Homer's Kidons who emigrated to Palestine and settling there along the chief river of the country gave to their river the name of Jordan in memory of their own Cretan Jardan.

Homer says that the Cretan king Minos was a descendant of Deucalion (the hero of the Universal Flood) and the beautiful Europa. Deucalion, together with his wife Pyrrha, were the unique survivors after some great catastrophe and Europa at one time was ravished by Zeus. Perhaps the myth concerning Europa hides the history of the conquest of Crete by some mighty prehistoric race. The queen Europa enters later on into the Cretan pantheon and there are two explanations of the meaning of her name : according to some ancient sources the word means ' the daughter of the Red Land ' and this translation corresponds to the Greek nickname for the Cretans, ' phoinix,' but the classical writer Hesichius declares that ' Europa ' signifies ' The Land of Sunset ' and therefore alludes to the western origin of the Cretan queen. Both etymologies agree on the most important point : they both imply the arrival of the Cretans from the West, and therefore from a certain Atlantic, or American, country. The American tribes often possess a reddish skin and, moreover, certain eastern shores of America, e.g. the shores of

Yucatan and Brazil, possess a soil rich in iron oxides and therefore are also red (the *terras roxas* of Brazil). Perhaps some red-skinned races inhabited Atlantis and later on immigrated into Europe. Probably the Cretans and Phœnicians belonged to the second wave of emigrants from Atlantis, which Lewis Spence identifies with the Aurignac race.

The history of the more or less known period of the Phœnician overseas expeditions is full of interest. In the second millennium B.C. the Balkan peninsula was invaded by the Achæan tribes who soon conquered Peloponnessus and some of the distant Phœnician colonies in the Black Sea region. In the twelfth century B.C. the Achæans attacked Troy, a state which was bound politically with Phœnicia and represented the northern rampart of the so-called Carian Union. After the fall of Troy the warlike new-comers began to dislodge the Phœnicians from Asia Minor, and the latter lost all their colonies on the Black Sea and in the Archipelago, and the might of the Land of Carou was shaken. Diodorus of Sicily, studying the very ancient documents found by him in the spared Phœnician archives, came to the conclusion that after the fall of Troy the most important Phœnician expeditions beyond Gibraltar began. They were provoked by the necessity to evacuate the population of Troy according to the engagements of the Phœnicians towards other members of the Carian Union. Simultaneously with the first of these expeditions also went out a Tyrrhenian one : the Tyrrhenians, or Etruscans, who inhabited the Adriatic shores, were apparently related to the Phœnicians. Later on our readers will see that the Phœnicians obtained settlers for their distant colonies from among the Carians, Ionians, Trojans, Tyrrhenians, and other small nations.

It is likely that the Phœnicians maintained relations with certain American countries up to the middle of the first millennium B.C., but after that epoch there began the decline of Phœnicia. Alexander the Great gave the Phœnicians a staggering blow when he destroyed their capital, the magnificent Tyre, but in order to annihilate Phœnicia it was necessary to destroy also its economic might which was based on the dominions overseas. According to Diodorus and some other historians Alexander ordered his Egyptian satrap, Ptolemy, to organize a powerful fleet and to conquer the Phœnician colonies beyond Gibraltar. The fleet was organized but, although it was duly sent and it is known that it passed the Straits, its further destiny is not mentioned in any of the works of the ancient historians. Several Mediterranean colonies of Phœnicians, such as, for instance, Carthage, existed independently for several more centuries until in their turn they succumbed to the sovereignty of the new-born Mediterranean power, the iron Rome.

The fate of Ptolemy's fleet would have remained unknown for ever, had it not been for an accidental find in Uruguay, which unexpectedly supplied a solution of this historic problem. The Brazilian scientist, Candido Costa, in his remarkable work *As Duas Americas* (p. 46), tells us that in 1833 a farmer discovered on the territory of his farm Dores, near Montevideo, a very ancient sepulture. On the surface of the soil was found an ancient slab with an inscription in an unknown alphabet, almost effaced by time. Under the slab was discovered a burial vault within which were found swords, a helmet, and an amphora with traces of ashes. The erudite Father Martins of Montevideo has established that the text is a Greek one and deciphered those words of the inscription which had remained more or less intact. Here is the translation of this fragment : ' Alexander, the son of Philip, was the king of Macedonia at the time of the 113th Olympiad. Here Ptolemy . . .' The remainder of the inscription has been obliterated by time. One of the swords is adorned by a human face, recognized by Father Martins as the profile of Alexander, and the helmet bears a representation of Achilles dragging Hector's body around the walls of Ilion. Many contemporaries of this discovery have affirmed that it was nothing more than a mystification, and some remain even to-day who are of this opinion. But it is hardly plausible to expect practical jokers to go to the expense of producing so many objects just for the sake of mystifying the population of Montevideo at that period.

C. Costa suggests that Ptolemy's fleet was brought by a storm to the coasts of Uruguay and found a temporary refuge in the vast bay of Montevideo. Another plausible explanation of the precious find suggests that the Phœnicians possessed a factory in the mouth of the La Plata, and the Greek-Egyptian admiral went there in order to attack the Phœnician ships. The amphora found within the vault contained, probably, the ashes of Greek warriors who had fallen during the sea-battle, but

C. Costa believes that the ashes belonged to seafarers, perished during a storm.

*   *   *

The Portuguese historians of the epoch of great discoveries relate that in 1461 on the island of Corvo (' The Raven's Island,' or in Spanish ' Cuervo '), which among the Azores is the nearest to America, was found an equestrian statue. It stood on the summit of a high rock, and the rider's right hand pointed towards the shores of the New World. On the rock were found inscriptions in an unknown alphabet. This statue is mentioned also by Sherif el Edrissi and other Arab historians ; the natives of the Azores, who still retain the recollection of it, call this statue 'Cadés' or 'Catés.' It is interesting that this word signifies, in the Quichua tongue, 'follow this direction!' Some years ago there were found on the island of Corvo Phœnician coins and in one grotto of the neighbouring island of São Miguel was discovered a stone slab engraved with the image of some building, probably of a temple. The publisher of the French review *Atlantis*, M. P. Le Cour, who recently visited the Azores, believes that it was the image of an Atlantean temple. This slab was exhibited some years ago in the Los Angeles museum of the Azores, a photograph of it was taken, but soon the slab disappeared. This photograph has been seen by many persons, and the scientist Vasco Bensaude, who lives permanently on the Azores, told M. P. Le Cour that in the archives of the archipelago he saw a description of this prehistoric slab.

The French writer, Chateaubriand, describing in the sixth volume of his *Mémoires d'Outre tombe* his sojourn in the Azores, writes as follows : ' evidently the Carthaginians visited the Azores because Phœnician coins were found on the island of Corvo. The first Europeans who came to Corvo found there an equestrian statue which pointed in a westerly direction .'

In the chapter nine of the *Chronicle of the reign of the king of Portugal, Don João*, written in 1560 by Damião de Goes, we read the following :

' The north-western island of the Azores, Corvo, is called by the seafarers " island of the Indicator," because they take their direction according to it. On the summit of this island in its north-eastern part was placed a statue of a rider on an unsaddled horse. The rider was hatless, and on his shoulders was a mantle in the Moorish style. One hand of the rider grasped the mane of the horse and the other indicated the west. When the king Don Manoel was informed about the statue, he ordered the painter of the court, Senhor Duarte D'Armas, to go to the Azores and make a picture of the statue in its natural size. When the picture had been received, the king sent a man in his confidence to remove the statue and transport it to Portugal. But this man returned from the Azores and reported that a thunderstorm had destroyed the statue and therefore he could bring to Portugal only the fragments of it: the head of the rider, his right hand, the horse's head, two horse's legs and a fragment of the horse's hip. This report was a lie: in fact the statue had been broken to pieces during the operation of removal thanks to the carelessness of the workmen. All the fragments of the statue were sent to the king and their further fate remains unknown. The chief notary of the king, Senhor Pero da Fonseca, visited the Azores in 1529 and heard from the natives that below the statue had been some inscriptions. Pero da Fonseca sent some workmen in order to take wax-impressions of these inscriptions, but the letters were much effaced by time, and the mould showed nothing distinct. Probably the statue, as well as the inscriptions, had been made by Norsemen, because they were accustomed to immortalize everywhere their sojourns.'

I cannot agree with Damião de Goes concerning the Norman origin of the statue and inscriptions on Corvo, because these bold seafarers did not immortalize their sojourns by statues. Moreover, the visit of Norsemen to the Azores could only have taken place between the ninth and twelfth centuries, i.e. a maximum of 600 years before the reign of Don Manoel : during such a short period the inscription carved on a rock could not be effaced. It seems to me that the statue and the inscriptions were Phœnician, unless M. P. Le Cour is right and they were Atlantean.

When Europeans visited the Canary Islands for the first time, they met there a very strange tribe of natives who called themselves 'Guanches,' a word which signifies 'men.' These Guanches themselves were still more astonished to see white men, because they thought themselves to be the unique representatives of mankind, which millenniums ago had survived a terrible catastrophe, which had destroyed everybody on the Earth. This catastrophe consisted of a terrific flood, which had inundated their fatherland, and they managed to escape only because the mountain tops, which are now the Canary Islands, remained above the waters. This mysterious aboriginal tribe was subdivided into two types: one white-skinned, and the other with a skin of brownish shade. The Guanches were beardless, but wore their hair long like Indians. The white-skinned Guanches were tall, whilst the others were below the normal stature. As to their degree of culture, it was a strange mixture of civilization with a semi-savagery: ignoring, for instance, the use of metals and clothes, employing only stone implements, yet the Guanches at the same time possessed the art of writing, some knowledge of astronomy, poetry, a refined legislation and complicated religious rituals. They had even the order of Vestals, like the ancient Romans, and generally esteemed women highly. The chronicles of the discovery of the Canary Islands describe the Guanches as a jolly, kind-hearted, and hospitable tribe who adored music and the dance. The alphabet of the Guanches as preserved to-day consists of letters similar to Semitic languages (Phœnician, Carthaginian, and Hebrew), but recently inscriptions written in other signs have been found on the islands. The Guanches very soon became extinct, or were assimilated by the Europeans, but the first missionaries sent to the Canary Islands, had time to compile in the fifteenth century a little dictionary of the Guanch language in Latin transcription: although this latter circumstance embarrasses the philological analysis of this language, nevertheless the linguists established a certain resemblance between the Guanch language and the dialects of the Berbers and Tuaregs, especially of the Hoggar tribe called Senhadja. Moreover, the influence of Arabic was established. This latter phenomenon might be explained by intercourse between the Guanches and the Arabs, who, according to Sherif el Edrissi, visited the Canary Islands before the Europeans. Therefore it is strange that the Guanches did not remember those visits and were amazed to see the Europeans. As to the resemblance between the languages of the Berbers and Tuaregs of the Sahara (the oasis of Hoggar) with that of the

Guanches, it could be explained by the hypothesis of a common origin of all three tribes. The origin of Berbers is also an ethnographic enigma and some scientists think that they, as well as Lybians ('the people of Lebou' of the ancient Egyptians), belong to the white race. In fact, the Europeans did not discover the Canary Islands: they were known millenniums ago and were called 'The Happy Islands' for their wonderful climate, fertility, and wealth. The king of Mauretania, Uba II (of the first century A.D.), left a description of the Canary Islands: he tells about their numerous population and their wealth. The present island of Tenerife, rich in plantations of date trees, was called in the old times 'Junonia' in honour of the goddess Juno, whose cult was much developed on Tenerife, but it is highly probable that the ancient authors intended in this case not the spouse of Jupiter, but the Phœnician goddess Tanit, the protectress of date-tree plantations. In fact, the words 'an oasis of date-trees' sound in the Berber language tchinit: this word much resembles the name of the Goddess Tanit.

Archæologists have found on the Canary Islands many remains of antiquity. On the Large Island, for instance, there was discovered a settlement of the cavern-men, which consists of several tiers of caverns in the rocks, and is called by the natives 'Atalaya': it is interesting to note that near Biarritz, in the country of Basques, there exists a mound with the same name. The French writer, Luc Durtain, visited Atalaya in the Canary Islands and has related that the natives there even to-day make clay vases much resembling the Indian vases of pre-Colombian America. Luc Durtain assumes that the present inhabitants of Atalaya inherited the shape and style of ornamentation of these vases from the extinct Guanches. Recently there were discovered in a grotto of the island of Tenerife, near San Miguel, sixty mummies, many ancient ceramics and lions' skins, the latter of which provoked the scientists to perplexity because lions never had existed in the islands, and the presence of their skins there could be explained only by trade with the Arabs. The Guanches mummified their dead, covering them with gum-resin like the old Egyptians and that mysterious nation whose sepultures were recently discovered in the Sahara by Count Byron de Prorok. The Guanches tattooed their bodies by means of special clay seals: analogous seals were found among the Neolithic layers of Thracia, Liguria, and Puglia. I personally have seen a rich collection of prehistoric seals in Quito (Ecuador): they are of steatite with various carvings. The proprietor of this collection, Mr. Ernesto Franco, dug them up in Esmeralda (Ecuador) from a depth of more than thirty feet, and the geologists consider that layer to be 20,000 years old. In the oldest tombs of the Canary Islands have been found skulls with certain anthropological peculiarities which, according to Professor B. Kubart, are similar to those of the Cromagnon race. This observation of Kubart's reminds one of the hypothesis of Lewis Spence, who believed that the Cromagnon race was nothing else than the first wave of emigrants from Atlantis, which invaded Europe about 25,000 years ago. The anthropological characteristics of the Cromagnon type are to be found to-day among the inhabitants of the Canary Islands: this phenomenon can be explained by the assimilation of the ancient Guanches by the European new-comers.

Two hypotheses exist concerning the origin of the Guanches: the Moroccan and the Phœnician. The first supposes the Guanches to have come from the South-western Morocco, and some peculiarities of this interesting extinct tribe favour it. Thus, for instance, according to ancient Arab authors, the Guanches ate dogs, a custom which still exists among the Berbers and the inhabitants of Tunis; even the name of the Canary archipelago derives, it seems, from the Latin word *canis* (dog). Further, the adherents of the Moroccan hypothesis indicate the resemblance between the Guanch language and the dialects of the Hoggar Tuaregs and of the Senhadja tribe. However, all these resemblances could easily be explained by the common origin of the Guanches, Senhadja, and Tuaregs: they could all have come from somewhere beyond Africa and later on settled separately on the Canary Islands, Morocco and Hoggar. I am of the opinion that the common fatherland of all three tribes was Atlantis: after its catastrophe one branch, the Guanches, remained on such land as survived the cataclysm and the two others emigrated to Africa.

The second hypothesis puts forward the Guanches as the descendants of the Phœnicians. The arguments in favour of it are as follows: the alphabet of the Guanches resembles the Phœnician and the colour of the skin of some of them was brownish, like that of the Phœnicians (*phoinix* in Greek). Some affirm that the Phœnicians at one time transported several thousands of Carthaginians and other inhabitants of North Africa into the Canary Islands and the Carthaginian admiral Hannon even founded a settlement (400 B.C.) on the West African shore opposite the islands. These facts indicate intercourse between the Phœnicians and the inhabitants of the islands, but are not sufficient to establish the origin of the Guanches : I am rather inclined to believe that the Phœnicians themselves and the Guanches had common forefathers in vanished Atlantis, because there are some indications of the Atlantean origin of the Phœnicians. In 1868, on the rocks in the surroundings of Las Palmas (Canary Islands), were found Phœnician inscriptions and six tall stone columns, which some millenniums ago had served as signal-towers for the ships entering the harbour of Las Palmas. Evidently this port was one of the most important ones used by the Phœnician navigators.

* * *

Some miles from Rio de Janeiro is situated a beautiful locality called Havea, and connected with the capital by a tram-line. Like all the surroundings of Rio de Janeiro, Havea is mountainous, and among its picturesque rocks one is very steep and difficult to climb. Nevertheless, excursions to this rock are frequent and the amateurs of alpinism overcome all its difficulties. The rock of Havea attracts tourists because on its summit, at the height of 2,754 feet, was found, in 1836, a very ancient cuneiform inscription. Each sign of it is about 3 yards wide and the whole inscription is perfectly visible from a considerable distance.

The shape of the neighbouring rock is also interesting : if you observe it from a ship travelling south, you see a colossal human head with a beard and a sharp-pointed helmet. The natives assert that it is the figure of the legendary giant Atlas, carved many millenniums ago. The figure is rather deformed by various erosive and abrasive processes and some efforts are necessary in order to see it well, but some people affirm that they easily recognize in this rock a human head. It is quite impossible to approach the Havea inscription closely : in order to do so certain auxiliary arrangements, such as, for instance, rope-ladders, would be necessary, because the last hold accessible to climbers is separated from the summit by a smooth vertical wall of rock. There is no foothold and therefore it is incomprehensible how the author of the inscription climbed up to the summit and worked there. One can only suppose that this rock was once covered with layers of alluvium which facilitated the climb. Later on, these layers must have been washed away by torrential rains.

The Brazilian scientists have produced several books concerning the Havea inscription, but it was the archæologist Bernardo da Sylva Ramos who, in his fundamental work about the prehistoric Brazilian inscriptions, translated and studied in detail the famous text. It is written in the cuneiform Phœnician alphabet, belonging apparently to the period of 887-856 B.C. and contains the following sentence : ' Badezir of the Phœnician Tyre, the first son of Jethbaal.' Badezir was the king of Phœnicia during 855-850 B.C., and his father, Jethbaal, reigned from 887 till 856 B.C. Thus the inscription might have been carved between 887 B.C. and 850 B.C. The Havea inscription is documental proof of Phœnician expeditions into South America and probably was carved in the neighbourhood of the colossal bust of Atlas in order to immortalize the name of Phœnicia and possibly also to acknowledge the Atlantean origin of their nation. Thus the age of the inscription must be not less than at least 2,780 years. Apart from this find, Professor Schwennhagen discovered in the Brazilian cities of Nictheroy and Campos, as well as in Tijuca (a summer resort of Rio de Janeiro), subterranean galleries of Phœnician origin, which served, probably, as warehouses for merchandise.

For a long time the Havea inscription was considered to be a petroglyph carved by some unknown prehistoric inhabitants of America. Other investigators believed it to be a freak of nature and still others, somewhat naïve, affirmed that this inscription was nothing more than the work of some mystifier or joker ! But during recent years about 2,000 prehistoric inscriptions have been found in Brazil. Many of them are in Phœnician, old Egyptian, and Sumerian, and others in unknown alphabets resembling Iberian, Carian, Etruscan, Cretan, etc.

Relations in prehistoric times between the Old and New Worlds must now be considered as a fact beyond doubt. Such an affirmation not long ago would have been met by scientists with amusement, and any petroglyph in the Phœnician language found in the Brazilian forests would have been considered trumped up. Thus the Havea inscription suffered from the same fate as many other similar discoveries : it is enough to remember the polemics that raged around the first cuneiform inscriptions found in Persia. At the beginning of the nineteenth century some scientists affirmed that such inscriptions represent nothing more than the fancy of architects, who liked to adorn their buildings with fantastic ornaments and the orientalists of 1840 sincerely believed that Nebuchadnezzar never had existed except as a purely mythological personality. Only the discovery of the inscription at Begistoun (Persia), written in three parallel texts in three different alphabets, gave the key to the cuneiform documents and laid a solid basis for Assyriology.

During my voyage through Northern Brazil in 1923–24 I met in the city of Bahia a certain French engineer named A. Frot. This gentleman has lived in Brazil for about fifty years and spent his youth in search for gold mines in the Brazilian virgin forests. But after having found some petroglyphs A. Frot abandoned his prospecting and began to study American prehistory and archæology. I must underline here this phenomenon : he who once has interested himself in archæology, will never abandon this most fascinating science ! Such is the charm of the past.

Not being an archæologist, M. Frot nevertheless did very much for this science : his discoveries in the Brazilian forests have proved a true revelation for archæologists and americanists. He discovered a series of inscriptions in various languages which have established beyond a doubt, that not only Phœnicians, but also the forefathers of the Egyptians, settled in South America. Frot even proved that the pre-Egyptians were of American origin. I had an opportunity of seeing a collection of photographs of some hundreds of Brazilian petroglyphs which were taken by M. Frot. Later on they were deciphered by orientalists and now we know their contents. They represent mostly descriptions of itineraries from Brazilian harbours to various gold-fields and prove that the Phœnicians and Carthaginians possessed many gold-mines in South America.

The inscriptions are generally stereotyped in character. Here is an example : ' therefrom you have to follow four days up this river. When you meet a hill with six palms on its top, you will find on the rock further instructions.' Similar inscriptions are scattered along all the routes, which finally led the novice to the gold-mines in the middle of the forests.

I maintained a correspondence with M. A. Frot for several years and he once informed me that he had discovered vestiges of Phœnician factories in the states of Parahyba and Rio Grande do Norte, wherefrom the Carthaginians sent groups of gold-diggers into the interior of the continent : some of them penetrated even into the present state of Goyaz. In 1926 Frot lived in this vast and almost unexplored state, where, while surveying a Carthaginian itinerary, he discovered its terminus. Unfortunately the mines themselves are situated among the virgin forest in an inaccessible place.

Later M. Frot wrote me a very interesting letter, which I give below in a brief English translation : ' The Phœnicians used in their South American inscriptions the same methods which were used by the old Egyptians at the earliest period of hieroglyphic writing. The same methods were employed by the Aztecs and by that unknown race which has left its petroglyphs in the Amazonian basin. The results of my investigations are so striking that I am afraid to publish them. In order to give you an idea of them I will say only that I possess proofs of the origin of Egyptians : the forefathers of Egyptians issued from South America and once formed three powerful empires. Two of them were founded in South America and the third on the Old Continent. The latter included North-western Africa, the Iberian peninsula and the islands of the ocean neighbouring Europe. The pre-Egyptians started their migration eastwards from the point at 57° 42' 45" West longitude from Greenwich (Frot does not give the latitude of this point) and this event is mentioned in an ancient Toltec document which I possess and which, besides the above information, contains also a short history of the pre-Egyptians. Moreover, I have discovered in Amazonia an inscription which contains an account of the voyage of a certain pre-Egyptian priest to what is now Bolivia.' The last words of this interesting letter from M. Frot apparently concern a discovery in the basin of the Rio Madeira, an inscription much discussed at that time in the Brazilian press. The deciphering of it established that at some remote period a group of pre-Egyptians moved to the Bolivian silver-mines.

I explain the hesitations of Frot concerning the publishing

of his works by the fear which many innovators feel when face to face with the conservatism and inertia of the representatives of academic science. Some of these would rather not at any price abandon their habitual theories. In fact, if the discoveries of Frot were accepted, many existing scientific theories concerning pre-history in general, and the pre-history of the Mediterranean races especially, would be radically changed.

After my return to Brazil in 1934 I tried to find A. Frot and visited his friend, a certain A. dos Anjos, who informed me that the Frenchman was actually in the unexplored Matto Grosso, where he had discovered some very ancient monuments, but he was unable to give his precise whereabouts. Very soon after this I left Brazil and thus lost touch with this remarkable man.

The above-mentioned Brazilian archæologist, B. A. da Sylva Ramos, belonged to the tribe of Tapuya Indians and spoke easily several native tongues: this circumstance facilitated extremely his work in the Brazilian wilderness. His collection consists of more than 1,500 photographs of Brazilian petroglyphs and he also received a hundred from Frot, as well as the key for the reading of some of the inscriptions. I hope to mention also the finds on the large island of Marajo in the mouth of the Amazon. This island, larger than the whole of Switzerland, divides the delta of this great river into two courses and possesses extensive cyclopic ruins of unknown prehistoric construction. Under them were discovered vast subterranean halls and galleries and the character of the walls is somewhat similar to that of the Etruscan ruins in Italy. The ceramics found amongst these Amazonian ruins bear sometimes inscriptions similar to Etruscan pottery and the style of ancient vases and ornaments also reminds one of Etruscan work.

According to Professor L. Schwennhagen (see his work *The Ancient History of Brazil*, p. 1, 1928), the Brazilian petroglyphs are carved on the rocks by means of metallic instruments, and the cavities have been filled with some exceedingly durable red matter. The chemist José Fabio analysed a small quantity of this matter and it turned out to consist of iron oxide mixed with some resinous substance. It is a remarkable fact that this red matter has resisted for millenniums the destructive influences of torrential tropical rains and the bleaching action of the sun. Professor Schwennhagen asserts that the majority of these

Brazilian petroglyphs represent Phœnician and Egyptian texts, the latter being executed in the so-called demotic writing. The presence of some Sumerian inscriptions indicates that among the Phœnician travellers there were also intellectuals, because the Sumerian language was used in Phœnicia only among educated people. I consider that several Latin inscriptions found in Brazil prove that they were made by Carthaginians in a comparatively late epoch, when the Latin culture had begun to penetrate into North Africa.

In the mouth of the river Parnahyba (please do not confound this name with that of the Brazilian state of Parahyba), in the Brazilian state of Piauhy, have been discovered interesting vestiges of the residence of the Phœnicians, enormous stone balls laid on the tops of the high rocks along the shore. It is probable that the Phœnician seafarers used these globes as signals at the entrance to the bay of Parnahyba. Perhaps such a globe was posted also at the entrance to the Straits of Gibraltar from the ocean, and this circumstance gave birth to the legend of Atlas, who supported the world on his mighty shoulders? Many ancient thinkers were aware of the spherical shape of our planet. The builders of the Great Pyramid in Egypt knew this perfectly well and it is likely that the inheritors of the Atlantean civilization, the Phœnicians, also knew of it.

We find interesting vestiges of the Phœnicians also on one of the coast islands in the Brazilian state of Parahyba : there are ruins of an ancient fortress, which probably protected the nearby Phœnician settlement. Although these ruins are very extensive, they represent, nevertheless, but one whole, an enormous building with many vast halls, large corridors and numerous galleries. The walls are more than 80 feet high, the length of the largest hall is 492 feet, and its width is 147 feet. One of the halls contains the fragments of a gigantic statue, probably of Baal, and the natives call this statue *sumé*. This word signifies in the Tupi language ' a great sorcerer, a chief priest, etc.' Is not this word connected with the name Sumer, that land which in the ancient times was known as the centre of religion and high culture ?

These ruins at Parahyba bear the historic name of *Sete Cidades* (Seven Cities), which is connected with a very ancient legend : the maps of the Middle Ages affirmed that somewhere in the ocean there exists a mysterious state of Seven Cities. Some geographers placed this state in ' The Happy Islands,' probably the Canary Islands. But when the latter were discovered and the State of the Seven Cities was not found there, geographers and seafarers began to seek the mysterious state more to the south and thus we can see in the medieval maps the *Insula Septem Civitatum* (' The Island of Seven Cities ') shown approximately lower than the latitude of the present Brazilian port of Recife (Pernambuco) in the then unexplored part of the ocean. Later on, when the Portuguese discovered Brazil and found on one of the coast islands of Parahyba the colossal ruins of the Phœnician fortress, they concluded that this was the mysterious *Insula Septem Civitatum*. The name of *Sete Cidades* has persisted from that time until to-day.

Some investigators have believed that these colossal ruins are nothing more than the results of a natural process of erosion of the rocks, but the presence of an evident plan in the building and of the fragments of a giant statue within it clearly prove that they are not a freak of nature. Moreover, it would be incomprehensible if the erosive processes had affected only this rock, while the others had remained intact !

CHAPTER VII

SOME millenniums ago, during the great westward migrations of the Asiatic tribes, the Cyclades islands of the Archipelago and the neighbouring shores of Asia Minor saw the appearance of a new nation called 'Carians' by the historian Thucydides. We know very little about them beyond the fact that they created a considerably developed civilization. We shall see later on that this Carian civilization was organically connected not only with the Phœnician culture, but also with the cultures of Crete and Cyprus and even with the Sumer-Babylonian culture.

Some historians believe that the Carians were related to the mysterious Pelasgi and, like the latter, were not of Aryan origin. The fact that the Phœnicians called themselves 'the people of Carou,' permits us to believe that the Carians of Thucydides were also related to the Phœnicians, inasmuch as they possessed many points in common. As the Phœnicians were Semites, therefore the Carians were perhaps also a branch of the Semitic race.

Ancient traditions record that some millenniums before our era, the Carians formed a State under the rule of a Chaldean magician, whose name was enveloped in mystery and has not survived. We only know that this name consisted of three taboo words the initials of which were K., A., and R. An artificial word Kar (Car) was formed from these initials and used as a conventional name for the magician-ruler. Eventually the tribes united under the rule of Kar began to call themselves Carians. The Chaldean origin of Kar seems to indicate Sumerian participation in some degree in the formation of the Carian State: in any case this circumstance causes us to suspect the cultural influence of the Sumerians in this particular corner of Near East.

Kar was the first law-giver of his people, introducing monotheism and founding the city of Halicarnassos (Hali-Kar-Nassos, or the 'Holy Garden of Kar'). During the life of Kar his empire was divided into two parts : Caria with the capital of Halicarnassos and Cara, or the present Cilicia, which apparently was a vassal state. There was a period during which Phœnicia, or the land of the Carous, was also a part of the Carian empire and thus all three states, Caria, Cara, and Carou, were at one time united under one common ruler.

The historian Diodorus considered Kar's times a true Golden Age in the history of mankind. The Carians, led by the mysterious Chaldean magician, made many useful inventions and discoveries, and their ships visited all the seas known at that time. Perhaps the legends concerning Happy Arcadia were nothing else than a dim remembrance of the prosperity of the prehistoric Carians and the term ' Arcadia ' was a distortion of ' Kar-Cadia,' or ' Kar-Adia,' or even of the Mesopotamian ' Akkadia ' ?

Kar, being a great politician and statesman, concluded alliances with some of the states in Asia Minor, and commercial treaties with Hobros (Cyprus), Crete, Sicily, and Sardinia. The best known of Carian political alliances was the ' Carian Union' (Caria, Troy, Ion, Phœnicia, and Crete) against their common enemies, the Achaians, but this alliance was concluded evidently some centuries after the death of Kar, at the epoch of the Trojan war.

The cultural activity of Kar abroad consisted in the diffusion of the Carian script, superior methods of agriculture, trade, etc. Kar sent into all countries priest-missionaries and ' cariatids,' i.e. priestesses, who taught womenfolk the art of weaving. The economic hegemony of the Carians among the prehistoric Mediterranean nations was very substantially supported by their cultural superiority, due to the activity of the legendary Kar. It is interesting to note that this enigmatical preacher, ruler, founder of a new religion, and social reformer, appeared on the Mediterranean shores almost simultaneously with similar leaders in other civilized countries, such as Zoroaster in Persia and Manou in Babylonia, and preceded Moses only by a few centuries.

It seems that the Carians were a very enterprising people and their trade expeditions penetrated far beyond the Mediterranean Sea. This assertion could be proved by numerous geographical and other terms possessing the syllable ' Kar,' or ' Car,' some of which are preserved until now. Thus we have, for instance,

Karnak in Egypt and Carnac in France (Brittany), the mountain and cape Carmel, Caramania (a part of the ancient Syria), the city of Carpassos (Cyprus), the island of Carpathos (Archipelago), Carniolia, Carinthia, Carpathian mountains, etc., etc. The Carian city of Carpassos (Cyprus) built, in ancient times, certain peculiar and capacious ships, able to contain as many as eight hundred passengers and to transport large quantities of merchandise. These ships were called 'carpassios' and this word, suffering various modifications in the course of time, reached us, in Russian as well as in other modern languages, in the words *karbas, barkas, bark, barque* (French), *barka,* etc., signify 'long-boats.' Perhaps the Spanish *caravella* and the Russian *korabl, korabel* are also the word *carpassios* distorted.

Perhaps even the name of Khartoum (British Sudan) and that of the island of Crete (Creta), as well as the word 'caravan,' derive from the name of the legendary magician, because Kar sent his emissaries and founded factories everywhere. Thus the name of the city of Khartoum could be translated by 'the work of Kar': it is interesting that the termination 'toum' (tum), which signifies 'work,' corresponds to the old German verb *thun,* or *tun* (to do), and in our days the German language possesses a series of words with this ancient termination: *Reichtum* (wealth), *Irrtum* (mistake), etc. All these words imply the idea of something accomplished or made.

The prefix 'Kar' (Car) in many terms lost its original significance and was transformed into a prefix signifying 'sacred.' Thus, for instance, the name of Carnac means 'a sacred city,' and it is known that both Carnacs, in Egypt as well as in Brittany, were religious centres. The ruins of the Breton Carnac, the city of the Druids, contain eighty dolmens, menhirs, and cromlechs. The other sacred name in ancient Gaul, Carnutum, signified in Carian an entire sentence: where the sacred laws were explained by Kar. 'In the language of the Abyssinian Gallas the word *cara* signifies " the sacred way." '

The energetic activity of Kar produced a strong impression on his people and later on the great reformer was deified. His economic activity gave many benefits to the neighbouring Phœnicia and the grateful Phœnicians also introduced Kar into their pantheon under the name of Mel-Kar, or Melcart, the god of trade. The cult of Melcart penetrated later on even into the neighbouring Hellas and Rome, where Melcart became Hermes, or Mercury. Alas, since the ancient Greeks could not conceive trade without cheating, poor Kar, now Hermes or Mercury, had also to become the protector of all thieves and swindlers.

The Lord of the Universe, whose cult was introduced by Kar, had no name except the cabbalistic ' Pan,' made up of the initials of the three mysterious words of which the name of Supreme Being was formed. Later on Pan joined the pantheon of the ancient Greeks in the capacity of the deity personifying the whole of visible Nature and inspiring her creative powers. Great Pan maintained his place in the Græco-Roman world for a long time, until he was superseded by the cult of the great Galilean. It was then that the famous phrase ' the Great Pan is dead ! ' was born. According to Christian traditions, this sentence was heard for the first time by the crew and passengers of the ship which carried Saint Paul to Italy. When this ship passed a solitary Mediterranean islet, the lamentations of numerous voices and a great cry : ' The Great Pan is dead ! ' reached the ears of the crew and passengers.

This god Pan was occasionally called Tu-Pan, which name, according to Professor Varnhagen, signified in the languages of the Pelasgi, Phœnicians, and Carians, ' the Divine Pan,' but the prefix ' tu ' by itself signified also ' a devout sacrifice.' The images of Pan represented mostly a faun with goatee and hoofs. The Christian priests of the early centuries A.D. fought energetically against the widespread cult of Pan and delegated his attributes to the devil in order to antagonize the Mediterranean population against the persistent Carian deity. Thus even to-day the goat's horns, the goatee, and the hoofs are as inseparable from the popular conception of the devil as they were in ancient world from Pan.

The goddess Cybele, who was believed to be the mother of Pan and later on of Kar, was also called ' Tu-Pana,' or ' Tu-Kera.' This religious conception of Universal Motherhood was, perhaps, a modification of an old Sumerian idea concerning Ishtar. It was personified in Phœnicia by Astarte, or Astaroth, in Persia by Anahit, or Anaitis, and later on by Kæres, or Ceres, by the Greeks and Romans. Some traditions of the Hindu Brahmins concerning the origin of the Gypsies affirm that the cult of

Astaroth in Phœnicia was brought into vogue there by the Gypsies, that mysterious tribe probably being of Atlantean origin. The cult of the Great Mother Cybele was one of the principal themes of the Crete-Minoan culture and no doubt the Egyptian Isis, as well as the Hittite goddess of fertility, were closely related to this very ancient conception.

Generally Cybele was represented as a mother with a baby in her arms, but sometimes this goddess appears alone, clothed in a long mantle and with a high tiara-like headgear. This was occasionally completed by a long sacred veil similar to that of the Carthaginian goddess Tanit, which hid the face of the goddess from vulgar eyes. Cybele was also often called Carmona, Kærmona, Kærimona, and Cærimona, and from this latter name derived our word 'ceremony' because the peculiar rituals of worship of Kar's, or Pan's, mother were called in antiquity 'ceremonies.' The order of the Vestals, i.e. of the maid-servants of the goddess Vesta, was probably an imitation of the order of Cariatids, the servants of the goddess Caria, the daughter of the divine Kar.

In course of time Cybele ceased to personify the idea of fertility and mother-love : Astarte and her later modifications, Aphrodite and Venus, were gradually transformed into goddesses of lascivious love only.

*   *   *

In Diodorus we find that the first Carian expedition beyond Gibraltar took place about 3500 B.C., and after that the Phœnicians, as well as the Carthaginians, ventured also to explore the Atlantic ocean. We cannot find in the works of Diodorus any description of the results of these Carian expeditions but now, thanks to the investigations in America, we begin to get some information on the subject. It is becoming clear that the trade voyages of the Carians ended in the colonization of some of the Caribbean islands and of the northern shores of South America. Perhaps, too, the Carians themselves were of American origin and their journeys beyond Gibraltar were nothing else than a series of visits to their ancient fatherland. These astonishing conclusions are based on many archæological finds in America and also on philological investigations. In this field the works of Professor L. Schwennhagen,

E. O. de Thoron, and Varnhagen are very useful. I recommend to my readers the article of E. O. de Thoron, 'Antiguidade da navegação do Oceano' (Vol. IV of the *Annals of the City of Para*, 1905), the *Antiga historia do Brazil* of Professor L Schwennhagen, and the book of Gustavo Barroso, *Aquém da Atlantida*. Besides these works, the book of Candido Costa, *As Duas Americas*, is also exceedingly interesting.

E. O. de Thoron affirms that he found proofs of the visit of the Carians to distant Ecuador: thanks to the deciphering of numerous American petroglyphs it has been established that at one time a Carian dynasty ruled in Quito. It seems that the Carians populated the north-western shores of the South America, and later on were assimilated by the autochtons of Ecuador. It is interesting to add that the Colombian scientist Miguel Triana affirms the origin of the highly-cultured Chibchas of Colombia from the Caribs of the Caribbean Sea, who are supposed by Professor Schwennhagen to derive also from the Carians. As Ecuador and Colombia are neighbour-states, it is very possible that the same migration-wave which brought the Carians or Caribs into Colombia, also populated ancient Ecuador. Miguel Triana proves the origin of the Chibchas by the anthropometric similarity of the skulls in the ancient sepultures of Facatativa (Colombia) and those of the Caribs, and by the study of a very remarkable mummy found in Guatavita (Colombia). More-over, the high cultural level of the ancient Chibchas (see earlier the legend concerning Bochica) permits us to suppose that the latter resulted from Carian influences. The astronomical know-ledge of the Chibchas especially induces us to believe that it was received by them from the ancient Carians.

It is a very remarkable fact that, everywhere in Central and South America, we find geographical and ethnographical terms which possess the prefix ' Car,' or ' Kar.' The sea which washes the northern shore of the South American continent is called the ' Caribbean' and its islands were populated at the time of Columbus by Caribs. The republic of Honduras is still populated by Caribs and Caras. The tribes Cariho, Caripuna, Cariou, Caraya, Carauna, etc., are scattered partly in Central and partly in Southern America. The oldest city of Venezuela, its present capital, is called Caracas and a whole series of localities in Northern Brazil possess names with the same prefix ' Car,' for instance: Cara, Carara, Carou, Cari, Cariri, Carai, Caraiba, Cario, Cariboca, Carioca, Caru-Tapera, Cariaco, Caralasca, Carova, Caricari, Cararaporis, Acarai, etc., etc. These examples are very numerous. In various regions of this continent we find the Guarani Indians, whose name, according to Professor L. Schwennhagen, derives from the Pelasgian *garra* (war), which also, it seems, originated the corresponding words in French (*guerre*) and in Spanish (*guerra*). L. Schwennhagen thinks that the Guaranis are descendants of the Carian-Phœnicians, who called themselves the ' warriors-peoples.' But on the other hand Gustavo Barroso believes that the word *Guarani* is distorted from *Carani*, which possesses also the famous particle ' Car.'

The following circumstance is also worthy of attention: all the Indian tribes whose names contain the prefix ' Car.' call the white men ' Cara,' although the Tupi word generally accepted by the Indians for white colour is *tinga*, which, according to Professor Schwennhagen, belongs also to the Carian and Pelasgian languages. Another circumstance is also interesting: Diodorus tells us that the Carians wore head-adornments made of feathers, and we know that all the Indian tribes, from Alaska to Patagonia, are accustomed to such adornments, especially in war-time. Perhaps this circumstance indicates the American origin of the Carians, unless, inversely, they learned this custom from the Indians during their voyages to America.

Discussing the Carian colonization of the Caribbean Islands, Professor Schwennhagen affirms that the Carians called these islands ' Antillas,' which name is distorted ' Atlantillas,' i.e. ' little Atlantis.' I cannot agree with the Brazilian scientist, because in the word ' Atlantillas ' we hear distinctly the Latin suffix ' illa,' while the Carian language should be nearer to the Semitic family and cannot possess the same structure as Latin.

Dim recollections concerning the past existence of Atlantis still persist among the natives of the Caribbean Islands and South America. Such, for instance, is the legend concerning the island Caraiba, which existed some millenniums ago, as affirm the natives in the Caribbean Sea. Professor Schwennhagen translates the word ' Caraiba ' as ' the land of the Carians.' According to this legend, seven tribes of the Carian race, after a terrific catastrophe, emigrated to this island, but these traditions do not indicate the land of origin of these seven tribes. They called themselves

' Cari,' but their priests changed their name into ' Tupi ' and ordered them to use the latter name, which signifies the ' sons of Tupan,' the great and almighty being who, according to the belief of the Tupis, rules the Universe. Is not this Tupan of the Indians the Carian Tu-Pan mentioned earlier ?

Many centuries B.C. the island of Caraiba was in its turn swallowed up by the sea : this second catastrophe is also mentioned in Indian tradition. The surviving Tupis emigrated to the South American continent, landing on the shores of Venezuela and founding there the city of Caracas. Some centuries later seafarers from a distant eastern country came to Venezuela and gradually transported almost the entire people of the Tupis into Brazil : only a small tribe of Tupinambas left some of its clans in Venezuelan territory. It appears that the Tupis landed on the island of Marajo in the Amazonian delta. The name of this island slightly resembling the name of the Upper Amazon (Marañon) was pronounced at first as ' Maraio,' or ' Maraion,' and only later was transformed by the Portuguese into ' Marajo,' which corresponds better to the spirit of their language. Professor Varnhagen is of the opinion that the words ' Mara Ion ' in the Carian language signified ' a great river,' but the word ' Ion ' sounds like the name of a certain small state of Ion in the Archipelago (Ionian islands) which at one time belonged to the Carian Union. Perhaps the explanation of another expert, Professor Schwennhagen, is more plausible. He believes that these newcomers to Brazil meant by ' Great Ion ' (Mara Ion) the country of their origin, i.e. the Ionian islands. Caru-Taperu, the name of a locality on the island of Marajo, again reminds us of the Carians : some years ago there were found prehistoric cyclopic ruins, which some scientists consider Etruscan, and others, Carian. The reader probably remembers the already-mentioned discoveries in Marajo of ancient pottery resembling much the Etruscan style, and also of Etruscan and Carian inscriptions.

Who were these mysterious seafarers from the distant East, who, according to the Tupi legend, transported the majority of their nation into the Amazonian delta ? They could either be the Carians or the Phœnicians, because both needed men for their American enterprises. Their friendship towards the Tupis could be explained by a common origin for all three nations, Carians, Phœnicians, and Tupis. Those clans of the latter who did not consent to emigrate again remained in Venezuela. Professor Varnhagen affirms that the Tupis of that country still preserve legends of the consecutive migrations of their fore- fathers. Some clans of the Tupis, both in Venezuela and in Brazil, call themselves proudly ' Tupinamba ' (' the true Tupis '). The legend of the Guaranis also mentions Tupinamba, the daughter of the prophet Roupave and the foremother of the Guaranis Indians.

The tribe known as Tupinamba still preserves some knowledge of astronomy, perhaps inherited from their distant forefathers, the Carians. As Thucydides calls the divine Kar ' a Chaldean magician,' it is clear that the legendary founder of the Carian empire must have possessed some knowledge of astronomy, because the Chaldeans were remarkable astronomers and astrologers. A missionary of the seventeenth century, Father d'Abbeville, published a highly interesting treatise concerning the astronomical knowledge of the Tupinambas and was rewarded with severe criticism from the French experts of his time : the erudite doctors of the Sorbonne could not conceive that ' a barbarous Indian tribe could possess any astronomical knowledge. . . .'

The religion of the Tupis appeared in Northern Brazil some millenniums before our era, coinciding apparently with the earliest Carian or Phœnician visits to the country. The Tupi language in itself is one of the most vivid proofs of a connection between the ancient civilizations of the Old and New Worlds. Its relation to the Carian and Pelasgian languages has been studied by Professor Schwennhagen, who finds that the language is really a Tupi-Pelasgian combination. The Tupi tribe known as Gheghes calls its own dialect *nhehen gatu* (a universal language) : this implies that the Tupi language in general was at one time very widely diffused and used probably by the Carians, Pelasgi, Atlanteans, and also certain American nations (Professor L. Schwennhagen, *The Oldest History of Brazil*, Part I, 1923). A further study of the Tupi language seems to show that the above-mentioned belt of civilized nations was connected also with Sumeria. Numerous words of the Tupi language are contained in the legislative text of the Sumerian king Urgana (4000 B.C.), which is preserved in the British Museum. The Carian language possessed a word *sumer* (chief of priests), which, transformed into *sume*, is still employed by the Tupis for the designation of priests, sorcerers, or even Christian missionaries and physicians.

Vestiges of the Phœnicians are very numerous in the Brazilian state of Piauhy : there has been discovered, for instance, ' The pyramid of Morvão,' a prehistoric building which probably was erected by the Phœnicians as a kind of necropolis. The earlier-mentioned tribe of Gheghes lives in Piauhy : its language *nhehen gatu*, or *nhehen catu*, closely resembles the language of the Albanian tribe of Gheghes. Such similarity of languages in two tribes who are separated from each other by such an enormous distance, but bear the same name of Gheghes, is striking. Doubt-less the Albanian and Brazilian Gheghes belong to the same tribe : at some time either Albanian clans emigrated to South America, or Brazilian clans went to Europe. But I believe that there is a third and more plausible solution : that all the Gheghes originated from Atlantis and eventually some of them emigrated to Brazil, and the others to Albania. Professor L. Schwennhagen considers that their language, the languages of the Tupis and Basques and even the Semitic tongues, are derived from a Pelasgi-Carian root. It is significant that Basques still call themselves the ' Euskara ' (Eus-Cara), a name which again reminds us of the Carians.

Some South American tribes possess traditions concerning their former fatherland : they affirm that their forefathers came from a certain ' Carou land,' which name is identical to that of the old Phœnicia. We venture to assert that the word ' Carou,' or ' Karou,' designated in very remote antiquity a country wherefrom issued not only the Phœnicians and Carians, but also certain South American Indian tribes. Some experts suppose that the Guaranis and Tupis either derive from the enigmatical Ibers, or that all these three tribes possessed a common origin. Later on the Ibers emigrated into the present Spain and the two other tribes went westwards to the shores of South America. Were this hypothesis justified, we could assert that the common fatherland of the Phœnicians and Semites in general, of the Carians, Ibers, Pelasgi, Guaranis, and Tupis, was Atlantis. In this case all the enumerated tribes would be nothing else than various branches of the great Atlantean race. We can find in the Tupi language words which sound identical with some Palestinian geographical terms, such as, for instance, the words *canaan, aramea,* and others. Guaranis of the Brazilian state of Ceara use a dialect full of words resembling Hebrew. The state of Ceara is situated in the north-eastern corner of the continent, right opposite the western shore of the African Sahara and like the latter is arid and often suffers from drought. The resemblance of the word ' Ceara ' and the Semitic ' Sahara,' combined with the similarity of the physico-geographical conditions and the situation of both countries, is striking : some scientists have even attempted to find in this coincidence a proof in favour of Wegener's hypothesis, affirming that at one time Ceara and the Sahara were one great desert.

Many names of Brazilian rivers and the Indian tribes who live along their banks contain the prefix ' Poti ' : as, for instance, Potijara, Potiguara, etc. Professor Schwennhagen recognizes in this prefix the Pelasgian word *poti* signifying ' a rivulet,' or ' an affluent.' Later on the Greeks adopted it in *potamos* (river). The same expert believes that the Quichuas, or ' Antis,' emigrated to South America from Atlantis. The Brazilian philologist E. O. de Thoron affirms that the Quichua tongue has a great deal of resemblance with old Egyptian, Greek, and even Hindustani. This gentleman has made a detailed study of this resemblance and has discovered numerous similarities and analogies between Quichua and the old Egyptian language. This similarity of languages in such distant races gives strong support in favour of the hypothesis of the American origin of the Egyptians (see earlier regarding the discoveries of Frot) and E. O. de Thoron is of the opinion that the Egyptians, as well as the Pelasgi, originated from America and Atlantis. E. O. de Thoron claims to have traced the origin of the Greek deities and their primeval significance. The Pelasgi have a tradition that their religion and gods came from an unknown race who inhabited a distant western continent : such a continent could either only be America or Atlantis. There are reasons to believe that the establishment of the Pelasgi in Peloponnesus and Crete and of the pre-Egyptians in the Nile valley occurred at about the same time and that this invasion of the Mediterranean basin by the Americo-Atlanteans was the third wave of emigrants from Atlantis which, according to Lewis Spence, swept across Western Europe. Here we must appreciate the striking resemblance between the vestures and sacred attributes of the old Egyptian

VESSELS RECONSTRUCTED OUT OF DEBRIS
(Museum of Lima, Peru.)

THE RUSSIAN ARCHÆOLOGIST E. JAKOWLEFF WORKING
ON THE RECONSTRUCTION OF ANCIENT VESSELS

PERUVIAN MUMMIES
(Each bag is a Mummy.)

priests and the vestures and attributes of the priests of certain South American tribes.

When Alvares Cabral landed on the spot where now stands the Brazilian capital, he met there Guarani Indians : they called this region ' Carioca.' The word ' oca ' signifies in Guarani ' home, abode' and resembles the Greek *oika*, which has the same significance. The Guarani word *cari* means ' white men ' and thus the whole expression ' Carioca ' signifies ' the abode of white men.' Such an etymology proves that at one time the region round Rio de Janeiro was inhabited by white new-comers. The earlier-mentioned Phœnician inscription on the nearby rock of Havea allows us to suppose that they must have been Phœnicians. These unknown new-comers called themselves ' the Cari ' and the Guaranis presumably adopted this term as a designation for any white man. The Brazilians still call any inhabitant of the capital, or its surroundings, ' carioca.'

The Ionian Islands of the Archipelago four millenniums ago were inhabited by the tribe known as Ionians, who formed the little state of Ion. The misty traditions of antiquity asseverate that the Ionians belonged to a Grecian race, but this supposition seems to be mistaken. The Ionians were allied to the Carians and Trojans, whose state was called Ilion (Il-Ion ?), although Trojans called themselves Dardans. When the Great War of Antiquity, sung by Homer, had been ended, the vanquished Dardans, together with other members of the Carian Union, Carians and Ionians, were obliged to seek a shelter from the wrath of the victorious Achaians in other countries. The Phœnician seafarers probably played a most important role in the evacuation of the vanquished peoples : they transported on their ships the numerous refugees of Ion and Ilion to various points of the Mediterranean basin. Thus the Phœnicians populated their numerous colonies with the refugees, who supplied them with cheap labour. The legends tell how the Trojan princess, Dido, founded Carthage and other refugees helped to start colonies in Spain and Southern France in a similar way. But it is now becoming clear that some emigrants from the Archipelago and Asia Minor emigrated even beyond the Mediterranean shores and that the Phœnician trirems carried many of them to America. Was not the appearance of the Carians on the South American shores due to this fact ?

We have already mentioned the archæological finds on the Marajo Island, and the conjectures of Professor Varnhagen.

Diodorus, recording the rescue of the Trojan refugees by their ancient allies the Phœnicians, adds that these refugees often gave the name of their mother-city Troy to their new settlements. In the light of this it is most significant that Brazil possesses a locality named Tutoya. This village is situated in the mouth of the river Parnahyba and the traditions of the natives affirm that it is the oldest settlement in Brazil. At first sight ' Troy ' and ' Tutoya ' do not seem to be absolutely identical, but Professor Schwennhagen explains that the sound ' r ' is difficult for Brazilian natives and they distort it at the first opportunity. The original and pure form of Tutoya must have been ' Toor-Troya.' The word ' toor ' signifies in Phœnician ' a capital,' ' a fortress,' and in fact we see among the ruins in Tutoya ancient vestiges of cyclopic fortress-like buildings. Thus we can consider it possible that Tutoya was founded by Trojan refugees. The Brazilian scientists trace in their country two more cities that were probably founded by Phœnicians and emigrants from other countries in the Carian Union : they are the present Turos in the state of Rio Grande do Norte and Torre in the state of Bahia. We can still hear the prefix ' toor ' in both names and many Phœnician inscriptions have been found in the surroundings of Torre.

The Carian deity Tu-Pan is still worshipped by almost all South American tribes as the almighty god Tupan. His cult is specially developed among the Paraguayan Guaranis, but at one time was extended also as far as the Pacific shores of the continent. Tupis assert that Tupan taught their ancestors agriculture and the use of fire. The nations of the ancient Peruvian empire portrayed Tupan in absolutely the same fashion as the Greek statues of Pan : the Peruvian Tupan was always represented as a faun with a goatee and hoofs. Simultaneously with the appearance of the Tupan's cult there appeared in South America also the cult of his mother, Cybele, or Kera. This last name was used wherever Cybele was believed to be the mother of Kar. When the first Portuguese missionaries in Brazil, the Fathers Manoel Nobrega and Anquieta, asked the natives : ' What is the name of this country ? ' they received the answer : ' Tupan Kere tan.' (' It is the land of Kera, the mother of Tupan.')

*   *   *

All that we know concerning the history of Guarani Indians is based only on a very uncertain foundation of popular tradition and myth. Such, for instance, are the local versions of the universal flood, mentioned by the erudite jesuit, Father José Guevara. There are two versions in existence : the first calls the hero of the Paraguayan epos Tume-Aranda, and the second, Tamanduare. The latter and his sisters, Guarasiave and Tupin-amba, were the children of a great prophet, Rupave, and together with two brothers Carive survived the Flood. The Carive brothers married the two sisters of Tamanduare. Guarasiave became the progenitor of the Guaranis, and Tupinamba of the Tupis. This circumstance shows clearly the relation between the Guaranis and the Tupis.

The Guarani legends tell that their forefathers inhabited a splendid capital, ' The City of Shining Roofs,' and Dr. Bertoni connects this circumstance with the legend concerning Atlantis, where the roofs, according to Plato, were covered by brilliant oreichalkos. But the first Spanish *conquistadores* took this Indian legend literally and thought that somewhere in the interior of the continent still existed a town with golden roofs. They even gave to this mythical Indian capital the name of ' El Dorado ' (' Gilded '). The covetous adventurers many times started the search for this capital, and their hazardous expeditions contributed very much to the enlargement of our knowledge of the New World. Perhaps the same Indian legends also gave origin to the tradition concerning the existence of a splendid prehistoric capital among the forests of the Matto Grosso : it is known that the unfortunate Colonel Fawcett, starting his last expedition to the Brazilian wilderness, intended to try and find this mysterious city.

Dr. Colman cites one interesting tradition of the Guaranis concerning their forefathers : the Indians affirm that their ancestors possessed a secret method of obtaining fire by means of a certain strange apparatus. This tradition does not refer to the common method, well-known among the wild tribes, of obtaining fire by the swift rotation of a pointed wooden stick in a wooden cavity, but specifies that the forefathers of the Guaranis obtained bright sparks, the description of which brings to mind the sparks of an electrical machine. In addition to this hazy information we should mention a discovery by certain investigators of large prehistoric buildings on the high Colombian table-lands : these cyclopean halls and galleries do not possess either windows or stoves, and it remains a mystery how these vast buildings were lighted and heated ? These regions are sometimes cold, but no traces or fires, or spots blackened by smoke, have been found anywhere in these ruins. The Colombian natives assert that the builders of these structures possessed a mysterious method of lighting and heating without fire. Perhaps those prehistoric races in Colombia and Paraguay were familiar with electricity ? !

In the surroundings of the Paraguayan locality called Paraguari, in the middle of a monotonous plain, rises an isolated rocky eminence called Tatoo-Cooa. Recently the Paraguayan writer N. R. Colman discovered there accidentally a very interesting artificial grotto, but unfortunately did not record its exact site and, when he went there again to make more detailed investigations, he could not find its entrance. Thus all that we know about this find of N. R. Colman is recorded from a recollection of his first accidental visit there, described in his book *Nande ipi Cuera*, written mostly in Guarani. This Paraguayan writer saw in the grotto the sitting statue of a naked Indian. The head of the statue was adorned with a kind of tiara and a triangle was carved on its forehead and another on its bosom. The apex of the upper triangle was directed upwards and the apex of the second one downwards. Although the Indian was sitting on a kind of throne, the over-all height of the statue was twice that of an average man. Its feet reposed upon a heap of spherical stones, some of them carved in a strange fashion. The walls of the grotto were covered with hieroglyphic inscriptions. Colman brought away some of the above-mentioned stones and made a picture of the statue, which is printed in his book. The author of *Nande ipi Cuera* believes that this statue represents the hero of many Guarani legends, a kind of local Hercules. The triangle on his forehead symbolizes spirit, and the other triangle, matter.

N. R. Colman in his book mentions also other monuments of Guarani prehistory. In the surroundings of Villa Rica, for instance, on the mountain of Ibitirusu, there is a subterranean gallery with its walls covered with ideograms and signs resembling Scandinavian Runic characters. In the cavern of Teyucare (' The Dragon's Grotto '), on the shores of the upper Parana, one can see signs, resembling Egyptian hieroglyphs, which resemble certain cyphers of the Mayas and the mysterious ideograms of the Paraguayan cinerary urns. On one mound in Yariguaa were discovered stones with inscriptions resembling the old Egyptian hieroglyphs and the enigmatical texts found in the Amazonian forests. The well-known South American ethnologist, Dr. M. Bertoni, affirms that at least one-half of the Yariguaa hieroglyphs is identical with the old Egyptian hieroglyphs.

All these finds and the study of the Guarani folklore led N. R. Colman to the conclusion that the culture of the Guarani race was at one time very high. It was apparently connected with other enigmatical cultures of prehistoric South America and with the pre-Egyptian civilization. The causes of the later degeneration of the local tribes are a very interesting problem : what was the catastrophe which destroyed the cultures of the native races ?

CHAPTER VIII

THE Etruscans, or Tyrrhenians, who came to the Apennine peninsula before the foundation of Rome and were apparently emigrants from some Western country, were famous as skilful metal-workers and metallurgists. Scanty information from ancient sources allows us to suppose that they were related to the Atlanteans.

The Indian tribes met by the Spaniards in the sixteenth century were also famous for their skilfulness in metallurgy. This knowledge of metal urgy was common to the Aztecs, Mayas, Peruvians, Caribs, and Chibchas. The Spanish chronicles tell us, for instance, about the magnificent garden of the Inca emperors in their capital Cuzco : this garden possessed numerous artificial trees and plants with stems, branches, leaves, flowers, and fruits made of brass, silver, and gold. This work was really artistic : silver butterflies sat on the golden flowers and lizards, snakes, and snails made of metal crawled upon the brass stems and branches. The Indians possessed a knowledge of methods of brass and copper hardening, and fabricated golden and silver statuettes and metallic automatons : parrots which moved their tongues and wings, and monkeys which not only broke nuts with their teeth but even spun with spindles. Cortez received from the Mexican emperor Montezuma a series of presents : there were mirrors of platinum, a metal which is difficult to melt, and several plates made of gold and silver strips in such a manner that it was impossible to detect the welded joints. Reading about these works of Mexican and Peruvian goldsmiths, one involuntarily remembers Plato's description of the metallurgical skill of the Atlanteans, who also created an alloy absolutely unknown to us, the mysterious oreichalkos.

The investigations of Professor L. Frobenius have proved the existence of certain curious analogies and resemblances between Etruscan antiquities and the antiquities of some American tribes. Moreover, anthropological analogies have been established in many cases. That well-known feature of primeval architecture, the so-called 'false vault,' which characterizes the Etruscan buildings, is to be found also among the ruins in America. I have spoken already about the discovery on the island of Marajo of ruins and ceramics resembling those of Etruscan art. Doubtless the Etruscans came to Italy from some Western country, and it is likely that this people formed a part of one of the migration waves which, arriving according to the theory of Lewis Spence during the last millenniums B.C., settled finally on the Apennine peninsula. But others consider that the Etruscans came from Asia Minor, because there are some affinities between the latter and the enigmatical Hittites. One cannot agree with this hypothesis on the ground that the Hittites themselves also probably emigrated from some western country. In any case Etruscan art developed independent of Asiatic influence : we can rather suppose that the sources of Greek and Roman art themselves must be sought in Etruscan art. Recently, near the ruins of the Etruscan city of Veii, there was found a statue of Apollo executed in a specifically Etruscan conception : this statue differs greatly from the corresponding statues in Greek or Roman style.

In spite of much that has been said to the contrary, the ancient hypothesis of the common origin of the Pelasgi and Etruscans still remains plausible. The race of the Pelasgi apparently inhabited a considerable stretch of the Mediterranean basin. According to Homer and other ancient authors the Pelasgi settled in Peloponnesus and Crete, but modern scientists have discovered their vestiges also in Italy, in regions formerly supposed to be purely Etruscan.

Homer calls the Pelasgi ' divine ' because, perhaps, they were much more civilized than the other tribes of the Archipelago, Hellas, and Crete. Did not the Pelasgi belong to the cultured Atlantean race ? According to the ancient tradition they were ' sons of Poseidon and Amphitrite,' the two principal sea-gods, and Poseidon, moreover, was the chief deity of the Atlanteans. Thus, Homer underlines the maritime origin of the Pelasgi, whose name also derives from *pelagos* (sea). This enigmatical nation bequeathed to its successors, the Greeks, its history which later on was transformed by the Hellenes and Latins into their mythology : the rulers and heroes of the Pelasgi became gods of the Greek Olympus, and the facts of Pelasgian history became myths concerning the innumerable Greek and Latin deities and their deeds.   Thus the Greek theogony is probably nothing else than a poetical account of the earlier history of the Mediterranean basin.

* * *

Among the ancient European nations there existed vague traditions of the migrations of their remote forefathers from the distant West.   Probably those peoples, who were loosely called by the ancient writers the ' Gauls,' consisted in reality of two absolutely ethnologically heterogeneous groups : of the Gaul-Celts, i.e. of the emigrants from the west, and of the ' Gaul '-Aryans, who later on came from Asia.   This misunderstanding was bequeathed by the classic historians to later writers and became gradually a source of considerable ethnological misunderstanding.

Some Gallic tribes of the time of Cæsar and Vercingetorix (the celebrated leader of the Gauls during their struggle against the Romans) claimed that their remotest forefathers came a long time since from a distant western continent, or large island, and were led by the great Hoo-Gadarn, called ' the Chieftain of Peoples.'   Hoo-Gadarn, according to the traditions and legends, was not only a leader and ruler, but at the same time a great enlightener of his subjects.   The legends relate that Hoo-Gadarn invented the plough and built the first sea-going ship. Apparently this legendary hero issued from some other race.

The same traditions and legends asserted that the Gauls, arriving to Europe, landed at the mouth of the Tagus at the point where Lisbon is now situated, and this spot therefore became known as ' Porto Galli ' (' the port of the Gauls '), a name from which derived the word ' Portugal.'

The Gaul-Celts very soon expanded throughout the European continent, penetrating even beyond its boundaries into Asia and Africa, and the science of toponymy (which studies the derivation of geographical terms) discerns the sojourn of the Gaul-Celts in various, sometimes widely separated, countries. The following are the most interesting examples.

The present Walloons (a district of Belgium, the inhabitants speaking mostly French and having much in common with the Latin race), for instance, were at one time called ' Gallons '

and their country, ' Gallonia.' Further, in antiquity and in the
Middle Ages, Wales was called ' Gæledonia.' Later on this word
became transformed into Caledonia and was adopted by the
ancient Scots for one of their regions. Two Galicias exist in
Europe; the Polish Galicia and the Spanish. A part of Con-
stantinople formerly reserved for Gallic prisoners is still called
Galata. It does not require much imagination to derive the
word ' Gælic ' from the name of the Gauls. Some investigators
affirm that even the name of the Abyssinian tribe of Gallas derives
from the Gauls, because this tribe possesses some features
resembling the corresponding Gallic characteristics. Dolmens,
found in the territory of the Gallas, resemble the Breton examples,
and the Gallas possess the same Gallic custom in valuing branches
of mistletoe which, according to Celtic belief, brings happiness
to the house. Some investigators believe that the word ' Celt '
itself derives from the name of the principal Gallic weapon,
gæleta, or *keleta*, a kind of hatchet. However, we must always
remember that linguistic resemblances represent a very uncertain
method of ethnological investigations. . . .

The hypothesis that the Gaul-Celts, arriving from Atlantis
together with the Celt-Iberians, settled in Europe 10,000 years
ago, is shared by the scientist Hirmenech, who affirms that not
only the Gaul-Celts, Armoricans, and Iberians were descended
from the Atlanteans, but even the Semites. Later on I will
dedicate a special chapter to the problem of the origin of the
Semites.

As to the probable remainders of the Atlantean race in Europe,
I shall mention the present Portuguese and Basques. The first
were called ' Lusitanians ' in antiquity because of the name of
their country, Lusitania (Portugal). Being in Lisbon in 1934,
I had an opportunity to hear an interesting lecture by Dr.
Domingos Pepulim concerning the origin of the Lusitanians.
This gentleman stated that although the origin of the Celts-
Iberians has not yet been established, Professor Mendes Correia
was of the opinion that the Iberian peninsula was colonized by
Atlanteans. The same hypothesis is shared also by Lewis
Spence, who affirmed that Western Europe suffered a series of
Atlantean invasions. According to Dr. Pepulim we must defi-
nitely reject the idea of Asiatic migrations to the Iberian peninsula.
He believes that Plato's Ligurians originated from the Iberian

peninsula and the term ' Celts,' which we find mentioned in the works of Hesiod, did not indicate any particular race, but all the tribes who inhabited Europe west of Greece. The name of 'Iberians' belonged in antiquity to all the tribes who lived along the river Ebro ('Eber') and also the Lusitanians or Portuguese were the direct descendants of the Atlantean colonists. In reality the Atlanteans were the 'Celts' mentioned by all ancient authors. The Portuguese, who are very distinct from the Spaniards and stand nearer to the Basques were, and still are, a very enterprising people and good seafarers, as also were the ancient Phœnicians and the mysterious Pelasgi, those 'children of the sea.'

Lewis Spence, in his book *The Problem of Atlantis*, suggests that the Cromagnon race emigrated from Atlantis about 25,000 years ago. Thus this race had to sustain a long and strenuous struggle against the inferior Neanderthal race which inhabited at that epoch the European wilderness. This struggle was finally ended in the triumph of the cultured Cromagnon. Thus we inherited from that epoch our tales about wicked giants and cannibals, who were nobody else than Neanderthal men. The well-known frescoes in the caverns of the Rhône (France) and of Cogul (Spain) belong apparently to the activities of the Cromagnon race, who came to Europe at the middle of the last Glacial Period, and were apparently a race of hunters. These artistic and very realistic paintings help us to reconstruct the life of mankind of 25,000 years ago. Mr. Morgan in his book about prehistoric mankind describes enthusiastically the monuments of art left by the Cromagnon race in the Magdalen caverns : in fact, these paintings and scanty fragments of prehistoric sculpture are wonderful creations. Apparently the primitive artists possessed a faculty which we have lost, namely the ability to render movement, and Mr. Morgan compares the expressiveness of these prehistoric painters with the art of Rembrandt himself. We can imagine the level of Atlantean art from such samples as these frescoes of Cogul.

Nine thousand years passed after the Cromagnon invasion and a new wave of emigrants rushed from Atlantis into Europe. According to Spence, 16,000 years ago the so-called Aurignac culture appeared on the western shores of the Old Continent. The new-comers contributed much to the civilization of prehistoric Europe : the Aurignac men introduced many useful inventions, animals, and plants.

Six thousand years more elapsed after the Aurignac invasion and, according to Spence, the third wave of emigrants from Atlantis rushed upon Europe. This was the Azil-Tardenos race, which appeared in the Iberian peninsula and in Western France about 10,000 years ago, and apparently contemporaneously with the destruction of Atlantis. The new-comers mostly settled around the Bay of Biscay, and probably Basques, Bretons, Irish, and even the Berbers of Africa are their descendants. It is very possible too that the profile found by Professor Baudouin on the Large Stone in Vendée (mentioned earlier) represents a man of this Atlantean race.

Some other scientists also derive the Basques from the Atlanteans : certain physical features of this people and distinctive peculiarities of the Basque language indicate their affinity with some Central American tribe, who are supposed to be of Atlantean root, but on the other hand the language of the Basques possesses many roots and sometimes entire words similar to Japanese and Georgian (Southern Russia). I was present when a former Russian officer of Georgian origin found himself able to talk with the natives of Vizcaya immediately upon his arrival in Northern Spain : he spoke Georgian, but the Basques understood this language. It is necessary to remind the reader that in antiquity Georgia was called ' Iveria,' a name almost identical with ' Iberia.' It is well known that the Spaniards and Portuguese often pronounce V instead of B and vice versa.

When in Guatemala, I often heard about one Indian tribe, living in the Peten district (Northern Guatemala) : this tribe speaks a language resembling Basque, and I have heard of an occasion when a Basque missionary preached in Peten in his own idiom with great success.

As to the resemblance of the Japanese and Basque languages, I once saw a list of analogous words with the same significance in both tongues and I was stupefied by the quantity of such words. The word *iokohama*, for instance, signifies in Basque ' a seashore city,' and everybody knows the great port of Yokohama in Japan. Both nations, the Basques and Japanese, are of low stature, both possess a square-built and strong constitution, and both are black-haired. But the skin of the Japanese is olive-coloured, their eyes are of Mongol type, and their skulls are sometimes decidedly prognathic, while the Basques are white, and their eyes, with jaws and chins, are similar to the Aryan type. The noses of the Basques are sometimes of eagle-type, like the Mayan ones, and the Japanese noses are flat. Moreover, the Japanese language has some analogies with the Malayan and Polynesian tongues : this circumstance, together with some physical particularities of the Japanese, induced many anthropologists to ascribe this nation to the Malayan race.

A very interesting Indian tribe called the Otomis lives in the neighbourhood of Tula in Mexico : these Indians speak the old Japanese idiom, and once when the Japanese ambassador to Mexico visited this tribe he talked with them in this old dialect.

Taking into consideration all these facts and observations, I would like to offer the following conjecture. It is likely that the emigration from Atlantis developed in two directions, eastwards. and westwards. The third wave of Spence brought, perhaps, the Basques into Europe and simultaneously a great number of emigrants from the unfortunate continent sailed in a westerly direction. Leaving some of its clans in the Mexican and Guatemalan territories (the Otomis and the Peten Indians), this western branch of emigrants spent many thousands of years on various Polynesian archipelagos and finally settled in the Japanese islands. Their prolonged residence among the Polynesian and Malayan tribes introduced many strange elements into the Japanese race and in the result gave a mixed type and a language rich in Malayan and Polynesian forms and roots. But the memory of their remote eastern fatherland remains to-day among the Japanese, and not in vain is the first legendary emperor of this nation, Jimmu-Tenno, believed to be the son of the Sun itself. . . . This myth is nothing else than the poetized recollection of the land where the Sun rises, of the sunk Atlantis : therefore the country itself, Japan, bears the proud title of the ' Land of the Rising Sun,' although it is clear, that the Sun rises for the Japanese somewhere in the east from their islands, i.e. in the direction of America. The Mexican enlightener, Quetzal-Coatl, arrived in Mexico from a certain eastern country called ' Tlapal-lan ' (' The Land of the Rising Sun '). Perhaps this was the title of the whole empire of the Atlanteans, and the Japanese, being offshoots of this great prehistoric nation, preserve this title for themselves until to-day?

It is likely that the Japanese settled in Asia simultaneously with another branch of the former Atlantean population, the present Coreans. The latter have some features in common with the Japanese, but are a very peace-loving and mild nation, quite the opposite of the proud, haughty, and war-like Japanese. Therefore I believe that the Coreans named their new abode, the Corean peninsula, by the name of 'The Land of the Morning Quietness' for these reasons.

*   *   *

CHAPTER IX

THE Phœnicians, Hebrews, and Arabs are the three chief branches of the great Semitic race which deserve particular consideration from a historian. I have already dedicated the several preceding chapters to the Phœnicians and now shall examine the scanty information we have concerning the origin of the Jews and Arabs. Reasons of space do not allow me to give any sort of exhaustive survey: I must limit myself to salient points pertinent to my inquiry.

I shall abide by the hypothesis adducing that the Semites appeared on the Old Continent as one of the migration waves from Atlantis, or from America. Probably the Akkadians and the enigmatical pre-Sumerians were the vanguard of this wave. Immediately after them came the Phœnicians and at the very end the Jews and Arabs. We shall not trouble ourselves with other comparatively small Semitic tribes which settled in Canaan and in the gaps between Palestine, Arabia, and Mesopotamia.

If we admit the hypothesis of the Atlantean origin of the Semites we can only marvel at the amazing reserve of vitality and cultural persistence of the population of the lost continent. Even a small portion of its migration waves was so vigorous that 12,000 years later its descendants continue to attract the attention of mankind.

Some tribes of Central and South America possess strange affinities with the Semites. We are surprised, for instance, to observe a similarity in the types of the natives of Yucatan and Peru with the Semitic race: the former sometimes possess true Jewish faces. The prehistoric sculptures of the Mayas and Peruvians give also many samples of this identity: you see sloping foreheads, eagle-noses, and sometimes stuck-out ears. Lord Kinsborough spent an entire fortune on publishing his *Antiquities of Mexico*, a magnificent collection of Mexican hieroglyphic inscriptions and pictures of ancient Mexican monuments. The author of this work attempts to prove that the

Aztecs and some other Mexican tribes are descendants of the lost tribes of Israel. It seems that the sole reason for such a bold hypothesis is the undoubtedly Jewish type of the figures on the Mexican monuments. We need not accept bodily this fantastic supposition, but certainly there is a kernel of truth in Lord Kinsborough's assertions.

Also, a certain resemblance can be discerned between the rituals of some American tribes and the Semitic rituals. The rite of circumcision, for instance, which existed among the old Egyptians, is not confined nowadays only to the Arabs and Jews, but exists also among certain American tribes. Circumcision is always executed by means of a stone knife and this circumstance shows the great antiquity of this rite : doubtless it was in practice during the Palæolithic Epoch.

During the last ten years several archæologists have been busy in the Near East investigating the problem of the origin of the Semites. These investigations have brought the conclusion that apparently the Semites originated from Arabia, which some millenniums ago was not a desert but a very fertile land : as a remembrance of that time one of the regions of it, Hadramaut, still preserves the name of 'Arabia Felix.' Archæological investigations have established that the Semites inhabited Arabia until about 5000 B.C. and thereafter, for some still unknown reason, moved to the north and to the north-east in a series of consecutive migrations. Nevertheless, much before these migrations some Semitic states, among which is remarkable the State of Akkad, or the enigmatical empire of Agadé, already existed in Mesopotamia. Moreover, we know, for instance, about one such Semitic centre in the northern part of Palestine, the Land of Ammurru, or the land of the Biblical Amorites, which maintained active relations with ancient Egypt. The cultures of prehistoric Semitic centres such as Jericho and Lahish already existed in the fifth millennium B.C., in the epoch of the northward mass-migrations of the Arabian Semites.

When the Semites, leaving Arabia, penetrated into Mesopotamia, they began to destroy the numerous and feeble native states, organizing in their place Semitic ones. We cannot yet say anything definite about the ethnical structures of those waves of emigrants : nevertheless it is plausible to suppose that the third one consisted of Hebrews, the fourth of Arameans and, as regards the Arabs, they did not leave their peninsula and remained in Arabia. However, the problem of the origin of the Semites is far from being solved, because we do not know whence they came to Arabia. Perhaps the investigations of americanists will throw light upon this interesting question.

The period of 5000 B.C. was remarkable for migrations by various nations. From the depths of the great Asiatic continent uninterruptedly streamed westwards hordes of barbarous and semi-civilized peoples. They passed over the Iranian table-land and the Caucasus and inundated the Near East. This west-ward stream was crossed by the Arabian Semites going northwards and eastwards, and therefore it is easy to imagine what a whirlpool of races and tribes there must have been at those spots which became the cross-roads of eastern and southern migrations. Not only were various races mixing, but this process of mutual assimilation acted also upon cultures and creeds. Thus the Semites received from without many ethnical and cultural foreign elements, including Aryan. Our remotest ancestors, the Aryans, still in a state of complete barbarity, wandered over the immense Asiatic prairies, while on the Mesopotamian plain already flourished the splendid cultures of Sumer and Semitic Akkad. The poetical and picturesque Biblical story of Cain and Abel probably symbolizes the conflict between the Aryan new-comers and the old Semitic settlers in Mesopotamia. We can see in Abel, pasturing his herds, the disordered throngs of Aryan nomads, who descended with their innumerable herds of cattle down the slopes of Hindukush and, pouring across the Iranian tableland, inundated fertile Mesopotamia. There they met Cain, the 'founder of cities,' as he is called by the Book of Bereshith, personifying the diligent and civilized Sumero-Akkadian agriculturist. Cain killed the nomad Abel, i.e. made a strong resistance to the attacks of the Aryan shepherds. The Hebraic version of this apparently Sumerian legend shows all its sympathies for the shepherd Abel, which can be explained by the Semitic animosity towards their Sumerian neighbours.

Westward and south-westward of Mesopotamia there sprang up at that epoch of migrations the cultures of the Semitic new-comers (Jews and Chananeans) and of the Egyptians. The Book of Bereshith calls these nations by the collective names of Sem, Chanaan, and Mizraim.

Goettner, in his *History of European Literatures*, suggested that the world's history resembles a fugue, in which the voices of various nations come one after another, like the instruments of an orchestra. It is a happy simile and I cannot help thinking that the first great accord of this orchestra of Aryan civilization was given by ' Cain,' that ' builder of cities,' of the Book of Bereshith, in the great Sumero-Akkadian half-Semitic civilization, accompanied by the distant voices of the remainder of the mysterious race from beyond the Pillars of Hercules. . . .

*   *   *

In Palestine have been discovered fragments of the so-called Moustier culture, which existed 500,000 years ago in Europe and the Near East. Between this remote period and the beginning of the Neolithic Epoch many millenniums passed and many human waves came into the world and vanished before the appearance on this historic scene of the first Semitic hordes. But until now all research in Palestine has failed to find any trace of epochs intermediate between the Moustier Period and the Neolithic. Thanks to the finds of Professor Garstang, who is working on the site of the Biblical Jericho, the Neolithic Period in Palestine is already well represented by various finds. Recently the museum of Palestine received from the expedition of Professor Garstang a collection of Neolithic statues : they are executed in a peculiar way in unbaked clay and possess eyes made of shells.

The archæological investigations in Palestine have corro-borated many ancient traditions and myths preserved by the Near Eastern nations. Moreover, these investigations have demonstrated that these Near Eastern countries lived an intensive political life long before the earliest events described in the Bible. Among the results of the excavations which justify some of the details of the Biblical narrations, it is very interesting to find proof that the biography of Abraham was written soon after the events described in the Book of Genesis. But I am of the opinion, as stated earlier, that the word ' Abraham ' is the collective name of an entire tribe ' Ibrim ' which later on came to be renamed ' Hebrews,' and the story of this famous patriarch is nothing else than the history of the migration of this tribe from Ur, i.e. from Mesopotamia, to the shores of the Dead Sea and Egypt.

In the ruins of a temple on the Sinai peninsula were found inscriptions in an unknown alphabet supposed to be the Hebraic of that epoch : this find led archæologists to suppose that the Jews during their wandering through the desert already used an alphabet somewhat similar to the Phœnician. In fact the books of Moses do contain references to writing and Moses is commanded by Jahveh to ' write these words,' or to ' write this on the gates and lintels,' etc. Sir Charles Marston discovered, on the site of the ancient Palestinian city of Lahish, several funeral urns of 1300 B.C. with inscriptions in the Sinain alphabet.

The traditions of Bereshith assert that the Ismaelites (Arabs) originated from Ismael, a son of Abraham, and his concubine and servant Agar. This tradition underlines on one side the common origin of the Jews and Arabs and on the other the lower origin of the Arabs in the eyes of Jews, the ' selected people of Jahveh.'

However, the same Bereshith, relating later on the story of Joseph, sold by his brothers into slavery to Ismaelitan merchants, implies that only three generations after Abraham the tribe of Ismaelites had already become so numerous that their caravans conducted a lively trade between Egypt and Palestine. It must be clear that Ismael alone could not have left any kind of tribe after only three generations (Joseph and his brothers were great-grandsons of Abraham). Therefore one is led to believe that here we are in the presence of the usual characteristic of traditions, which invariably baptize by the collective tribal name the legendary personality of its forefather. Thus I believe that Abraham and Ismael, as well as Isaac, Jacob, and all his sons, are nothing else than the names of primeval Hebrew and Arab tribes. The story of the banishment of Agar and Ismael from the house of Abraham indicates, in my opinion, an ancient and deep animosity between the Hebrews and Arabs.

*   *   *

The first book of the Pentateuch of Moses, or the Book of Genesis, is usually called ' Bereshith ' from the first words of the Hebrew text which mean ' at the beginning.' The date and the authorship of this remarkable book have for a considerable time occupied the attention of orientalists. Sir Charles Marston supposes that no legends of the Book of Genesis are more recent than 2000 B.C., but most likely this is an underestimate because it seems that the unknown author of Bereshith did possess some information, or at any rate traditions, concerning remotest periods of the Earth.

Although tradition ascribes to Moses the authorship of Pentateuch, and it is very likely that some of its chapters have really been written by this remarkable man, it is difficult to accept him as the author of the whole Pentateuch. This applies more specially to Deuteronomy, which describes the circumstances of Moses' death, which could hardly have been narrated by himself. A careful study of the comparative chronology of Bereshith and Egyptian sources also limits the range of Moses' authorship: as far as one can see, Moses was able to compile the whole of Leviticus and the last chapters of Genesis which deal with the first patriarchs. As to the first and the most remarkable part of Bereshith, it was apparently compiled by unknown annalists. The Book of Numbers and Exodus were probably definitely written on the basis of temple records in Jerusalem and popular traditions at a much later date—perhaps in the times of the pontiff Ezra.

The first and the smaller section of Genesis, dealing with the creation of the world and the first people, is distinctly different from the following chapters, which concentrate upon the origin of Israel and the events leading up to the patriotic mission of Moses. The first chapters of Bereshith are remarkable for their depth of thought and breadth of generalization, while the rest of the book presents a poetical and often touching story of Israel. On the whole, Genesis is one of the most remarkable literary achievements of all time. As Bereshith uses the name of the god Jahveh, it is called 'Jahvist' to distinguish it from other versions of Genesis.

For many centuries the Christian world considered Bereshith to be the oldest written monument, although, strictly speaking, there was no doubt that humanity had possessed documents of even greater antiquity. The author of the Book of Numbers hints at the existence of such ancient books (ch. xxi, verses 14–15 and 27–30).

Among the first patriarchs mentioned in Bereshith the

personality of the just Enoch is particularly interesting : he led such a pure and sinless life that Jahveh took him to heaven alive. The word ' Enoch ' means in ancient Hebrew ' initiated ' (see Tempestini's Dictionary of Hebrew). Hebraic, Arabic, Ethiopian, and even Chinese tradition insists that the just Enoch wrote a cosmogony, which was known under the name of the ' Book of Enoch.' According to Tempestini, the same traditions ascribe to Enoch the invention of writing and the compilation of the first treatises on arithmetic and astrology. Undoubtedly all these tales are based upon fact : apparently in remote prehistoric times there existed a great scientist, moralist, and astrologer named Enoch (i.e. initiated into the mysteries) who left after him works of which survived only the above-mentioned Book of Enoch. It is very possible that the sudden disappearance of Enoch himself originated the legend of his removal to heaven before his death.

According to tradition, the Book of Enoch was taken by Noah into his ark and thus preserved for posterity. We find hints of this book in the Epistles of the Apostles Peter and Judas and in the works of Christian authors, as, for instance, Origene, Procopius, Tertullian, Lactance, St. Justin, St. Ireneus of Lyons, Clement of Alexandria, etc. The sectarian Manicheans quoted texts from this book and the Christian writer Eusebius (see the fourth and ninth parts of his book *The Preparation of a Christian in the Spirit of the Gospel*) affirms that Abraham, being in Egypt, learned much from the Book of Enoch. It was for a long time considered lost, but in the eighteenth century Bruce brought from Abyssinia its Ethiopian version, which later on was translated into English by the Archbishop Richard Laurence.

The Ethiopians, or Biblical Midianites, affirm that Moses learned much from the Book of Enoch, which was given to him by his father-in-law, the Ethiopian priest-magician Jethro, and later on incorporated some of the knowledge thus acquired into Bereshith. Perhaps the Book of Enoch served as a prototype for all the other versions of Bereshith. The Ethiopian version of the Book of Enoch (not to be confounded with the well-known apocryphal Gospel of Enoch) may represent one of the oldest vestiges of a mysterious culture which many millenniums ago flourished on the Gabesh tableland. For a long time it has been known that very ancient manuscripts are kept in the Abyssinian monasteries and the oldest church libraries.

Until 1934 the Codex Sinaiticus, which belonged to the Imperial Library in St. Petersbourg and later on was sold by the Bolsheviks to the British Museum, was considered to be the most ancient version of the Pentateuch of Moses. But in 1934 another copy of the Pentateuch was discovered which not only is older than the Codex Sinaiticus, but, being written only 30 years after the Jewish occupation of Chanaan, may even be the first and the most authentic text of Moses. This important discovery was made at the time when the Prince of Wales, the future King Edward VIII, visited the poor Samaritan synagogue of Nablous (Sichem of antiquity). Then the rabbis as a special privilege showed him this ancient manuscript, which bears a so-called *tashkil*, or chronogram, which runs as follows : ' I, Abisha, son of Phinees, son of Eleazar, son of Aaron the pontiff, God bless them, wrote this book on the mount of Garizim, 30 years after the occupation of Chanaan by the children of Israel. Jehovah be praised ! ' Thus, the ' Abisha manuscript,' as this codex is called, can be dated about 1600 B.C., while the Codex Sinaiticus cannot be much older than A.D. 350. The authenticity of the Abisha manuscript was carefully verified and some supporting documents were found in a Manchester library. It is to be hoped that the British Museum will buy this precious manuscript before it tempts some wealthy collector, or that at any rate it will be photographed.

* * *

Most historians agree that the Jewish compilers of the Jahvist Genesis borrowed some of their data from the Sumero-Babylonians. I have dealt already in detail with this subject, as far as the Universal Flood is concerned, and the question now is to establish the epoch at which the borrowing occurred. King, for instance, thought that this happened in the seventh century B.C., but the find of the Abisha manuscript of the sixteenth century B.C. destroys this supposition. Probably Moses, or some other unknown author, arranged the Sumero-Babylonian legends which were in circulation at that time among the Jews, or borrowed them from the Egyptian priests, who had considerable connection with Sumero-Babylonian literature. We see from the Bible that Abraham and his father Tharra at one time lived in Ur and so, perhaps, their tribe took with them to Egypt traditions, or maybe even documents, recording the Sumero-Babylonian tales. In support of this supposition I quote a Babylonian myth which has much in common with Bereshith's story of original sin :

One of the Tell el Amarna tablets contains a Babylonian myth about Adapa, whose father, the God Ea, has forbidden his son to eat anything offered by the god Anou, because he suspects that the food of Anou is a ' food of Death.' But Ea's suspicions are unfounded : in reality Anou is offering to Adapa the ' food of Life,' being desirous of making him immortal and learning from him some of his secrets. Adapa's obedience to his father's command deprives him of a chance of becoming immortal.

The cult of Bel, or Baal, who personified the sun, was widespread in the Near East. The dim traditions of prehistoric peoples tell about Bel, a great leader and reformer, who colonized Mesopotamia and established there a priests' hierarchy similar to the Egyptian system which, however, appeared many centuries later. The legends concerning the origin of Bel affirm that this god was the son of Poseidon and Lybia, which may indicate that Bel came from Libya, which at that time was a part of the kingdom of Poseidon, the great maritime empire. Later on, as happened so often in antiquity, the founder of the Sumerian empire, Bel, was deified and became the symbol of the Sun.

A number of Greek authors, beginning with Homer and ending with Plato, record the existence of the great empire of Poseidon beyond the Pillars of Hercules. Other data, some of it already mentioned in this book, indicates that this powerful empire greatly influenced the life of the Mediterranean prehistoric peoples and the life of the nations of the Near East. This empire was apparently created by highly cultured Atlanteans soon after the end of the last Glacial Period. Once we admit the existence of this Atlantean empire, we may easily ask ourselves whether it was not Atlantis which passed on to the Sumerians and other nations of the Near East the legends which later on became the foundation of Genesis.

Some commentators explain that the Biblical legend con-

cerning Adam and Eve symbolizes the Atlantic catastrophe:
as Adam and Eve were thrown out of Paradise because, tempted
by Satan, they ate the forbidden fruit of the tree of Knowledge,
so the Atlanteans lost their prosperous island because they
studied the ' forbidden sciences,' i.e. magic and occultism. They
become proud of their knowledge and of their materialistic
progress and therefore were punished by God.

Very likely the Garden of Eden was situated somewhere on
Plato's continent and the legends concerning it, like the legends
of the Happy Arcadia of the Pelasgi and Greeks, are an inheritance of Atlantean-American antiquity, brought by prehistoric
emigrants to Phœnicia, Mesopotamia, and Egypt. The angel
with flaming sword, keeping Adam and Eve out of Eden, indicates,
perhaps, the fact that the garden of Atlantean Eden was situated
in the neighbourhood of some terrifying volcano.

We find a similar legend among the Phœnicians, who probably
brought it from the distant west. Some time during the last
century in the ruins of Tyre there was found a very ancient
Phœnician coin which bears the picture of a solitary tree with
a serpent winding around it. Archæologists immediately assumed
that this represented the Biblical Tree of Knowledge. This
supposition was supported by the recent finds in Ras Shamra of
tablets recording a detailed story of Adam and Eve very similar
to the Biblical one.

There is a Greek legend which credits the Phœnician hero
Cadmus with the invention of the alphabet. The name ' Cadm,'
pronounced with a light aspiration, like ' Hadm,' and ' Adam '
with accentuation on the first A, are almost identical, and we
are justified in thinking it possible that they belong to the same
personality. Adam obtained from the forbidden fruit the light
of knowledge for his posterity, and the Phœnician Cadmus,
or Cadm, enlightened mankind, giving to it the elements of
writing, i.e. the source of knowledge.

Adam and Eve may symbolize the ancient Atlanteans, who
lived in wealth and contentment in the earthly Paradise, or
Atlantis, until they irritated God by their evil studies and
practices, which to-day might be termed by occultists black
magic, and were expelled from their fatherland when it was
destroyed by an earthquake and volcanic eruptions. The
insidious devil in the shape of a serpent may be a remembrance

of ophiolatry (the cult of serpents), practised by the Atlanteans. We must note that the serpent symbol is found everywhere on the prehistoric monuments of Mexico and Central America.

According to Genesis, the first man bore the significant name of Adam, which means ' red,' or ' made of red clay.' Such a name makes one think that this story originated with a red-skinned race, i.e. an American one, or with Phœnicians, who were called by the Greeks ' phoinix ' (red), and who in their turn might have been distant descendants of the Atlanteans. The latter, according to traditions of the Mayas of Yucatan (see the Book of Chilam Balam of Chumayel), were red-skinned.

The French scientist Devigne noticed that the expression ' sacred tree ' is very similar in many languages. It is enough to quote together ' um ' of ancient Egyptian, ' hom ' of ancient Persian, and the Mayan ' om,' or ' hom.' This similarity deserves further investigation. The Hindus and Iranians worshipped the Spirit of the Sacred Tree, called ' Haoma,' and a mysterious beverage of the same name, which word sounds almost like ' soma,' the sacred Hindu beverage.

Some scientists believe that the creation of the world in Bereshith corresponds chronologically (5508 B.C.) to the beginning of the Pharaonic Period in Egyptian history. Thus, the unknown author of Bereshith in his picturesque language probably defined as ' Chaos ' the time preceding the establishment of state order in Egypt.

The coincidence of certain of the chronological dates of Bereshith with Egyptian ones could be easily explained by the education which Moses received from Egyptian priests. Thus, the differences in chronologies were probably introduced by Moses purposely, for reasons of a political and religious character. On the other hand, as the definite version of some Jewish sacred books was compiled during the Babylonian captivity, there is the possibility of Sumero-Babylonian influence. Genesis dates the creation of the world at 5508 B.C., while the Egyptian chronology begins the First Dynasty at 5004 B.C., thus making a difference of 500 years between the creation of the world and the beginning of pharaonic Egypt. Some investigators believe that all the first patriarchs, ending with Noah, were none else than the first pharaohs, although the periods of life allotted by Bereshith to the patriarchs do not correspond to the length of reign of the various pharaohs. According to these theorists, the first pharaoh Mena (Menes of the Greeks), the founder of Memphis, was the Biblical Adam. The wife of Mena, Shesh, corresponds to the Hebraic Isha (Eve). The first son of Mena was called Teta-Kent ('criminal'), which brings to our mind the Kanighi (Cain) of Bereshith, who slew his brother. The twentieth pharaoh of the First Dynasty was Nofru, i.e. the Noah of the Bible, and his son was Khufu, or Cheops, i.e. Ham of Bereshith. We know from the Bible that the son of Ham, Mizraim, settled in Egypt. If we accept the above hypothesis and recognize Nofru for Noah, we shall find that the Universal Flood occurred 1656 years after the creation of the world and that during these 1656 years there reigned only twenty pharaohs, which is an evident absurdity. A certain amount of contradiction can also be noticed on the genealogical tables found in Egyptian royal tombs. The genealogical table of Abydos is considered to be the most exact: it was found in the mausoleum of Seti I, who, according to some Egyptologists, reigned at the time when Joseph, the son of Jacob, was sold by the Arabs into slavery. The table is engraved upon a rock more than 80 feet underground, but the British Museum possesses an exact copy. This table is nearer than others to the Biblical genealogy and begins with the pharaoh Mena.

* * *

Among the mediæval legends concerning the unknown in the depths of Africa and Asia, the most remarkable are the following: the legend about the fabulous kings Gog and Magog, the tradition concerning the kingdom of the enigmatical priest John, and the cycle of legends concerning the whereabouts of Paradise. On the last subject a whole literature has arisen and almost all theological dissertations, cosmographies, and maps have mentioned Paradise. All conjectures concerning its whereabouts were based on the verse 8 of the second chapter of Bereshith, where it is said that the Lord planted a garden in Eden, in the East. The Book of Genesis (ch. ii, verses 8–14), in describing the site of Paradise, says that a river issued from Eden dividing itself into four rivers: Phisson, running through the auriferous Land of Havila, rich in *bdolach* and onyx, Gihon (Geon), watering the Land of Kush, Hiddekel (the Tigris), and the Euphrates.

Some medieval commentators on this passage of Bereshith advanced the hypothesis that there are two Paradises, one existing on the Earth and the other—a spiritual one—in Heaven. The medieval theologians competed in the refinement of their dialectics in each defending his beloved theory concerning Paradise. The masses of the population, however, were eager to get more information concerning the earthly, more accessible, paradise. According to popular belief, this resembles partly the Moslem conception by the abundance of various fruits, delights, and pleasures, and by the absence of the necessity of working. The common people believed that in Paradise exist the source of eternal youth and live speaking birds, among which is the famous legendary Phœnix. On the Day of Universal Resurrection the blessed were to be accepted into this Paradise by its guardians Enoch and Elias and the tradition concerning the latter is connected with the tradition about the coming of the Antichrist.

The mediæval writer, Saint Althelmus, said in his poem, *De Laude Virginum* (p. 13, verse v), the following :

> '. . . Heliam colit, ut superis in sedibus Henoch,
> Quem rapuit quondam divina potentia coeli,
> Lurida ne mundi pateretur damna nefandi,
> Idcirco simul ad belli certamina cruda
> Contra Antichristum gestant vexilla Tonantis
> Omnia de nigris surgent cum corpora bustis
> Clausae per campos et tumbae sponte patescunt
> Dum salpix crepat, et clangit vox clara tubarum
> Adveniant Deo, qui cunctis praemia pensat,
> Seu pia perfectis, seu certe saeva profanis . . .'

('. . . He respects Elias and Enoch, living in heaven, who were once raised up by the Divine Will with the purpose of liberating men from the sight of terrible crimes of the sinful world. Therefore they will carry the banners of the Thunderer at Doomsday, when the tombs will open themselves everywhere, when the dead will rise out of them, when the last trumpet of the Archangel will resound and the trumpets of angels will announce the coming of Lord. He will render their due to all men : a blessing to the perfect and a cruel punishment to sinners. . . .')

Enoch and Elias, according to the medieval creed, guard the interior side of the entrance to the Paradise, but the gates without are guarded by an angel with a flaming sword. The tradition adds that Christ will give them as an assistant the Apostle St. John in order to combat the Antichrist. When the latter tries to penetrate into Paradise, St. John will help the angel to keep out this most undesirable guest.

Other traditions say that the Tree of Life from Paradise served for making the Holy Cross and that out of the sword of the angel was prepared the spear with which was pierced the flank of Christ. When this sword was taken from him, the disarmed angel let into Paradise the souls of blessed people, resurrected by the Saviour from the subterranean kingdom.

The words of the Bible concerning the easterly position of Eden were understood by some commentators to signify that Paradise was situated in Virgil's Elysium, i.e. outside the Earth. This abode of the righteous was supposed to possess its own atmosphere, its own soil, and even its own starry heaven.

Theophilus, the archbishop of Antioch in the second century, believed that the River Gihon (Geon) of the Biblical Paradise is nothing else than a great Ethiopian river, the tributary of which is the Nile. At that epoch Ethiopia was often confounded with India.

Cosma Indicopleustes says that the Earth is surrounded by an ocean, but beyond it there is another Earth, also surrounded by another ocean, and this latter is connected with Heaven. Just at the point of this connection is situated Paradise. Its four rivers penetrate into the Earth and, running under the earth-crust and both oceans, rise again on to the surface of the Earth.

Saint Gregory of Tours, in the sixth century, supposed that the Nile runs from the east towards the Red Sea and affirmed that this mighty river was so long that its sources were in India, where the Earth merges into Heaven at the spot where Paradise is situated.

Isidorus of Sevilla affirmed in the seventh century that the Nile was the Biblical Gihon.

A certain Mosis, a scholar of the tenth century, affirmed that Paradise was situated in an inaccessible eastern region, beyond high mountains and unnavigable wide seas, otherwise it would have been occupied long ago by the greedy rulers of the Earth. Adam, being of giant stature, waded across these seas and thus reached Palestine, where he died.

Michael Psellus, a mathematician of the eleventh century, wrote a treatise concerning the whereabouts of Paradise. This work contains all the legends which were in circulation at that time about Eden.

Dante says that Paradise is situated upon the summit of the Purgatory Mountain, but generally borrows his information from the above-mentioned work of Cosma Indicopleustes.

Even Christopher Columbus advanced a hypothesis concerning the whereabouts of Paradise: the great seafarer thought that it should be somewhere along the Orinoco !

However, most of the medieval cartographers place Paradise in the neighbourhood of India. When the Epoch of Great Discoveries began, the seafarers described enthusiastically the blessed islands of the Atlantic Ocean, and the contemporaneous cartographers began to place Paradise on their maps mostly near the Canary Islands.

Let us study a little the Biblical data concerning the whereabouts of Paradise. Two of its rivers, Hiddekel, or Tigris, and Euphrates, are well known to us, but we cannot trace either the Land of Havila, or the rivers of Phisson and Gihon. The Land of Kush could be one of the Egyptian provinces, although it is really too remote from the Tigris and Euphrates. Also we do not seem to be able to trace any native onyx in ancient Babylonia. The mentioning of the Tigris and Euphrates can be explained by the additions introduced by the Babylonians themselves out of national pride, but the use of other mysterious and contradictory geographical terms is very puzzling. I am inclined to think that Gihon and Phisson are the names given in the original version of the story of Paradise, always allowing for distortions such as are likely to be introduced after thousands of years' currency. At any rate Eden did not exist in Mesopotamia. Incidentally, I have visited the locality of Gurneh in Mesopotamia where, according to the traditions, Eden was situated : it is a miserable Arab settlement in the middle of the monotonous alluvial plain. The district is so absolutely barren and devoid of vegetation that the thought of the magnificent gardens of Eden remains far from the mind of the spectator. . . .

As regards the Lands of Havila and Kush, we must admit that they did exist somewhere in antiquity. The very ancient Hindu manuscripts mention the Land of Havila, very rich in gold, and so remote from Hindustan that midday came there when midnight was in India. This would imply geographically a difference of 180° of longitude, placing the mysterious land somewhere in Mexico, a notoriously auriferous country. On the other hand, if we identify Havila with the Biblical Ophir, the philological investigations will give some foundations for the belief that Havila was in Peru.

But once we admit the identity of Havila with Mexico, we can assume that the legend of Eden with Mexican geographical terminology was adopted by the Atlanteans and passed on through the Phœnicians to the Near East.

Very likely some tribes, surviving after the Atlantean catastrophe, settled in the valley of Nile and on the territory of the present Abyssinia ('the Land of Kush'), baptizing their new abode with the names of their lost home-land. The original Land of Kush probably was situated east of Mexico on the lost continent, which conjecture would agree with Genesis in placing Paradise to the east. The Land of Havila was probably situated also in this part of the world and, perhaps, nearer to the American shores. Later on the Sumerians, adopting the Mexican story (or Atlantean legend) of Paradise, added to it the names of their own rivers Tigris and Euphrates, but in the original tradition were mentioned only the rivers Fisson and Gihon, which existed on the lost continent. This reasoning is supported by some indications of American folklore. Eventually, when the Mexican-Atlantean legend became widespread in the Near East, the term 'Havila' was relegated to some auriferous district of the Old Continent, to Hadramaut in Arabia, for instance.

Dr. Herrmann is against the above supposition, but his conjectures should be mentioned in order to complete the account of the present state of investigations concerning Genesis. Herrmann, in his interesting *Die Erdkarte der Urbibel*, attempts to throw fresh light upon the problem of the situation of Eden, to establish the nature of the Universal Flood, to interpret the meaning of the Biblical term 'Ophir,' and to penetrate the mystery of Plato's Atlantis. While the German scientist is not able to give a definite solution of any of the above problems, a short survey of his conjectures would not be out of place in my inquiry.

His investigations concern chiefly the toponymical data presented by two very ancient books : ' The Book of Jubilees ' and ' Asatyr ' (' mystery '). The Book of Jubilees, sometimes called the ' Little Genesis,' is considered more ancient than Bereshith, and its geographical conceptions betray the influence of the Phœnicians. Studying this book, Herrmann came to the conclusion that the mysterious Gihon of Bereshith was nothing else than the Nile, the river of Ham, and that therefore the site of Eden should be sought in Abyssinia. At the same time the erudite historian quotes the opinion of the Hebraist Jahuda, who affirms that to the ancient Egyptians Eden was a mysterious subterranean country situated to the extreme west. This opinion of Jahuda lends a support to my hypothesis of the Atlanto-American origin of Bereshith.

The ancient Samaritan book of Asatyr led Herrmann to select the oasis of Hadramaut in Arabia Felix as an alternative for the site of Eden. The mysterious river of Fisson, watering the Land of Havila (' where gold is '), would be then nothing else than the torrent Wadi el Roummah, which in ancient times carried its auriferous waters through the present Nedjd, and now in some places disappears under the sands. Nedjd is still rich in gold, precious stones, onyx, and fragrant vegetable pitch, and, according to Herrmann, is the Land of Havila, credited by Bereshith with abundance of onyx and *bdolach* (the aromatic secretions of certain plants). This supposition is supported also by the fact that the ancient Hebrew documents gave the name of Eden to the whole of Arabia, including the western shores of the Red Sea and even Abyssinia. Herrmann discerns the word ' Eden ' in the name of the present British Colony Aden. When the Book of Jubilees mentions the inundation of Eden, it implies, according to Herrmann, that the local Abyssinian flood was extensive enough to submerge also the Yemen and the Arabia Felix of the ancients, i.e. the region of Eden.

Convincing as are the arguments of Dr. Herrmann, they do not take into account the results of the excavations in Mesopotamia (by Langdon and Woolley) and the legends of the natives of America. Apart from the usual distortions which ancient compilers introduced into their texts owing to patriotic considerations, or simply through ignorance, we must remember that there were many floods in various regions of the Earth and the descriptions of them were probably grafted upon the original Atlantean version of the Universal Flood.

Herrmann, believing that the Bereshith story of the Universal Flood is only an Armenian version of the Gilgamesh legend, thinks that the mention of Ararat was added by an Armenian compiler, and that the flood was purely local and took place in Abyssinia. The Book of Jubilees incidentally mentions that Eden was also submerged by the Flood. As far as the duration of the Flood is concerned, various opinions differ considerably. The Sumerian version speaks of six days, the Jahvist Genesis estimates its duration at forty days, and the Book of Enoch allots to it a whole year. Modern archæologists reckon the duration of the Flood in centuries.

*   *   *

Lord Kingsborough, in his *Antiquities of Mexico*, informs us that at one time there was common among the Toltecs the picture of a serpent with the head of a woman winding around a solitary tree standing in the middle of a space bordered by other trees. The Spanish missionaries of the time of the Conquest understood this woman-serpent to symbolize the first Woman in the Garden of Paradise. Some years ago Guatemalan archæologists found an ancient copper tablet with a carving representing a snake winding around a tree, in close conformity with the story of the Bible.

A myth of the North American Pahoute Indians tells about the god Hinuno, who quarrelled with other gods and, therefore, was cast out from Heaven. Then Hinuno became the god of evil. Mexican legends have a story about a god, or a spirit, who rebelled against the Supreme Being. The name of this spirit was Sootan, or Shutan—a striking analogy with the Semitic and Christian Satan, or Shatan (Shaitan), of the Moslems. Perhaps it was the name of some powerful vassal of the Atlantean empire, who rebelled and was exiled to a remote colony in the Old Continent. Eventually the legends of the Semites and Indians transformed this ancient revolutionary into the mighty spirit of evil.

The sixth chapter of Bereshith tells us that once upon a

time the ' sons of God ' (' the sons of Light,' i.e. some cultured race) descended upon Earth and, captivated by the beauty of daughters of men, entered into union with them and thus created a progeny of great and glorious giants called the ' Giborim.' We find a similar story in the myth about the Greek Titans, who rebelled against Zeus and attacked Olympus. One of them, Prometheus, ' brought to men fire from heaven,' i.e. enlightened mankind, and was punished for this crime by Zeus. This tale of rebel giants is repeated also by Mexican traditions, which speak about the giants called Kinams, who at one time ruled the universe. Ramayana tells about the ' Rakshas,' or giants, who, being under Ravana, the king of demons, fought against the People of Monkeys (perhaps the Veddahs, the primeval races of Hindustan) and were defeated by the king Rama. The Codex Popul-Vuh also mentions the dreadful giants who at some time tried to master the world. The Book of Enoch describes in detail the war against cannibal-giants, who were 300 elbows high and would have eaten everything upon the Earth.

The universality of this legend may indicate its origin: it is probable that these powerful giants, fabled to be familiar with magic, and sufficiently proud of their knowledge and daring to defy the Almighty Himself, were nobody else than the Atlanteans

The Indian historian of Mexico, the famous Ixtlil-Xochitl, relates that after the Universal Flood men were busy inventing methods by which they could save themselves in case of a recurring of the wrath of the gods.

Therefore the ancestors of Aztecs decided that the best thing would be to build a tall tower on the top of the Great Pyramid of Cholula, erected at a remote period by the giant Shelua. This intention of the Aztecs displeased the gods and they mixed the languages of the builders of the tower, struck the unfinished structure with terrific thunderbolts, and destroyed what was left of it by dropping from Heaven an enormous stone (doubtless a meteorite) shaped like a toad.

This legend of the Aztecs much resembles the story of the Tower of Babel mentioned in the Book of Genesis. Lewis Spence considers that the Biblical story of the Tower of Babel

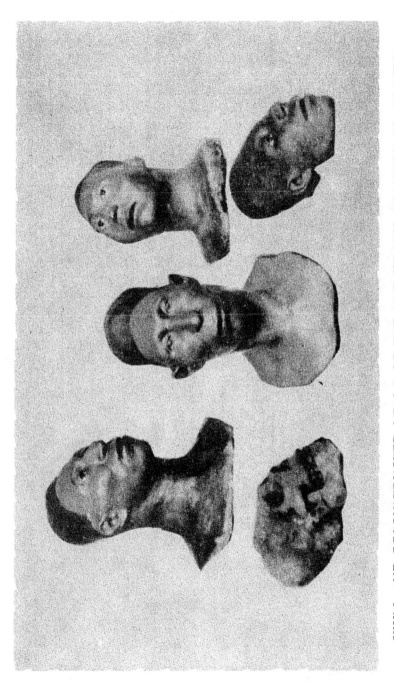

SKULL AND RECONSTRUCTED HEADS OF THE PREHISTORIC INHABITANTS OF PERU

(Museum of Lima.)

RECONSTRUCTED FIGURE OF THE SO-CALLED 'MAN
OF PARACAS IN HIS WAR-CLOTH

refers to some cyclopean Atlantean construction. As far as the ' mixing of languages ' is concerned, I deem myself justified to discern in it disorders which may have easily occurred amongst the workmen of the various heterogeneous tribes who would be gathered for the construction of some exceptionally great prehistoric building.

The Biblical legend of the creation of the world finds its counterpart in the remarkable story of the Quichua Indians of Peru, which begins with the following words : ' In the beginning there was only water and Chaos was the ruler, while the Great Spirit soared above the waters.' This is practically a repetition of the first words of the Book of Bereshith.

The world-creation myths of the Muskoghen Indians (the tribes of the Creeks, Choctaws, and Seminoles) say that the Great Esaughetuh created men out of clay and divided the land from the waters, over which hovered doves. In this legend we find again a strong resemblance to those of the Book of Genesis.

The story of Quiché Indians concerning their hero Zipancu, for instance, is related by the famous Codex Popul-Vuh with much the same details as the story of Samson in the Bible, or incidentally, in the Sumero-Babylonian solar myth of Shamash.

An Aztec legend explains that once upon a time the gods lived in a terrestrial paradise, which was a splendid garden full of trees bearing magnificent fruits and with fragrant flowers. Multicoloured birds sang charming melodies and the gods listened to them, spending their time in happy inactivity. But there was a drawback which caused discontent among the gods : a darkness reigned upon the Earth. The native legend does not explain how the gods could enjoy the bright colours of the birds and flowers in darkness. . . . Thus, the gods decided to create two luminaries, one for the day and the other for the night. In order to create them it was necessary to sacrifice two gods, but none of them was willing to commit suicide and so they decided to draw lots. Tecu-Tzitz-Tecatl, the richest and most powerful god, and Nana-Otzin, the poorest and weakest, were selected by fate.

Both gods were sent to the summit of the Great Pyramid of

Teotihuacan, which now is called the Pyramid of the Sun, each to light there a fire in which they were to burn first their possessions and then themselves. The rich god threw into the fire the multicoloured feathers of the quetzal (a very rare bird), precious objects, gold, and fragrant copal, but, when it came to throwing himself into the flames his courage gave out, and after four attempts he renounced it altogether and thus lost his opportunity of becoming a sun. But the poor Nana-Otzin, who had only the green thorns of cactus to offer, valorously leapt into the fire, was burnt, but immediately was resurrected in the heavens in the shape of the brilliant Sun. When the first god saw this, he promptly threw himself into the fire. He also was burnt, but was resurrected only as the Moon, the light of which, however, was at first almost as bright as sunlight. The gods corrected this by throwing a sparrow on to the satellite, which reduced the moonlight and left several dark spots on the disk.

In this very naïve and somewhat contradictory Aztec legend we can trace some points of analogy with the Biblical legend of the first men, if we consider Adam as a symbol of the Sun, fertilizing the whole of nature, and Eve, as a symbol of the mild Moon. As the happy Mexican gods lived in a paradisiacal garden, so the first immortal and godlike men of Bereshith inhabited a beautiful garden and were not obliged to work for their food. As the two Mexican gods, one strong and the other weak, sacrificed themselves in order to procure light for the other gods, so the first men of Bereshith, the strong Adam and the weak Eve, lost their immortality in order to procure the light of knowledge for posterity.

Incidentally, the Satan of Bereshith, on inviting Adam and Eve to learn the difference between Evil and Good, speaks of the gods (in Hebraic, *elohim*), instead of God, which shows that this book was not written by such a pronounced monotheist as Moses and that this legend was born amongst a polytheistic people. The same plural ' gods ' (*elohim*) is found in the first verse of Bereshith, which says that ' in the beginning the gods created . . .' etc. No exegetic subtlety could efface this clear indication of the polytheistic outlook of the author of Bereshith.

So much for the analogies of the two legends. I must point

out, however, that the Mexican legend completely lacks the profound philosophy which underlines the narrative of Bereshith. Bereshith explains in its story that great knowledge does not bring happiness to men, knowledge being really allotted to the gods alone, and that men, like animals, can obtain happiness only by the sheer joy of life. A striving for knowledge on the part of a creature is an act of rebellion against the divine will and is punished by destruction or death. Later on, a thousand years before the birth of Divine Light and Love, a Jewish king, despairing at the apparent futility of existence, exclaimed : ' Whoever multiplies knowledge, multiplies sorrow ! '

The source of light, the Sun, was often symbolized by. the Toltecs, Mayas, and Aztecs in the image of a more or less conventionalized feathered serpent. Quetzal-Coatl and Cuculcan, the enlighteners of Central America, were also often symbolized by winged serpents. Bereshith likewise has a serpent, the spirit of Evil, who directs Adam and Eve along the road of Knowledge, i.e. light.

Brasseur de Bourbourg knew of another Aztec legend, which is even nearer to Bereshith and assured us simply, that ' in times immemorial there was a paradise on Earth, inhabited by the gods. When the gods tasted of the forbidden fruit of the sacred tree, they were expelled from paradise.'

One feels that, behind the texts of Bereshith, Asatyr, the Book of Jubilees, and the traditions of the various peoples, is hidden under the veil of millenniums some single truth, common to them all. Apparently, at some time, there existed a great centre which furnished cultural, cosmogonic, theogonic and mythological inspirations to all the prehistoric peoples. Many millenniums ago the great Atlantean culture stretched from Mexico to Babylon and probably even further, into India and distant Indo-China. This culture created a range of sacred codices of mythology and primitive philosophy, some of which have survived to our days. The same culture collected a treasury of knowledge concerning the phenomena of nature and particularly empirical knowledge, such as medicine, the forecasting of the weather, and magic in its various forms. This led to the creation of the whole epic world, populated by gods, giants, dwarfs, luminaries, animals, and invisible good and evil spirits.

To-day we still find the New World, Egypt, Asia Minor, and India endowed with magnificent monuments, often cyclopean in their technique and pyramidal in their conception. They are architectural reminiscences of this splendid prehistoric culture. . . .

CHAPTER X

THE most interesting hypothesis concerning the origin of the Egyptians and their culture is the Ethiopian one. First of all I must explain that the term ' Ethiopia ' has not always been confined to present-day Abyssinia. Secondly, it is necessary to note the hypothesis of Professor Leo Frobenius affirming that at one time Northern Africa served as the cradle of some great prehistoric culture.

We have already seen that, according to L. T. Ojeda, many terms of the Mediterranean toponymy are nothing more than the ' duplicates,' or repetitions, of geographical names of places sometimes very distant from their earlier homonyms. According to Ojeda, some catastrophe which caused the inundation of the prehistoric Mediterranean depression and the formation of a sea in its place destroyed a series of countries which possessed names identical with many present-day ones. The survivors escaped to various countries and gave to their new homes the names of their fatherlands. Thus, if we accept the hypothesis of L. T. Ojeda, then, whenever we deal with geographical terms presented by ancient authors or traditions, we must always make sure whether we are dealing with a locality in the Mediterranean depression, or with its homonym of post-catastrophe times. But this differentiation is very difficult and in the case of myths sometimes even impossible. According to P. Le Cour the word ' Ethiopian ' (' Eti-ops ') signifies ' sun-burnt,' and shows that the inhabitants of ancient Ethiopia were dark-skinned even if they were not negroes, and lived in a hot climate. At first sight all the above seems to apply to the modern Abyssinians.

However, it turns out that two Ethiopias were known to ancient authors, such as Diodorus Siculum (*Historia*, lib. iii, cap. i), Homer (Iliad, i, 424), Hesichius, and Eustate, who all differentiate between Eastern and Western Ethiopia. Diodorus affirms that the ancient Egyptians took their hieratic writing,

sculpture, and some of their other knowledge from the
Ethiopians. The Ethiopians themselves have a tradition supporting this statement. Theophrastes, in his biography of the
famous magician Apollonius of Tyana, relates that the latter,
after his education in India and Egypt, came to Ethiopia in
order to enlarge his knowledge by learning from the Ethiopian
mystagogues. The same Apollonius, according to Theophrastes,
claimed that Pythagoras learned from Egyptian priests only
what the latter themselves had learned from the Ethiopians.
Very possibly the prehistoric Ethiopian culture was superior
to that of their neighbours. Unfortunately none of the quoted
authorities specify which of the two Ethiopias they had in
view, except Homer, who says distinctly that the Olympian
gods went to a feast in Ethiopia far beyond the ocean. Virgil
(Aeneid, lib. iv) supplements this information by stating that
the Sun sets in Ethiopia, where the giant Atlas supports the
Universe on his mighty shoulders. Scylaxus of Coriandre
records that the Phœnicians maintained an animated trade with
the Ethiopians of the island of Cerne, situated beyond the
Pillars of Hercules. Some authorities believe that Cerne, or
Ogygia, belonged to the group of the Canary Islands, often
visited by the Phœnicians, but I do not see how the Ethiopians
could get so far. This tradition of the western situation of
Ethiopia survived into the Middle Ages : at least, we observe
that one of the medieval maps calls the Southern Atlantic
' Oceanus Ethiopicus.'

Other ancient authors are even more specific and identify
Ethiopia with Atlantis. Diodorus, for instance, in discussing
Western Ethiopia, states that it was populated by the Atlanteans.
Pliny's words are also worth quoting : ' Universa vero gens
Ætheria appellata est deinde Atlantia, mox a Vulcani filio
Æthiopia ' (Hist. Natur. i, 6). They mean : ' In fact the whole
country was called Ætheria from the name of Vulcan's son.'
Pliny explains that originally Ethiopia was called Ætheria, or
Æria, and later on, Atlantia. One wonders whether Æria does
not derive from the word ær (air, in Greek æther), or from æs
(copper). The name of Vulcan's son was Æther.

In this connection it is interesting to note that the Latin
writer Aulus Gellus affirmed that the name ' Æria ' was once
used both for Africa and Crete. This strange coupling of

Africa with Crete may indicate that in the day of Aulus Gellus the primitive meaning of the term ' Æria ' had already been forgotten; at the same time there probably still existed in the epoch of Aulus Gellus a tradition of some Mediterranean catastrophe which had separated the island of Crete from the opposite African shore. Perhaps the waters of the ocean which rushed into the Mediterranean depression after the breaking of the Gibraltar isthmus flooded the lowlands between the Egyptian shores and the Cretan tableland.

Moreover, the wife of the giant Atlas, according to tradition, was called ' Æthra.' This circumstance is also an indication in favour of the hypothesis placing ' Æthiopia ' in Atlantis. We have to remember that the poetical language of myths often calls the more or less large countries, or colonies, ' wives,' and the small provinces ' daughters ' of the mother country. Thus, for instance, Homer calls the nymph Calypso, living in the island of Ogygia, ' the daughter of Atlas.'

The above facts lead us to the conclusion that in antiquity the name of Ethiopia was given to a region of Atlantis. This region was populated by dark-skinned people and possessed a fine climate (good ' air '). Therefore ' Æthiopia ' is probably more correct etymologically than ' Ethiopia.' When catastrophes overwhelmed Atlantis, the population of this region escaped like many other refugees to Europe and Africa. One would add that the migration wave, which comprised these ' Ethiopians,' must have included also the Gauls, because these two peoples seem to have had a certain connection. I have already mentioned the similarity of their menhirs and superstitions and the presence of the tribe called Galla in Abyssinia. For a certain time these ' Ethiopians ' inhabited the mountainous Atlas region and from there migrated to Abyssinia which they named ' Ethiopia ' in remembrance of their lost fatherland. These dark-skinned new-comers were much more cultured than the aborigines of Egypt of those days and Diodorus did not exaggerate the cultural role of the Ethiopians in Egypt. It is also not at all impossible that not all the original Ethiopians escaped in the same direction: some fractions of Atlantis might have temporarily survived the catastrophe and furnished shelter to Ethiopian clans. Such a fraction was probably the island of Cerne mentioned by Scylaxus of Coriandre, or the Ogygia of Homer,

the residence of Calypso, ' daughter of Atlas.' The testimony of
Diodorus and other authors of antiquity brings to our mind
the conjectures of certain atlantologists on the same subject.
They believe that the Egyptians borrowed from the Atlanteans
their god Osiris and the idea of the existence of the soul after
death. ' The astral double ' was known to the Egyptians as
the ' ka,' and it is interesting to note that the Book of the Dead,
probably also borrowed from the Atlanteans, indicates that the
Land of Amenti, or the abode of the souls, was situated far
away to the west from Egypt, beyond the Pillars of Hercules.

The recent discovery of a very ancient sphinx in Abyssinia
has lent unexpected support to the hypothesis which presumes
Ethiopian influence on the development of ancient Egyptian
culture. The very fact of this piece of sculpture being more
primitive than those of ancient Egypt, in my opinion, gives all
the better support to the Ethiopian hypothesis. In fact, were
the Abyssinian sphinx superior to the Egyptian, it would have
indicated that the Ethiopian artists had borrowed an Egyptian
conception and perfected it.

The existence of the Abyssinian sphinx had been known, or
at any rate suspected, for a long time. It was mentioned by
the Frenchman Lefevre, who visited Abyssinia in 1843, and
another French traveller Romond, in 1909, heard from natives
of this monument. Lefevre even specified that the sphinx was
cut out in a rock overhanging the Ardibbo lake in the Argobba
mountains, and that its pose seemed to indicate an intention of
leaping into the lake.

In 1937 the Italian administration of the Uollo district of
Asmara province decided to verify these reports and the sphinx
was really found near Angiarro, situated in the Uollo-Callu
district. The sphinx is roughly hewn in volcanic rock and
occupies an area of about twelve square yards, resting on an
enormous pedestal. The head and the front paws are carefully
finished, but the remainder of the figure is only blocked out.
It is plausible to think that the presence of two superimposed
rocks gave to the primitive artist the idea of using the top one
for the lion and the other for the pedestal. Although the lion
is lying down, there is sufficient movement in its figure to make
it seem ready for a spring. The officials who inspected the

sphinx came to the conclusion that the back of the statue is not a work of art at all, but a natural rock, accidentally possessing the shape of a lion's back. The head of the statue resembles a lion and is adorned by a conventionalized tuft of hair. The ears are small, the teeth are sharp, and the eyes are made so well that they give life to the whole statue. The maneless neck is long out of all proportion and reminds one of a reptile. The front paws are finished with claws. In spite of its crudeness, the style of the whole figure resembles Egyptian art.

The monument is overgrown with moss and lichens and seems to be very old. Under the front paws are visible four hieroglyphs, so far undeciphered.

The natives call this monument ' Sil-Denghia ' ('a stone figure'), and say that it was made very long ago by a white artist to the order of some ancient king. At one time the Abyssinian sphinx was used to mark the boundary between Argobba and Uolla-Callu.

*   *   *

Owing to the recent discoveries made in Central and South America, it is now possible to develop the Atlantean hypothesis of the origin of the Egyptian culture still further, tracing the origin of the pre-Egyptians themselves to America.

The fact is, that in many countries of the New World have been found traces of a prehistoric race which had much in common with the pre-Egyptians. G. Hurley and E. Valcarcel, for instance, affirm the Andean origin of pre-Egyptian art and culture. Richard Marsh found in the virgin forests of the Matto Grosso the remains of a culture very similar to the early Egyptian and an identical discovery was made in Venezuela by Dr. Requena. The Frenchman A. Frot found in the Brazilian forests a whole series of petroglyph texts, which seem to establish positively the eastward migration of pre-Egyptians from South America.

Even without any other proofs, the explorer among American antiquities is invariably impressed and puzzled by the evident resemblance between the prehistoric buildings of Mexico and Peru and the architecture of ancient Egypt. This resemblance is particularly vivid in the case of the American pyramids and majestic portals such as the famous doors of the Tihuanaco

Sun Temple in Bolivia. Egypt was not the only country to build pyramids : they form a sort of ' pyramid belt,' which begins in Armenia (the discovery of the Russian archæologist Professor Marr in Ani) and Mesopotamia with its zikkurats, passes through Egypt and, after the Atlantic gap, continues through Yucatan, the Mexican tableland, Guatemala, and San Salvador. The pyramids built by the Toltecs and Mayas are orientated in a most precise fashion and their astronomical significance is beyond doubt. This circumstance brings to our mind the latest discoveries concerning the structure of the Great Pyramid at Gizeh. The French General Langlois, in his articles in the *Revue Scientifique* of 1935, tells us about a mysterious prehistoric race which preceded the appearance of the Toltecs, Mayas, and other cultured peoples in America. This mysterious race, possessing great mathematical and astronomical knowledge, built many pyramids which were exactly orientated. Sometimes this very orientation has enabled us to date the buildings themselves and to place them between our era and 3000 B.C. at least. I might add here that I personally consider some of the American pyramids to be of much greater antiquity. The Great Pyramid of Teotihuacan, for instance, was undoubtedly built many millenniums before our era. Probably in America, as well as in Egypt, there have been cases of imitation of very ancient monuments, and the Toltecs, Mayas, etc. have erected pyramids, copying their ancient predecessors and without realizing the significance of the imposing monuments of the great vanished race. Some of the vague Indian legends say that the great pyramids of the New World (such, for instance, that of Cholula) were built by giants of unknown origin, who eventually perished in a great catastrophe with floods and earthquakes. The picturesque language of the Orinoco Indians terms this epoch ' the days when forests were flooded ' (' Catenamanoa ').

The resemblance between prehistoric American, Egyptian, and Babylonian buildings is sometimes amazing. The famous step pyramid of Sakkar in Egypt is plainly a copy of Mexican pyramids and Babylonian zikkurats.

The characteristic trait of American prehistoric and Egyptian monuments is the tendency to impress the spectator by their magnitude. Their builders strove to make them last for ever, and they attempted to achieve this either by using the pyramidal form or by employing enormous monoliths. This predilection for the colossal influenced also a whole range of cultures, beginning with the Mesopotamian cultures in the East and ending with the Breton in the West of Europe. Throughout this belt, from Central America to Babylonia, prehistoric architecture is characterized by geometrical simplicity in design, which produced sometimes an unparalleled beauty and the maximum of durability.

The kinship of prehistoric American and ancient Egyptian cultures is demonstrated very eloquently in the ruins of Palenque, Ocochingo, the Mitla palaces, the Xochicalco, Teotihuacan, and Sihuatan pyramids, by the decorations of the Sun Temple of Cuzco, by the monolithic portal of the cyclopean temple-observatory of Tihuanaco, and by many other monuments throughout Central and Southern America. Here it is interesting to note that A. Poznansky and R. Mueller have come to the conclusion that the ruins of the city and port of Tihuanaco date at least 13,000 years B.C.

Incidentally, the knowledge hidden in the details of the structure of the Great Pyramid at Gizeh was probably acquired by the Egyptians from the Atlanteans, because this knowledge, attracting at present a good deal of attention, shows a level superior to that usually found in Egypt. The central position of the continent in the Atlantic Ocean probably contributed to its predominant role in the civilized world of those days: its influence in the west stretched as far as Yucatan and Mexico and, in the east, as far as the Mediterranean basin and Babylonia. Later on we will see the wealth of knowledge displayed in the construction of the Great Pyramid at Gizeh, which was built in all probability under the influence, if not the direct supervision, of the Atlanteans. Besides the Great Pyramid and those of Gizeh, there are in Egypt several dozens of smaller pyramids, but neither the Pyramid of Kephren, next to the Great Pyramid in size, nor any other of the pyramids in Egypt, have displayed so far any interesting peculiarities of construction, and unlike the pyramid of Cheops, they usually contained the sepultures of their royal builders. Contrarily to the Great Pyramid, which was erected for scientific and mystical purposes, these structures were built at a much later period as mausoleums, imitating the shape of the mysterious monument.

The most prosperous period of Atlantean history was probably characterized by emigrations of the superfluous population to distant European colonies. These emigrants were replaced by pre-Egyptians and other tribes issuing from America. The pre-Egyptians, originating in South America, probably in Brazil, slowly traversed during several millenniums the territories of Peru, Bolivia, Ecuador, Central America, and Yucatan, creating along their route several states with indelible Egyptian traits. From America, through Atlantis and Northern Africa, the pre-Egyptians finally reached Lybia and Egypt and settled down along the Nile, which in those days probably discharged itself into a great swampy region between Gizeh and the now submerged low tableland south of the present Archipelago.

The pre-Egyptians probably stayed among the Atlanteans for a long time, until seismic or volcanic phenomena, or some other reason, drove them to the Old Continent. Then they traversed the territories of the present Morocco, Tunis, and Lybia and, perhaps, even a part of Abyssinia (Ethiopia) before they settled along the Nile. It is also possible that some of the pre-Egyptian clans went farther and, crossing the Red Sea, continued their migration through Arabia, Hindostan, Indo-China, and Indonesia. This may explain the recent discovery in New Guinea of a mysterious tribe resembling the ancient Egyptians.

* * *

The resemblances between prehistoric Mexican and some other American monuments and those of ancient Egypt are so striking that Mexico is often called ' American Egypt.' The chief points of resemblance are the pyramids and the hieroglyphic writing. But besides the exterior resemblances of certain American cultures with the Egyptian, I should mention some not less important analogies in ceremonies, religious rites, and mythology.

The anointment of the Chibcha *zipa* (king) in Colombia, for instance, resembles the coronation ceremonies of the pharaohs. Circumcision amongst the prehistoric Americans in certain countries was accomplished with the same ceremonies as in ancient Egypt, including even the use of a flint knife. H. Onffroy de Thoron also points out a distinct resemblance between vestments and religious attributes of the priests of some South American tribes and those used in ancient Egypt.

Egyptians believed that the firmament was sustained at four points of the horizon by four so-called Canopic deities, the children of Horus, and portrayed these spirits on the urns with the viscera of the dead. The American Mayas also believed that the spirits Can, Muluc, Ix, and Cauac support the four cardinal points and gave to each of these spirits, or Bacabs, a colour of its own : the eastern spirit was red, the northern, black, the southern, yellow, and the western, white. The visceræ of dead Mayas were also deposited in four urns with images of a corresponding Bacab on each.

The myths of the Ipurines, Andean Indians related to the tribes of the Antis and Quichua-Aymaras, resemble very closely the myths of Orpheus and Eurydice and partly the Osiris and Isis cycle.

Archæological finds resembling sometimes even in details Egyptian *objets d'art* are very common in Latin America. In this respect certain statues (among which is interesting particularly that of the goddess Xochipilly) in the National Mexican Museum remind one vividly of some Egyptian ones. The hairdress of ancient Mexican busts is very often analogous to the character-istic fashions of ancient Egypt. Two statuettes found in San Salvador reproduce exactly Egyptian mummies, except for the mysterious inscriptions on the pedestals. Wolf-headed statuettes, very similar to the Egyptian Anubis, were found among the ruins of the remarkable Sihuatan pyramid in San Salvador. This proves the existence of zoolatry among the builders of this prehistoric edifice, a unique instance of animal-worship so far discovered in America. The statuettes of Franco's collection in Quito (Ecuador) present many instances of Egyptian aspect in hairdress, beards, attire, and the breast-ornaments of priests. The curious fact of the presence of a bearded race in prehistoric America is borne out once more by the statue of ' The Bearded Man ' of the Tihuanaco ruins which alone survived the vandalism of the Spanish conquerors in Bolivia.

The layer of lava covering the prehistoric Mexican city near San Angel, the so-called ' Pedregal,' often yields stone scarabs absolutely identical with those found in Egyptian excavations. This prehistoric city was buried by the eruption of the volcanoes

Ajusco and Xitle about 8000 years ago. The thickness of the lava layer of Pedregal is 5½ yards and it is amazing to think that such a small crater as the neighbouring Xitle could, together with Ajusco, throw out such a great quantity of lava. . . . On the borders of Pedregal, in the locality of San Angel, galleries with a little archæological museum inside are cut in the lava. One can see in this museum the semi-carbonized and petrified corpses of the prehistoric inhabitants of Mexico. It seems that they belonged to some cultured race because among the finds you can see well-worked ceramics, artistic adornments, fine statuettes of gods, etc., and the aforementioned astounding stone scarabs.

Some scientists affirm that this 8000-years'-old race belonged to the so-called Mounds Builders and, in order to prove this assertion, mention the pyramid of Peña Pobre in Tlalpam, near San Angel. This pyramid, believed to be 11,000 years old, is a barrow faced with stones and identical to the known mounds in Texas. Other scientists suppose that the Peña Pobre pyramid was erected by the cultured tribe of Tarasques which at one time inhabited the Anahuac tableland. I have visited this monument, although it is not easy to approach it because it is surrounded by swamps and thick shrubs.

The autochthons of the New World are beardless and probably have been so since time immemorial. We can only suppose that at one time a bearded race did exist in America and eventually either died out, or emigrated. On the other hand some ancient Egyptian frescoes portray a mysterious redskin race ' Mazinti,' of a beardless Mongoloid type which may have been intended to represent some tribe of the original fatherland of the pre-Egyptians in America. I have said already that the mythological Egyptian Land of Amenti, or the abode of the dead, may symbolize the former fatherland of the pre-Egyptians and it is significant that the sign of ' Tau,' ornamenting the boats which carried souls to the Land of Amenti, can be found also on the Palenque bas-reliefs in Mexico.

Finally I should mention the discovery by Dziuk of white Indians on the Darien peninsula in Panama. These Indians wear a practically Egyptian hairdress and, in the opinion of some explorers, they resemble very much the ancient inhabitants of the valley of the Nile.

*   *   *

However, the most striking fact supporting the hypothesis of the American origin of the pre-Egyptians is the presence of hieroglyphic writing in New World prehistory. Here a short account of these hieroglyphs will not be out of place.

All the Aryan peoples and most of the others use alphabetical writing in which every sound is represented by a sign, or a group of signs. The remainder of humanity uses a cumbersome and old-fashioned pictorial method. Even in remotest times mankind was conscious of the necessity of fixing thought on some durable material and attempted to do so by a series of drawings. Thus, for instance, in order to record such an idea as ' the enemy was vanquished,' a series of little men was drawn, or carved, on a rock and the primitive artist did his best to show that they were falling under the blows or arms of other little men. Gradually the desire to shorten work led to the simplification of the drawings. For instance, the Chinese hieroglyph *jen* (man) still resembles a man with widely spread arms and legs. This simplification of primitive pictograms, or ideograms, was the first step towards the invention of a proper alphabet.

The process of the evolution of writing underwent many different stages, one of which was the hieroglyphic stage. Hieroglyphs sometimes still resemble the primitive pictograms and sometimes are simplified sufficiently to become symbolical signs, but are never a real alphabet. This fact creates a great difficulty for the investigators of texts in unknown languages. Their first duty is to discover to which type of writing belongs the newly-found inscription. As very often such texts are composed of a mixture of pictograms and hieroglyphs, the experts are frequently confronted by an impasse.

The hieroglyphic texts of ancient Egypt attracted the attention of European scientists only at the very end of the eighteenth century. The archæologists of those days believed that they were dealing with real and perfect ideograms, and tried, without result, all possible systems and keys, until Champollion conceived the brilliant idea of treating these texts as a sort of alphabetic writing. By a lucky accident Champollion discovered the famous Rosetta stone inscribed with three parallel texts. Two texts were given in hieroglyphics and the third in Greek. The last text included the name ' Ptolemy,' and Champollion found its equivalent in the hieroglyphic version. This permitted him to decipher the name of Cleopatra, and produced the meaning of fifteen hieroglyphs, which accelerated the deciphering and eventually enabled Champollion to read the whole of the text.

The contemporaries of Champollion relate that the discovery of the secret of the hieroglyphs so impressed him, that he shouted 'found!' and, throwing the sheet of paper with the finished translation to his brother, swooned and remained unconscious for five days. We can well understand this. Without his discovery we would have still been obliged to rely on the scanty and vague information of ancient writers in our studies of Egyptian history. Champollion, in his book on pharaonic Egypt, specifies that the priests of Isis used three kinds of writing : simple and clear (demotic), symbolic (hieratic), and hieroglyphic. Heraclites refers to them as 'speaking,' 'meaning,' and 'hiding.'

As far as the hieroglyphs of Mexico and Yucatan are concerned, they have attracted the attention of students since the middle of the last century, and have puzzled both them and the layman alike by their resemblance with Egyptian and also with Chinese writings.

In this connection it is interesting to remember the hypothesis that some of the nations under the immediate cultural influence of the Atlanteans possessed writing, and in such instances, as with the Mayas and Egyptians, we sometimes see analogies striking enough to cause us to deduce a common origin. That this influence was far-reaching we see from the fact that some investigators found resemblances between the Mayan hieroglyphs and the primitive Chinese trigrams of the legendary emperor, Fo-Hi. Probably the Phœnicians also created their alphabet by simplifying ideograms, borrowed either directly, or still more likely indirectly, from the Atlanteans. Such a supposition is all the more plausible, because we can see attempts at such simplification in rock inscriptions throughout the world. Many such ideograms display hints of the simplification process, tending towards the creation of hieroglyphs and the eventual birth of an alphabet proper.

For a long time all attempts to decipher the Mexican texts halted before overwhelming difficulties. The mysterious signs of the Toltecs, Aztecs, and Mayas consist of complicated arabesques and drawings usually enclosed in square frames.

It was necessary first of all to establish whether these signs were hieroglyphs, letters, or syllables. This was all the more difficult, because there was no Rosetta stone in America.

The hieroglyphic writing of the Toltecs, Aztecs, and Mayas was used apparently throughout Central and Southern America, but the Spanish conquerors burned thousands of written documents and nobody took pains to obtain an explanation of the hieroglyphic system from the frightened native intellectuals. By the time the Europeans had begun to come to their senses, it was too late: only a few manuscripts were saved, and it was not possible any longer to find a native, who could, or would, translate them, or explain their workings. Only in the nineteenth century were the ancient Mexican manuscripts, or codices, first subjected to systematic study. After many years of all sorts of research and guess work, the philologists were able to decipher the numerals and incidentally to discover that the Mayas possessed considerable astronomical knowledge. Their astronomy was closely connected with their religious beliefs, as is usual throughout the history of humanity. The ancient inhabitants of Yucatan and Mexico kept detailed records of their astronomical observations. These have enabled us to discover a certain amount regarding their chronology. Professor Luddendorf, for instance, by studying the Mayan records of sun eclipses, has established that their culture is at least 5000 years old. The dates of the eclipses are fortunately known to us, thanks to the exactness of the ancient Chinese and Chaldean chronicles. Professor Fritz Reck affirms that the Aztecs were quite familiar with the movements of the planets and that their works on astronomy and astrology very much resemble the Chinese systems. Even the calendar of the Aztecs resembles the Chinese. As a matter of fact the idea of some connection between the cultures of Central America and China is not a new one and the similarity between the monuments of prehistoric Mexico and China has impressed the americanists for the last hundred years, although so far no explanation of it has been offered.

In 1936 the Viennese Anthropological Society was startled by the announcement of Professor Fritz Reck to the effect that, after seven years of work, he had succeeded in deciphering some of the Mexican manuscripts. He was referring in particular to the famous Codex Vindobonensis, which was offered to Cortez by the emperor Moctezuma, and to six other manuscripts. Considering that in all there are only about twenty Mexican manuscripts in existence, some very good work seemed to have been done. The chief difficulty in the deciphering of these mysterious hieroglyphs consisted in determining the order in which they should be read. Various peoples use various methods in this respect. The Aryans, for instance, write from left to right, the Semites vice versa, the Chinese and Mongolians in general use the vertical system, and a few tribes also the so-called ' boustrophedon,' which consists in alternation of the direction and writing along a line, similar to the route of an ox ploughing the field. Reck discovered that the Toltecs, Aztecs, and Mayas, instead of using any of the above systems, had one of their own, which consisted in fancy changes of direction of the written lines. These fancy lines, resembling somewhat chess horse-moves, were arranged according to cabbalistic rules. Thus, the reading of these hieroglyphics requires a good deal of mental gymnastics, and some americanists hold that this aspect of the writing reflected also on the mentality of the Mayas themselves.

Apart from this peculiarity, we find much resemblance between the single hieroglyphs of prehistoric America and those of ancient Egypt. Le Plongeon, for instance, indicates at least thirteen Maya signs which are identical with the Egyptian signs of analogous meaning, and Dr. Bertoni finds the same of half of the Yariguaa hieroglyphs (Paraguay) of the Guaranis. The Yariguaa hieroglyphs probably represent the southern boundary of an autochthonous American race in many ways akin to the civilization of the Nile valley. Inscriptions in Egyptian style are particularly numerous in Brazil, in the virgin forests of Amazonia, and in the Matto Grosso.

Apart from the similarity of Quichua roots and expressions with the corresponding Egyptian ones as established by H. Onffroy de Thoron, we have the work of A. Frot, who has proved beyond doubt that at one time the pre-Egyptians migrated from South America to the north-east.

Thus, it is now clear that some millenniums ago the ancestors of the ancient Egyptians abandoned the country of their origin in America. A section of these migrants settled in the territories of the present Peru, Ecuador, San Salvador, Mexico, etc., but the majority probably went to Atlantis. Their sojourn in this centre of prehistoric culture enriched the knowledge of the pre-Egyptians, and this fact explains the high degree of culture shown by them in the valley of Nile and their knowledge of the 'forbidden sciences'—astrology, magic, etc. Probably the ancient Egyptians borrowed their occultism bodily from the Atlanteans, who, according to traditions, were adepts in hermetism.

It seems that at some time while Atlantis was still in existence, a great migration wave came through it from the New World to the Mediterranean shores. Perhaps the learned Atlantean engineers accompanied the group of migrants which went to Egypt and either built there the Great Pyramid and the Sphinx, or at least prepared plans and calculations for their eventual construction.

The similarity between the general traits of the Egyptian, Sumerian, Mayan, Toltec, etc., cultures, architecture, and religio-astronomical ideas makes the Atlanto-American hypothesis of the origin of Egyptian civilization much more weighty than either the Caucasian or the Sumerian hypotheses.

Abbé Moreux believes that the Sumerians were familiar with optics. They could obtain such knowledge only from the mysterious prehistoric race of pyramid-builders, who were such proficient astronomers, geometers, and astrologers. Some of the ancient sepultures of Lybia (on the route of the pre-Egyptians towards Nile) have yielded optical lenses, made of glass, or some similar material, showing that a prehistoric race which dominated the Mediterranean world culturally and, perhaps, politically also, was advanced enough to use, if not telescopes, at any rate some sort of optical instrument. We should note that, long before Galileo, the Chinese used rock-crystal lenses, and even now in China you can come across spectacles made of this material.

Perhaps the Sumerians inherited from that mysterious race of pyramid-builders the duodecimal system and the knowledge of the Zodiac with its, for us enigmatical, terminology. It was probably from that race also that the Sumerians, Egyptians, Toltecs, and Mayas acquired the calendar systems. Many investigators have discovered grounds for a belief that this mysterious prehistoric race is identical with Plato's Atlanteans. While I adhere to this plausible hypothesis, I feel justified in amplifying it and speaking of the 'Atlanto-Americans.' In my modest opinion the recent discoveries of A. Frot, Richard Marsh, and others, warrant such an amplification.

* * *

It is necessary at this point in my inquiry to make a short survey of certain African territories, which in prehistoric times may have seen the passage of the pre-Egyptians, before their final settlement along the Nile. This survey is particularly important, because there is a possibility of pre-Egyptian influence upon local autochthonous tribes on the one hand and of African influences upon the new-comers on the other.

Until the end of the Great War the efforts of investigators were concentrated upon the Nile valley and, thus, for the rest of Africa we possess practically only the material discovered during the last twenty years. Of particular interest among this material are the discoveries of Professor Leo Frobenius, of Count Byron de Prorok, and the discovery of traces of the so-called ' Asselar Man ' in the Sahara.

The last is especially interesting, as it shows the existence of a Neolithic culture in North Africa about 20,000 years ago, or even earlier. An enigmatical race at that epoch inhabited the Eastern Sahara and a part of Western Sudan. It is well known that the Sahara dried not long ago and that certain regions of it were still fertile at the time of the Roman emperors. In the epoch of the Asselar Man the whole of the Sahara must have been inhabitable, and consisted of vast grassy plains and luxuriant forests, traversed by rivers and containing extensive swamps.

The fragments of primitive implements, found near skeletons of the Asselar race, show a connection between this Neolithic culture and the primeval inhabitants of the Iberian peninsula. This connection is also borne out by the resemblances noticeable in Asselar and Spanish prehistoric paintings, portraying chiefly war and hunting. Contrarily to the opinion of Lewis Spence, who derives the Cro-Magnon race from Atlantis, the French scientists, who discovered the Asselar culture, hold that Asselar Man was the ancestor of the Cro-Magnons. So far, however, I see no valid evidence preventing us from agreeing with Spence.

Professor Leo Frobenius believes North Africa to be the cradle of some great prehistoric culture, and describes in his remarkable works the archæological finds he was able to make in Africa. Besides the interesting finds in Jorubaland and on the Gold Coast, where he found a bronze statue of the god Olokun (the African Poseidon) and the traces of some prehistoric nation, he describes, valuable frescoes, statuary, ceramics, and ideograms in numerous caverns of North Africa. All this material proves that at one time the Black Continent was the home of a comparatively elevated culture and Professor Frobenius supposes that some regions of North-Western and Northern Africa at one time were subjected to mighty cultural influences. In fact from my personal interview with the collaborator of Frobenius, Professor Obermayer, I was able to glean that Professor Frobenius is inclined to seek the cradle of human culture in Africa, instead of Asia, and to derive the prehistoric culture of the Old World from the mysterious race which once populated the fertile regions of the Sahara.

The prehistoric paintings of North African caverns are of great artistic merit and resemble the Cro-Magnon frescoes of Cogul (Spain). They are sometimes life size and are remarkable for their bright, apparently mineral, paints. Frobenius found likenesses of extinct animals and birds. Some of the paintings prove that certain animals, still existing, such as elephants and buffaloes, were much larger then than now and thus show the great antiquity of the paintings themselves. Some of the drawings show attempts at simplification and symbolization, which eventually were to give birth to ideograms and later on to alphabets. We must not forget that not so long ago the Greek *alpha, beta, gamma,* and the Jewish *aleph, gimel,* etc. etc., were nothing else than simplified pictures of the heads of the bull, goat, ram, camel, etc.

The archæological expedition of Count Byron de Prorok discovered in 1932 the mausoleum of Tin-Hinan, supposedly a prehistoric queen of the Tuaregs. This mausoleum is situated in the Saharian oasis of Hoggar, in the western part of the desert, approximately on the parallel of the Canary Islands. The body of the queen, shrouded in silk, was in an excellent state of preservation. Her head was adorned by a golden diadem, studded with stars, made of precious stones, and her hands and feet were covered with golden and silver bracelets, also ornamented by precious stones. A beautiful statue and many precious objects were found near the mummy of Tin-Hinan. The skull of the queen is remarkable for its harmonious proportions and indicates her origin from some advanced race. Some data permits us to place the reign of Tin-Hinan at several millenniums before our era.

Count de Prorok is also convinced that the Sahara at one time was the seat of a flourishing civilization. Although he does not hazard to connect this civilization with the Atlanto-Americans, he finds it necessary to point out the similarity of objects found in Tunis with many discovered in the prehistoric ruins of Mexico. Particularly striking is the resemblance between the flint implements found in two so widely separated regions.

Professors Gauthier and Reigass have established that in antiquity a caravan route led from the Sudan through Hoggar to the Mediterranean shores. They investigated a part of this route in 1934 and in the mountains, beyond the dried torrent of Dierat in a cavern, and upon the neighbouring rocks, found remarkable frescoes. Besides the drawings cut into the stone many of these prehistoric pictures are real paintings done in ochre. In spite of their tremendous age, the colours are still vivid, and the technique and expressivity are remarkable. Warriors armed with darts and shields are the most common subject of these paintings. Some of the figures are represented as riding in war chariots and (possibly) gods, or leaders, are painted in life size. Most of the figures are either headless, or else possess canine heads or phantastic masks. There is a possibility that the figures with canine heads are intended to represent baboons, so numerous in these regions, and whose heads distinctly remind one of dogs. Even in our times the natives of these regions imagine the baboons, who rob their fields, to be an inimical and well-organized tribe.

All this may imply a religious-mythological meaning for the pictures and indicates a complex mythology and, therefore, a comparatively high culture among the prehistoric inhabitants of the Sahara. The animal kingdom is well represented by the subjects of these paintings, in which we see hippopotami, giraffes, wild bulls, elephants, and rhinoceroses. From this we can infer that the Sahara at one time was a great grassy plain, covered here and there with thick forests and marshes and not lacking in rivers and lakes. The pictures of Dierat resemble the

Palaeolithic frescoes in Spain, and can probably be ascribed to the same epoch.

Professor Gauthier believes that the prehistoric inhabitants of the Hoggar were nobody else than the ' inconquerable ' Garamants of Tacitus and other classical writers. Some investigators believe that the Garamants borrowed their culture from the Creto-Mycenians, or from the ancient Egyptians. A certain amount of information concerning the prehistoric population of Southern Lybia and the Sahara came to us from the Romans, and their records from the time of the Emperor Augustus show that the relatively safe littoral strip of Lybia was hedged in by numerous courageous and wild tribes of the desert, causing much worry to the Roman authorities. A spark of rebellion burst into a conflagration very easily in northern Africa, and the Romans had to fight and to come in contact with many tribes, concerning which they have left us some information and some fables.

In connection with the Dierat paintings it is interesting to mention the tales of some adventurous traders who dared to penetrate into the dangerous region and who spoke of terrifying Blemias, Satyres, Augiles, Ægypanes (half-men, half-goats), Troglodites (snake-eaters), cavern-men, and blood-thirsty Atlants, who lived under an eternally clouded sky and cursed the Sun at sunrise and at sunset, etc. Of all these mythical and real tribes, the Garamants, who inhabited the Fazania oasis (now Fezzan), are of particular interest to us. They are still a mystery to contemporary ethnographers, but we know from the ancients that the Garamants were a war-like tribe possessing war-chariots and a peculiar advanced culture. They could weave, used metal alloys, and possessed elements of writing: their *tifinars* (petroglyphs) still exist on the rocks near Fezzan, and depict the Garamants in their war-chariots with numerous rams with peculiar horns. These ideograms are especially numerous in the Hoggar. The chief occupations of the Garamants were agriculture, cattle-breeding, war, and pillage. In any case it is clear enough that some thousands of years ago the Hoggar was inhabited by a people organized into a state and possessing a certain degree of culture.

CHAPTER XI

THE Great Pyramid at Gizeh, or the Pyramid of Cheops, is sometimes called the ' Bible in Stone.' The following inscription was found in one of its inner corridors: ' I am the herald and the witness of (the will) of God. He created me with human feelings and deposited a mystery within me.' Apparently the author of this inscription wished to speak in the name of the pyramid itself.

It is interesting to note that Isaiah (ch. xix, verses 19–20) mentions the erection in Egypt, near its boundaries, of a monument and altar dedicated to God and witnessing to His glory. The Jewish prophet probably had in view the Pyramid of Cheops.

A considerable section of the public believes the pyramid to be a symbol of the destiny of mankind and that every inch of it symbolizes a definite event. Some have found a striking identity between Biblical data and indications furnished by the pyramid. C. Barbarin affirms that the system of inner corridors and chambers is arranged in such a way that every branch of them, every length, every slope or prominence, etc., has a profound, exact, and eternal significance. Colonel Garnier (*La Grande Pyramide, son constructeur et les Prophéties*, 1905), affirmed that the main gallery of the pyramid symbolizes the succession of historic events of past and future, and saw in this gallery a prophecy of a great war for 1913, making a mistake of only one year. . . . Garnier also affirmed that the builders of the pyramid foresaw the advent of Christianity and recorded a prophecy of it by the suitable disposition of the galleries, the various stones, etc. Alexandre Moret (not to be confounded with the astronomer Moreux) says in his *Dieux et Rois d'Egypte*, that the ancient Egyptians, thousands of years ago, knew of the coming birth of Christ and the details of His life and death, such as the Last Supper, etc. C. Barbarin says that the calculations and prophecies of the pyramid call our epoch the ' Epoch of

Chaos,' and specify that this epoch ends on the 15–16 September 1936, giving place to the new Theocratic Epoch. Our failure to notice this transition (we are writing these lines in 1937) is explained by the fact that no turning-point in history is ever noticed by its contemporaries. . . . Perhaps this point is under our eyes, but we are not able to discern its importance. Further, C. Barbarin (*Le Secret de la Grande Pyramide*) finds that while the pyramid supplies exact dates of future events, it omits any specification of them. The mathematician Léa Mayou offered a hypothesis which explains that the disposition of the corridors and chambers of the pyramid is a symbol of the ' mystery of the Upper Nile (beyond the Sixth Cataract) ' : the galleries represent the tributaries and the chambers the great lakes or sources of the Nile. This hypothesis, however, was severely criticized by G. Maspero. The pyramid theory was thoroughly investigated by Maspero, Colonel Garnier, C. Lagrange, Piazzi-Smyth, D. Davidson, C. Knight, X. Wedge, X. Aldersmith, W. Kingsland, B. Stuart, and many others, among whom Davidson and Dr. Aldersmith were very active together from 1910 to 1914, comparing the chronology of the pyramid with Biblical chronology. After the death of Dr. Aldersmith, Davidson continued the investigation and published a voluminous work abundant in mathematical and astronomical calculations. Habermann made an exhaustive study of the pyramid in search of the historic, religious, and prophetic data it contains.

The entrance corridor of the pyramid, beginning on the level of its sixteenth step, descends for $30\frac{1}{2}$ yards, and then branches off into two galleries, one of which continues to descend and the other ascends towards the centre of the building. The descending corridor ends in the Underground Chamber, excavated in the living-rock foundation of the pyramid. This corridor symbolizes the fall of man into darkness, unable to find the way of Truth. The Underground Chamber is 100 feet below the first step and, while it has a smooth ceiling, its floor is rough and uneven. The Egyptian texts explain that this Chamber symbolizes madness. The ascending corridor at a certain point branches off into a horizontal passage, leading to the Queen's Chamber, but the main gallery continues upwards, its height increased suddenly to 27 feet (with a width of not more than a yard). The length of this section of the ascending gallery, which leads to the King's Chamber, is 52 yards, and its width is greater at the floor than at the ceiling. Above the King's Chamber there is a whole series of rooms, one over the other, the purpose of which was apparently to protect the King's Chamber from above.

The pyramid is an edifice evidently erected with some scientific purpose, and its name derives from the Coptic *pirimit*, or *piramit*, which signifies ' the tenth measure in numbers.' The Great Pyramid has had for a long time the reputation of preserving great scientific secrets and immense treasure. The Caliph Al Mamoun gave orders in A.D. 820 to his men to search for treasure which was supposed to have been hidden within the pyramid by its builders. For several months the workmen in vain tore off the top of the pyramid and the facing-stone on its northern side at the level of the sixteenth step, seeking for an exterior entrance into the Inclined Gallery. They never managed to find the door, formed by an enormous monolith rotating on an axis, but at last a stone fell with a peculiar noise within the pyramid and unexpectedly a breach was opened. The workmen penetrated into a corridor with regularly spaced limestone monoliths and so into the King's Chamber. There was found there only an empty granite sarcophagus without a lid.

The ensemble of the data furnished by the pyramid gives us much to think about. First of all it must be clear that its builder was a first-rate mathematician, because it is not easy to incorporate so many remarkable astronomical and geodetic data into such a simple task as the construction of a pyramid with a square base. It is clear that not only was π known to the builder, but also that he attached to it enough importance to wish to immortalize it in his structure. This mysterious builder knew about terrestrial eccentricity, the length of the polar radius, the dimension of the orbit of the Earth, the distance of our planet from the Sun, the phenomenon of the precession, the exact duration of the sidereal year, and the weight and density of our planet. It is also evident that he knew the surface of our globe, possessing probably maps, or geographical globes, not inferior to our own. We know definitely from the ancient documents that not only had the ancient Egyptians no such knowledge, but even the Chaldeans, those first astronomers, never attained to such heights of science. The question, where did the prehistoric builder of the pyramid obtain such knowledge, is not easy to answer. Abbé Moreux, for instance, abandoned any scientific attempt to explain this miracle and ascribes the knowledge shown by the builder of the Great Pyramid to divine revelation. . . .

We shall, however, attempt a scientific explanation of this miracle. First of all it is necessary to fix, at least approximately, the epoch of the construction of the pyramid. Certain conjectures permit us to suppose that it was built between 2654 and 2592 B.C. Usually, on the strength of Herodotus's testimony, the construction of the pyramid is ascribed to Cheops (second half of the third millennium B.C.), but this can be admitted only if we assume the existence in the Egypt of Cheops' time of plans and calculations inherited from some greatly cultured race. The supposition that the pyramid was built by some cultured people inhabiting the valley of the Nile immediately before the arrival of the pre-Egyptians, so far has not been borne out by any archæological discovery, and what we know of Badrian culture (the most ancient in the Nile valley) makes such a supposition impossible.

On the whole I am inclined to adopt a provisional hypothesis and consider the pyramid to have been built in a very remote epoch, probably during the post-Glacial Period. As is not rare in Egyptian history, Cheops, probably, simply ascribed to himself the construction of the pyramid. As regards the above-mentioned astronomical conjectures, corroborating, as it seems, Cheops' authorship of the pyramid, it is essential to remember that this data is not of a very precise nature. I can support my doubt by the following detail in the arrangement of the chambers of the pyramid.

If one stands in the lowest underground chamber, one can see the Polar Star, or that present so-called Pole of the Universe, through a narrow inclined corridor, leading outside. The Pole of the Universe changes its position in recurring cycles of about 25,796 years, and thus every position of this Pole is always repeated after about 26,000 years. Now it is practically at the Polar Star, but it is possible that at the time of the building of the pyramid the Pole of the Universe was situated in Alpha Draconis (seen also through the above-mentioned corridor), ' in the neighbourhood' of the Polar Star. This circumstance may indicate the epoch of the construction of the pyramid, because it is evident that the builder intended to place the observer in such a position that the latter could see the Pole of the Universe through the inclined gallery. Thus it is quite feasible that the pyramid was constructed about 30,000 years ago. . . .

We should, in my modest opinion, ascribe the construction of the Great Pyramid to an unknown race which inhabited the valley of the Nile many millenniums ago and possessed a culture not inferior, and perhaps even superior, to our own. This race possessed extraordinary knowledge in the realms of mathematics, astronomy, and geophysics, and built the pyramid in order to immortalize their achievements and perhaps also for mystic purposes.

Herodotus gives many details concerning the construction of the pyramid, but all his information was apparently borrowed from the Egyptian priests, or from the traditions which circulated at that epoch among the Greeks. As regards the details of the construction found in the inscriptions within the pyramid itself (as, for instance, the quantity of food-supplies for workmen), they could have been added by the Egyptians of Cheops' time either from hearsay, or out of their own imagination.

According to Herodotus, 100,000 workmen were busy for more than 20 years with the construction of the pyramid and every three months the exhausted workmen were replaced by new ones. The Egyptian priests told Herodotus that before the construction it was necessary to build a special road for the conveyance of materials and the construction of this road alone took about 10 years of work. Herodotus also describes the machines appropriated for the lifting of the monoliths of which the pyramid was built. The pyramid was also faced with enormous blocks of limestone. The hieroglyphic inscriptions describe the method of its construction under the guidance of an architect. The monoliths were dragged on a sort of sledge, pulled in its turn by numerous gangs with very strong ropes.

To-day the pyramid consists of 203 ranges of stones, disposed in steps 1 yard high. The platform on the top of the pyramid is 6 yards square.

*   *   *

The Great Pyramid is remarkable for its mathematical and astronomical elements which doubtlesss were intentionally incorporated by its builder. A detailed study of the structure will convince any investigator that the wealth of mathematical, geometrical, and astronomical data concealed within it is not accidental, but has been produced intentionally after numerous and complex calculations, made by somebody possessing an astounding amount of knowledge.

Its orientation is exact to within 4′ 35″, and this circumstance has astonished the astronomers greatly. . . . Much complicated work was necessary in 1900 before the astronomers of that time could calculate the distance of the Earth from the Sun, which quantity was to be made an astronomical unit. As the result of these calculations the distance of our planet from the Sun was fixed at 90,000,000 miles. The margin of error in the estimation of Moreux was equal to 42,000 miles. The scientists of those days did not know that it was enough to multiply the height of the pyramid by 1,000,000,000 in order to get this distance equal to 90,000,000 miles.

The diagonals of the base of the pyramid, if extended towards the Mediterranean, will coincide with the eastern and western boundaries of the Nile Delta. The meridian of the summit of the pyramid divides the Delta neatly into two equal sectors, whose central angles are equal to 45°. This meridian is an ideal one, because it traverses more land surface than the others, and divides the inhabited surface of the terrestrial globe (the so-called *æcumena*) into two equal parts. The summit of the pyramid is situated in 29° 58′ 51·22″ of north latitude. This circumstance at first sight does not seem significant: the moment, however, we remember that the apparent position of the Polar Star is invariably 1′ 8·78″ out, owing to the phenomenon of atmospheric refraction, we see what was in the mind of the builder. If we add the value of the refraction, i.e. 1′ 8·78″ to 29° 58′ 51·22″ we get exactly 30°, and we realize that the mysterious builder of the pyramid, guiding himself by the Polar Star (or by a corresponding point in the constellation of Draconis), wished to centre the pyramid upon the thirtieth parallel. This parallel is remarkable for the fact that it separates a maximum of the land of our planet from the maximum of the ocean surfaces. Apparently the builder wished to record permanently the distribution of the continents and oceans of those days, and we can see that this distribution has remained almost the same until our own times.

Not the least interesting detail concerning the orientation of the pyramid is the following : the reflection of the sunrays from the sides of the pyramid indicates almost exactly the equinoxes and solstices and therefore, the sowing-time. The northern side of the pyramid is lighted at sunrise for some moments during the period from the spring-equinox till the autumn-equinox. During the remainder of the year the southern side is lighted from sunrise till sunset. This phenomenon fixes the moment of the equinoxes within 12 hours. When the stone-facing of the pyramid was intact, this phenomenon of the ' missing shadows ' must have been still more pronounced and was noticed by the ancients. The Latin poet Ausonius writes :

> '. . . quadrata cui in fastigio cono
> Surgit et ipsa suas consumit puramis umbras.'

(' the pyramid itself swallows the shadow born on its summit.') This phenomenon has now been explained by Professor Pochan, who discovered that the northern and southern sides of the pyramid are not true planes, but dihedral angles of 179° 50'. Thus, in plain speaking, the sides in question have been hollowed out to the extent of 94 centimetres, insuring a rapid disappearance of the shadow of the sunrise at the equinoxes.

The unit of measurement used by the builder of the pyramid was apparently the so-called pyramidal, or sacred, elbow divided into 25 pyramidal inches. Amazingly enough these inches are the same as the English. 10,000,000 sacred elbows make 6,356,600 metres, which is the length of the polar radius of our planet with a probable error not greater than 0.01 of a millimetre, or 0.003937 of an inch. As the polar radius is a more constant quantity than an earthly meridian, therefore the sacred elbow is a more reliable unit of measurement than the metre which is 1/40,000,000 part of the Paris meridian. Thus, the metrology of the builders of the Great Pyramid is incomparably superior to our own and, to quote the words of the astronomer Abbé Moreux, the English have been quite right not to part with their ' archaic ' system of yards, feet, and inches. The sacred elbow of the ancient Jews is also the same as the pyramidal one. 100,000,000 sacred inches

represent the exact length of the arc described by our planet along
its orbit in 24 hours. This, in metres, will give a number which
can be divided exactly by 2π.

The central King's Chamber of the pyramid contains a large
oblong box of red granite. For a long time it was believed
to be a sarcophagus, but we now know that it never contained a body and its purpose is purely symbolical. Its
dimensions contain much and various data. Its gross
volume, for instance, is equal to 138,000 cubic sacred inches,
or four English quarters, exactly double its capacity. This
granite box can contain exactly 2,500 lbs of water, and this
is another illustration in favour of the English system of measurements and weights. The number of cubic sacred inches,
expressing the capacity of this box, was apparently a sacred
number in Egypt. The ancient Jews, who learned much from
the Egyptians during their captivity in Egypt, also held it in
mystical esteem. The Bible and a few simple calculations will
show us that the capacity of the Hebrew Holy Ark corresponds
to the capacity of the granite box in the pyramid. According to
the information given by the Books of Kings, Solomon made
a great vessel of red copper, calling it the ' Copper Sea,' and
placed it in the temple of Jerusalem : the volume of this vessel
corresponds exactly to the volume of the mysterious granite box.
Various mathematical operations with the elements of dimension
of this box give us scientific data, such as, for instance, the
density of the Earth, etc.

It is interesting to note that the builder of the pyramid gave to
it such proportions that in every measurement of it we find either
the first four simple numbers (2, 3, 5, and 7), or their multiples.

The area of every side of the pyramid is equal to the square of
the height of the pyramid itself, which peculiarity was observed
by Herodotus. The sum of the diagonals of the base in sacred
inches is 25,800, which is nearly equal to the period of the
precession of the point Gamma (the point of spring-equinox).
The weight of the pyramid is exactly one quintillionth (according
to the English system one thousand billionth) of the weight of our
planet. If we multiply the average density of the stone used as
material for the pyramid by the volume of the pyramid itself,
expressed in cubic pyramidal elbows, the result will be a number
beginning with 552, and 5·52 is the density of our planet in

relation to water. The perimeter of the base of the pyramid is equal to 1015 yards and the overall height of the building is 161·55 yards. The perimeter, divided by double the height, will give a quotient equal to 3·1415, which is nothing else than π within 0·0001 of exactitude. The remarkable circumstance about this is that π was worked out within 0.0001 of exactitude by Europeans only in the fifteenth century after much research, while the builders of the pyramid already knew it millenniums ago !

The length of the inner antechamber of the pyramid in sacred inches, multiplied by π, gives 365·242 . . . which is the length of the so-called tropical year, to within 0·001 of the length of the tropical day. The length of one side of the base is 366 sacred elbows, which is the number of days in a leap year. The proportion between the area of the base and the area of the vertical section of the whole pyramid is 3·1416, i.e. π to 1. Double the length of any side of the base is 3·1416 times greater than the height of the pyramid, which proportion gives us again the famous number π.

According to William Kingsland and Morton Edgar, the side of the base of the pyramid is 9131·025 inches long, while, according to other investigators it is 9131·416 inches. This last figure is the number of days contained in 25 years, which allots to each sidereal year 365·25664 . . . days—a difference of only 30 seconds with the year adopted by modern science. Further, it was found that 9131·416 inches are equal to practically 1/480th of one equatorial degree.

At this rate the total length of the equator line would come to 24903·86181 miles, which quantity is only 1·5 miles more than the measurement adopted by modern science. If we divide the length of the equator as given by the pyramid, by π, we will get the diameter of our planet equal to 7927·1 miles, which quantity is only 0·5 miles longer than the measurement calculated by the modern astronomer Sir James Jeans.

The total length of the equator of our planet, as given by the pyramid, comes in inches to 1,577,908,684. This number is the number of the days contained in the so-called ' Day of Brahma' (see *The Secret Doctrine*, by H. P. Blavatsky).

The following calculations are also very interesting : the length of the equator of our planet in feet gives the number of days in 360,000 years, and in yards, the same number for 120,000 years.

All these calculations, based upon the length of the sides of the base of the Great Pyramid, provoked a lively controversy in the press. Davidson, for instance, affirms that the length of the side of the base is only 9131·25 sacred inches and Sir Edmund Beckett on the contrary estimates it at 9132 inches.

In the estimation of Sir Flinders Petrie, practically seconded by the Egyptian Survey Department, the northern side of the base of the pyramid is 9131·416 inches, the western is 9133·4 inches, and the eastern and the southern sides are only 9119·2 and 9125·7 inches respectively..

William Kingsland discounts some of the above measurements because they are taken between the outer edges of the plinth on which the pyramid rests, and not between the corners of the pyramid itself. William Kingsland also rejects the sacred elbow and the pyramid inch, calling them the inventions of Piazzi-Smyth.

*   *   *

But I repeat, whatever are the results of these polemics, the mass of information incorporated in the Great Pyramid gives us a majestic picture. . . . Such data could be incorporated in a monument such as the Great Pyramid only by a nation whose culture was far superior to the Egyptian. In the solution of the problem of the origin of the pyramid builders is hidden also the solution of the origin of Egyptian culture and of the Egyptians themselves.

CHAPTER XII

THERE are in Mexico the ruins of a prehistoric sacred city which apparently in that country had the significance that Mecca possesses for Moslems, or Lourdes for Catholics. This city is called 'The Archæological City of Teotihuacan,' and is situated in San Juan de Teotihuacan, about 50 kilometres from the capital. The district surrounding these ruins is called 'The Archæological Zone.' The word 'Teotihuacan' signifies 'the city where prayers are offered to God.'

Even as late as the end of the last century nobody suspected that the range of hills in the vicinity of San Juan de Teotihuacan contained beautiful prehistoric monuments. Quite by accident was discovered first the Great Pyramid of the Sun, and later on the Pyramid of the Moon, followed by the uncovering of the temples of Quetzal-Coatl, Tlaloc, and others.

The Sacred City, as represented by the now uncovered ruins, is the most recent of ancient cities buried in this locality under thick layers of alluvium. Excavations of the cultural layers under the ruins of the Sacred City have brought to light numerous ceramics of a type similar to those found in the earlier-mentioned ruins of San Angel and Tlalpam, destroyed and covered by lava during the volcanic eruptions of 8000 years ago. However, even the upper cultural layer is of very considerable antiquity. The Toltecs with their magnificent and refined culture came to Teotihuacan long after the oldest city had been abandoned by its original inhabitants. The new-comers built their temples over the semi-ruined buildings of their predecessors and such superstructures are particularly noticeable in the case of the Quetzal-Coatl temple, of the so-called Temple of Agriculture, and of the frescoes covering the walls of the above-mentioned buildings. Eventually there came a moment when the Toltecs were obliged to leave Teotihuacan to ferocious, and then barbarous, Aztecs. The latest arrivals in their new home strove to imitate the buildings they found there, but never succeeded even in approximating to the beauty and the elegance of architecture of their predecessors. Most of the buildings and ruins now seen in the Sacred City belong to the Toltec and Aztec periods and there are hardly any vestiges, save the pyramids, of the oldest pre-Toltec culture. It seems that the Toltecs, threatened by the Aztec invasion, covered the best buildings with a thick layer of cement and an ultimate layer of loose earth. The next owners of the land, the Aztecs, simply built their city on the hillocks thus formed, never suspecting the existence of the architectural treasures beneath. At present only a small portion of the Sacred City has been excavated from the artificial hills and it is safe to say that future excavations reserve many surprises for archæologists. During the excavations here it is necessary to remove first a layer of earth, often a yard thick, and then a layer of cement over a foot in depth. One can only wonder how the Toltecs managed to spend the enormous amount of labour necessary for the burying of their whole city ! Some consider that this work must have been carried out by slaves or prisoners of war. In this case the number of the latter must have been extraordinary. The area of the Sacred City is considerable, amounting, as it does, at least to 6½ square miles. The general planning and the details of the buildings are very symmetrical, and the streets issue in regular order from the main avenue, which is about 55 yards in width and ends in a spacious square surrounded by important buildings.

The pre-Aztec Teotihuacan was remarkable for the beauty and grandeur of its buildings, as, for instance, the Temple of Quetzal-Coatl. The characteristic features of this architecture are the combination of the step pyramid with a rectangular prism crowning it, with numerous staircases and peculiar frescoes depicting scenes of everyday life and mythological subjects. The bas-reliefs portray human figures, animals, and plants which occasionally are conventionalized. Among the bas-reliefs those of the Temple, which represent a feathered serpent, are remarkable, and among the high-reliefs is a very interesting one which portrays some monster with widely open jaws. Its head resembles much more the head of some prehistoric lizard, e.g. dinosaur, than that of a serpent.

The Great Pyramid of the Sun is 126 feet high and occupies

an area of 440,000 square feet. It really consists of five truncated pyramids, one on the top of the other, arranged in steps. The Pyramid of the Moon is of similar structure and is 46 yards high and occupies an area of only 176,000 square feet. Scientists variously estimate the date of the building of the Great Pyramid from 2000 B.C. to A.D. 900, but I think that it is safe enough to date it about 5000 B.C.

The whole Archæological Zone is traversed by an ancient paved road which is called ' The Road of the Dead,' because, according to the traditions of the natives, the numerous barrows bordering it are ancient graves.

*   *   *

From time immemorial the peninsula of Yucatan has been inhabited by the Mayas, who at one time were masters of almost the whole of Central America and created a refined and remarkable culture. The colossal buildings erected by the Mayas are all the more amazing for us because this nation was very limited in its technical means. The Mayas, for instance, had no wheels, and all the materials for their gigantic structures were transported by sledge. These resemble those still in use in the islands of the Azores and Madeira. The Mayas were acquainted with bronze and gold, but had no iron, and all their implements were either of wood or stone. Therefore the Mayan achievements amaze us even more than those of Egypt and Babylonia.

Mayan writing was developed not less than the Chinese, and Mayan astronomy was so advanced that their calendar was not less exact than our own, although it was much more complicated. I had an opportunity of admiring the delicate colours and complicated drawings of the Codex Troano-Cortezianus in the Archæological Museum of Madrid, one of the few codices of the Mayas which has survived from their rich literature. A comparison of Mayan designs and frescoes with the later Mexican drawings shows that the latter are more awkward, crude, and lacking in perspective, but richer in colours. Some Mayan frescoes, such, for instance, as the Tulum frescoes, are definitely artistic.

The state organization of the Mayas was astoundingly perfect and their army was organized under the supervision of special officers. The colossal Mayan pyramids were built not only for religious purposes, but also for astronomical and chronological purposes. Involuntarily here one remembers that the Great Pyramid at Gizeh also contains much astronomical data in its geometrical proportions. The investigation of Central American pyramids (especially the pyramid of Oaxaca) has demonstrated that there is a close connection between the city-planning of the Mayas and the orientation of nearby pyramids. All the chief Mayan buildings had the façades disposed strictly east to west. This rule was observed not only in Yucatan, but also in Guatemala and in the Mexican State of Chiapas, although some façades in the latter localities show a slight deviation. Cities built on the same parallel, such as Chichen-Itza and Tenayuca, possessed in their central places pyramids whose bases have a remarkable feature : their diagonals form with the corresponding meridians the same angle of $17°$. Investigations of the Mayan pyramids have demonstrated that they were used also for chronology and that the Mayan year began on the 26 July.

T. A. Joyce shows that the area under the cultural influence of the Mayas was very large and considerably more extensive than that once covered by the culture of the ancient Greeks. While the latter, comprising Crete and the colonies of Asia Minor, stretched along the meridian for $8°$ and along the parallel for about the same distance, the Mayan culture was spread over $20°$ along the meridian and over $10°$ along the parallel. In fact, it was bounded on one side by the Pacific and on the other by the Mexican Gulf, a zone stretching from Honduras to the River Panuco in Northern Mexico.

The peninsula of Yucatan and most of the Guatemalan territory are still populated by Mayas with an occasional sprinkling of other American tribes. Among the latter, the Nahoa tribe is worthy of attention, since there was a time when it created a peculiar and developed culture. Some anthropologists affirm that the Nahoans and Toltecs invaded Central America about A.D. 800 and T. A. Joyce, for instance, believes that the Toltec hegemony ended about A.D. 1100. But others believe that the Toltec empire was founded in the second century B.C. and ended about A.D. 400. However, the dates of Mexican chronology so far are a subject of controversy. The americanists divide the known history of the Mayas into two epochs : the Ancient Empire and the New Empire. The first was at its height at about 500 B.C. and in those days comprised even Çopan of the present Honduras. But in the fourth century B.C. the Mayas abandoned Copan and from this epoch began the period of the New Empire.

As regards the great monuments of Mayan architecture, opinions vary also: while some experts consider them as belonging to the first century A.D., others think that these astonishing buildings must have been erected in the third century B.C. T. A. Joyce believes that the megalithic structures of Lubaantun (British Honduras) are much older than the Ancient Empire. Recent discoveries of Dr. F. Blohm in Yucatan have forced archæologists to place the beginning of the Mayan culture 500 years earlier than was previously accepted, and I believe that future finds will compel us to realize that the Mayan culture is older still. But already the amazing resemblance, and even similarity between certain Mayan drawings and the oldest Hindu art permits us to a certain extent to accept this view. In the Codex Troanus, for instance, we see the picture of a god with the head of an elephant, holding a bunch of rays. A big snake is lying near the feet of the deity. This Mayan drawing very much resembles the episode in the Rig-Veda, describing the fight of the sun god, Indra, with the serpent Vritra. Another picture in the same codex represents a further episode of this battle depicting Indra pouring rain on the head of Vritra. One can find in this codex also images of the Hindu god, Ganesha. Many drawings, bas-reliefs, and ceramics which are to be found in the Mayan ruins irrefutably prove a certain kinship between Mayan and Hindu art and mythology: the images of monkeys, for instance, on Mayan vessels are identical with those on Hindu. Dr. Maudsley found in the Copan ruins a drawing much resembling the drawings in the temples of Cambodia and Java. And inversely, one of the ornaments in the Javanese temple of Boro-Boudour is identical in headgear with the Copan statues. Incidentally, the emperors of Annam in Indo-China wear the same head-gear. The elephants' ears which serve as an ornamental motive on the buildings of Indo-China are the same as those on the high-reliefs of Honduras. There can be no doubt that at a remote epoch Mayan culture was influenced by Asia.

Among the numerous prehistoric monoliths existing in

Baul and Pantaleon (Guatemala), two are particularly remarkable for their artistic qualities. One of them is a colossal high-relief representing a human head with a curious head-gear. This monolith is 24 feet high and its lower part is buried so deeply in the soil that the chin of the head touches the ground. The face is full of expression, the eyelids drooping, the lips tightly closed, the cheeks hollow, the nose slightly flattened, and the supraciliary arches very prominent. On the whole the type of this face is neither Indian nor Mongolian. The back of this monolith is flat and covered with still undeciphered hieroglyphs. The other monolith is also 20–24 feet long, but it is horizontal and represents a strange animal with an enormous head and very short front paws. The mouth of the monster is open and a human head is visible inside the cavity. The pedestal of the monolith is covered with hieroglyphs.

In Quirigua, another locality of Guatemala, there exists a monolith representing some king or chief priest. The statue, draped in an embroidered mantle, is at least 12 feet high, and its head is adorned with a magnificent tiara. The face of the figure does not belong to the usual Mayan type and resembles rather some Roman emperor. . . .

We have already mentioned that the little Central American republic of San Salvador is exceptionally rich in various monuments of remote antiquity. The artistic objects of Sihuatan, for instance, come from the oldest, still undetermined, culture, and are remarkable for their technique and execution. This art might be credited to Nahoan culture, but one must not lose sight of the fact that, although the Nahoas had totemistic beliefs, they did not practise zoolathry, and in the oldest culture of Sihuatan, zoolathry was so developed that it has no equivalent anywhere in America, being comparable only with the animal-worship of ancient Egyptians. This analogy between ancient Egypt and oldest Sihuatan is not limited to religion, but extends also to works of art. The wolf-headed Sihuatan statuettes, for instance, are very similar to Egyptian statues of Anubis (Anmibé). This and other analogous finds in various countries of Central and South America lend a solid support to the hypothesis of the American origin of the pre-Egyptians.

A very interesting monument among the Sihuatan ruins is the recently-discovered large pyramid. It was found quite accidentally under a thickly overgrown hill and, as there are many similar hills in this locality, it is reasonable to hope that they also may contain pyramids. The uncovered pyramid is orientated very exactly, its height is 60 feet and its base is formed by a rectangle of 60 by 39 yards. Like the very ancient Mexican pyramid of Peña Pobre, the bulk of the Sihuatan pyramid is built of earth and rubble, while its facing is made of stone, arranged in steps, like the famous Sakkarah pyramid in Egypt. Perhaps the most curious feature of the Sihuatan pyramid is that, in spite of the universal use in ancient San Salvador of measures based on the length of the human foot and step, every geometrical element of the whole building consists of an exact number of metres, without any fraction. Local archæologists calculate the age of the Sihuatan pyramid at about 2500 B.C.

In addition to the ruins and the pyramid, I have seen in San Salvador some very curious finds. There were discovered, for instance, two statuettes, absolutely identical in appearance with Egyptian mummy cases, with inscriptions on the pedestals written in some unknown alphabet resembling cuneiform writing. These statuettes are now in the possession of the Archbishop of San Salvador, who affirms that the inscriptions on their pedestals are written in Chaldean. It would be interesting to obtain an expert opinion on this point.

In the locality of La Liberdad exists a large stela of 257 square feet, covered by a text resembling very much Mongolian or Tibetan writings : at any rate such was my personal impression of this unknown alphabet.

I have also seen in the collection of Mr. Justo Armas, in San Salvador, a manuscript on palm-leaves which was obtained from an Indian living in Chiquimulca. The Indian affirmed that the manuscript had been in the possession of his family for several centuries. The palm-leaves on which the manuscript is written had evidently been treated in a special way and the text, consisting of long lines, was apparently arranged in hexameters and made up of rounded letters. It is similar in its general appearance to manuscripts I have seen in ancient Buddhist monasteries in Ceylon.

But probably the most interesting find made in San Salvador is a clay dish belonging to a local amateur archæologist. The designs scratched on this dish portray a group of palms, and some

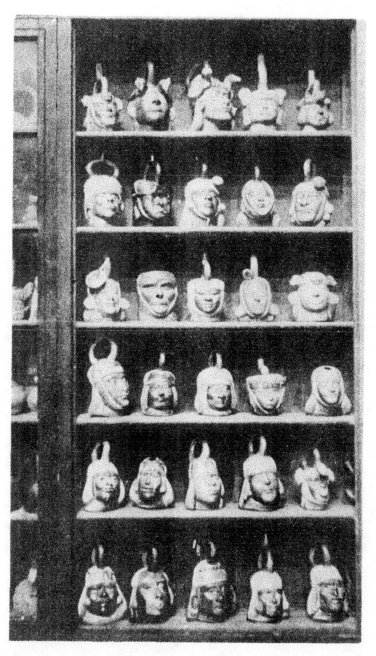

THE SO-CALLED PORTRAIT HEADS OF THE PRE-
HISTORIC CULTURE IN PERU
(Museum of Lima.)

TWO PERUVIAN MUMMIES A MOTHER WITH HER
CHILD

(Museum of Lima.)

men flying over them in curious machines. Behind the latter seems to be a trail of flame and smoke. Mrs. Osborne, a noted americanist, believes that this dish comes to us from a very remote epoch, when Central America possessed a great culture, and that the drawings on the dish represent flying machines in use ! Of course, this picture may be simply an illustration of a fairy tale, but one cannot help taking into consideration the high level of Atlantean culture and the possible significance of the Cretan myth about Icarus.

*   *   *

One of the latest Mayan codices is the famous Book of Chilam Balam from Chumayel, which was certainly compiled before the Spanish invasion of Yucatan. I have had an opportunity of meeting Señor A. M. Bolio, who was the first to decipher and to translate into Spanish this remarkable manuscript. A Mayan Indian by birth, Bolio is a remarkable linguist and a passionate student of the history of his people. In my opinion, modern science is lucky to count amongst its followers a representative of the great Mayan race, fond of his people and at the same time endowed with all the erudition of a modern philologist. It would have been impossible to find a more suitable investigator for translation of the Book of Chilam Balam and for the rendering of its mysterious significance into a European language.

For the purpose of my inquiry the fifth chapter of this book is particularly interesting. Bolio discerns in it dim indications of some great catastrophe which overtook our planet and concerning which the priests and the chroniclers of the Mayas seemed to preserve comparatively distinct recollections. In fact, Bolio is willing to go further and in our personal conversation he often expressed a conviction that the fifth chapter of the Book of Chilam Balam contains a description of the cataclysm which destroyed Plato's Atlantis. Like the former vice-president of U.S.A., General Charles G. Dawes, Bolio presumes an organic connection between the Mayas and the race which at one time populated Atlantis. General Dawes holds the opinion that after the catastrophe of Atlantis the Mayas colonized Yucatan and other countries of Central America and that the prehistoric monuments of Yucatan are an illustration of the style of Atlantean

architecture. It is interesting to note here that the Mayas themselves still preserve traditions concerning the arrival in Yucatan
of their remote ancestors from an eastern land, which later on
had been swallowed up by the ocean.

The Book of Chilam Balam is one of the most important
Mayan manuscripts so far discovered, especially as it was written
in the Latin alphabet instead of in hieroglyphs. The document
represents a collection of texts from various epochs, written
in various styles, although an Indian, Juan José Hoil, a native
from the locality of Chumayel, is generally accepted as its
author. His authorship is based on an inscription on page 81
of the manuscript with the date of 20 January 1782, although it
is possible that besides J. J. Hoil, other Indians contributed to
the compilation of the famous book. This manuscript was found
in Chumayel (Yucatan) in the 'sixties, being offered to the
Bishop don Crescencio Carrillo y Ancona, the noted historian of
Yucatan, and then was photographed and published by the
Philadelphia University. After the death of the bishop the
manuscript was presented to the Cepeda Library in Merida
(Yucatan). Unfortunately, in 1916, the manuscript disappeared
under mysterious circumstances and all our studies have now to
rely upon the facsimile made by the Philadelphia University.
Very probably some patriotic Mayan removed the precious
manuscript from the possession of the unlawful, from his point
of view, proprietors.

Most of the text of this book is of a mystical character, but it
contains also a description of various events of Mayan history
and some condensed chronological tables, or the so-called
' series of Catouns.' Some passages contain interesting religio-
symbolic formulas, used for the consecration of priests, and the
end of the manuscript gives quotations from the predictions of
the famous prophet, Chilam Balam, and other lesser prophets.
The name of Chilam Balam, who was once a chief priest of the
Mayas, is ordinarily applied to all books of prophecies and, in
order to distinguish them, the name of the city where the book
was written is always added. Therefore the manuscript translated
by A. M. Bolio bears the name of ' The Book of Chilam Balam
from Chumayel.'

Doubtless some passages of this book are simply ancient songs
and poems, transmitted orally from one generation to another

before the arrival of the Spaniards. When the Mayan priests had learned the Latin alphabet they made a secret record of these ancient poems. By rendering them into Latin script the priests apparently wished to preserve them from the fury of the conquerors, who destroyed everything written in ' devilish ' hieroglyphs. Thus was prepared by the priests a new collection of Mayan books which have been preserved religiously by their proprietors. The Mayas still show a great respect for their *yanalte*, i.e. books, in accordance with their ancient traditions, which requested a sacred and mystic respect for every written line.

Although the penmanship of the Book of Chilam Balam is excellent, the deciphering of it is very difficult, owing to the intentionally haphazard method of spacing and punctuation. While some words are divided into several parts, others are joined together, forming one long word. Considering the difficulty of the Mayan language, these artificial difficulties render the reading of the book doubly complex. Moreover, at the epoch of the compilation of the manuscript, those Mayan sounds which were lacking in Spanish were transcribed by conventional combinations of Latin letters. These combinations are different to-day. Finally, the manuscript lacks the first pages, which were lost before it was acquired by the Bishop don Crescencio. Thus, the first and very difficult work for Señor Bolio was to sort out and and put in order the text.

The Spanish translation of the book is difficult to understand, because it is full of obscure and even apparently absurd passages. However, the reader must remember that the psychology of the Mayas, is quite different from the psychology of Europeans and especially modern Europeans. Bolio found that many deep esoteric passages of the book could not be rendered in all their inner meaning, because of the poverty of the Spanish vocabulary. The mystical conceptions of the Indians are difficult to understand and, when they are three hundred years old and the meaning of ancient formulas and allegories is lost, the text becomes to us a sort of acrostic. Undoubtedly the author of the book belonged to the caste of priests and expressed his ideas in obscure allegorical language, the key to which no longer exists. This language was never at any time familiar to the common people and, when the priests disappeared, no trace of it was left and the modern translators have to do a good deal of guessing. Linguists affirm that the true sense of any Mayan text can be obtained only after much trouble and patience. Bolio selected the following most fitting passage from the Book of Chilam Balam as a forenote for his translation : ' Each one of them speaks in his own words and thus it happens that they do not understand each other. But everything will be explained. Not everything that is written here is evident. The time when everything will be explained is not known yet, but those who know come from our great Mayan race. They will understand what is written here and the day will come when it will be evident to everybody. Then everything will be explained.' Bolio believes that those accustomed to mystical, esoteric, and occult texts are more likely to understand the Book of Chilam Balam than matter-of-fact archæologists and historians.

*   *   *

The fifth chapter of the book, composed in a magnificent, somewhat Biblical and at the same time primitive, style, in spite of its obscurity makes the reader feel that he has before him a description of certain great calamity of remote antiquity. Here is the most interesting passage of this part of the book :

' During the Eleventh Ahau Catoun, Ah-Musen-Cab came out in order to close the eyes of Thirteen Gods. His name was unknown to all. Only his sisters and children mentioned it among themselves, but also were not allowed to contemplate his face. This occurred, when the Earth began to waken. Nobody knew what was to come.

' And the Thirteen Gods were seized by the Nine Gods. And a fiery rain fell, and ashes fell, and rocks and trees fell down. And He butted trees and rocks against each other.

' And the Thirteen Gods were seized and their heads were cut off, and their faces were slapped, and they were spat out, and weights were placed upon their shoulders.

' And their Great Serpent was ravished from the heavens, together with the rattles of its tail and also with their quetzal feathers. And beans were taken, minced with their seed and their heart, minced pumpkin seeds, minced great pumpkin seeds and minced beans. And One, Who is eternal, clothed them and bound everything together and ascended to the Thirteenth Heaven.

' And then their skin and pieces of their bones fell here upon the Earth. And then their heart hid itself, because the Thirteen Gods did not wish to leave their heart and their seed. And the arrows struck orphans, aged ones, widowers and widows, who lived, not having strength for life.

' And they were buried on the sandy shores, in sea-waves. And then, in one watery blow, came the waters. And, when the Great Serpent was ravished, the sky fell down and the dry land sank. Then Four Gods, the Four Bacab, destroyed everything. And in the moment, when the anni-hilation was finished, they settled in their places the Yellow Men.

' And the first White Tree rose in the North and a white-breasted bird sat on it. And a rainbow appeared as a sign of the destruction below. When the first White Tree rose, the first Black Tree also rose and a black-breasted bird sat on it. And the first Yellow Tree rose and, as a sign of the destruction below, a yellow-breasted bird sat on it. And the steps of the Yellow Men, those who seem yellow, were heard.

' And the Great Mother Seiba arose amidst recollections of the destruction of the Earth. She rose straight up and elevated her head, begging for herself the eternal foliage. And by her branches and by her roots she called to her Lord.'

In similar expressions the fifth chapter of the book continues to describe the further details of this enigmatical catastrophe, but lack of space and the difficulty of the special terminology of the text oblige me to limit myself to the quoted passage.

Now we shall go over it with the help of Señor Bolio's commentaries. ' Ah-Musen-Cab ' is the Mayan spirit, governing the eastern section of the subterranean world, and his name in literal translation means ' The Secret Red of the Earth.' The cardinal points have special colours with Mayas : white is, allotted to the north, yellow to the south, black to the west and red to the east. Since, according to the Mayas, there are three planes—the heavenly, earthly, and subterranean, each with their own cardinal points, the Mayan cosmogony possesses twelve cardinal points. Four spirits, or Four Bacab, rule the earthly plane, or the surface of the Earth.

The twelve cardinal points, disposed in three stories, have a common centre, which is symbolized esoterically by the Seiba tree. This symbolical tree, the Great Mother Seiba, reaches with its roots the centre of the Earth and with its summit—all the thirteen heavens, which are reduced to seven by some americanists. The souls of men ascend the trunk of Mother Seiba until they reach the place of eternal bliss, where they merge into deity. Therefore ' thirteen ' symbolizes in the Mayan esoteric teaching the centre of the world.

The ' Winged,' ' Feathered,' or ' Great ' Serpent, covered by quetzal feathers, is an expression often found in Mayan texts and interpreted in various ways. According to some americanists, it represents Quetzal-Coatl, or Cuculcan, the great enlightener of the Central American nations, eventually deified by Indian tribes. The quetzal is the most beautiful and also the rarest bird of Latin America, resembling partly a parrot and partly the New Guinea ' bird of paradise.' The republic of Guatemala, which protects this rare bird by severe legislation, has incorporated it into its coat of arms. According to other americanists, the Great Serpent symbolizes sometimes the forces of Nature and human life. Whenever the author of the Book of Chilam Balam wishes to mention some great misfortune, or death, he uses expressions such as: ' the Great Serpent was ravished,' or ' thrown down.' The Great Serpent is portrayed in the shape of an ordinary rattlesnake. One archæologist has offered still a third explanation : he told me that originally in the Toltec cosmogony the Great Serpent denoted the constellation of the Ursa Major and later on any celestial body, star, planet, and especially a comet.

The phrase of the book, ' this occurred, when the Earth began to waken ' signifies, according to Señor Bolio, the beginning of a certain great epoch in the history of the Mayas. But I consider that this phrase simply means that the catastrophe occurred during the spring. However, we must admit that it also could be interpreted as indicating the beginning of some epoch in the life of the whole Earth, such as, for instance, the post-Glacial Period.

The ' Thirteen Gods ' and the ' Nine Gods ' indicate apparently two cosmic groups of forces : the first group consists of the protectors of the Mayas and the second takes care of the whole planet. '9' and '13' are the sacred numbers of Mayan occultism.

The Mayas call themselves the 'yellow people,' but one must remember that 'yellow' is a vague term in the Mayan language. It is applied, for instance, to a special clay found in Yucatan, which is, however, distinctly of a red colour. At the same time the Mayas call Europeans 'red people,' because the latter came from the east, symbolized by red.

'Seed,' or 'seeds,' should be understood as 'humanity, mankind, etc.' In the Book of Bereshith the expression 'Abraham's seed' signifies also a whole race, namely the Jews.

Many features of the Mayan calendar-system have been definitely established, such as, for instance, the term 'Catoun,' a score of years, which was always marked on a special slab. Instead of months the Mayas had periods of 20 days each. Every Catoun was ended by a special day, called Ahau and numbered progressively from one to thirteen. The number of Ahau applied also to the whole corresponding Catoun. The Mayan calendar was drawn in the form of a circle, or 'Wheel of Catouns,' and it started always with the Eleventh Ahau. On the whole, however, the Mayan chronology and calendar are very complex and the authorities sometimes do not agree on the interpretation of Mayan dates.

The first chapter of the Book of Chilam Balam contains a passage which must be regarded as a very valuable indication of the change of the Mayan solar calendar into a lunar one. This change was made at some moment in Mayan history and the passage tells about this event in the following terms : '. . . it is the name of Catoun, which ruled, when Catouns and Ahaus were changed, the Eighth Ahau.' This change of calendar coincided with the destruction of Itzaes's culture by invaders, who belonged to the Nahoah race and introduced religio-astronomical reform. The very ancient solar cult at that time began to mix with lunar rituals. This calendar reform contributed much to a further complication in Mayan chronology. One wonders whether this change of calendar was not induced by some startling phenomenon in the solar system.

I propose to venture to interpret the description of the enigmatical catastrophe mentioned in the fifth chapter of the Book of Chilam Balam by eliminating and clarifying some of the obscure lines of the Mayan author. For convenience I quote first Bolio's interpretation :

'During one of the Mayan calendar-cycles the Red subterranean spirit came out of his underground abode in order to deal a blow at the Thirteen Gods, who take care of the Mayan people. This event took place at the very beginning of a remarkable epoch. But everything that occurred happened entirely unexpectedly : the cosmic group of the Nine Gods assaulted the group of Thirteen and defeated it. Fiery rain and ashes fell, the Earth trembled, rocks crumbled, and trees were destroyed. The Great Serpent, the symbol of light and life for the Mayas, disappeared from the sky. Men perished in great numbers and their souls departed to the Thirteenth heaven to join the deity. The Earth was flooded and the sky fell upon the Earth. The Earthly spirits Bacab destroyed everything. When the destruction and the annihilation had been accomplished, the spirits Bacab began to arrange the people of Maya. At first everything was settled in the north, then in the west, and last in the south. Then the Mayas began to settle anew. They repented and turned their prayers towards the Almighty.'

I have already mentioned the interesting parallelisms between the texts of the Book of Bereshith and those of the Book of Chilam Balam concerning the great catastrophe. These parallelisms give us the idea of a common source for both books. Such an idea is supported especially by some details in the story of the Book of Genesis of the Universal Flood, and in the description of the enigmatical catastrophe in the fifth chapter of the Mayan manuscript.

The reader will find below my own interpretation of this chapter : I attempt to elicit possible cosmic facts hidden under the cover of the Mayan mythology :

During a very remote epoch, probably at the end of the post-Glacial Period, a catastrophe occurred within the solar system. For some unknown reasons the satellite of our planet was pulled away from it into space. This occurrence was accompanied by a range of events which caused a destruction of a considerable section of humanity. An enormous meteorite fell upon the Earth, violent earthquakes occurred and the surface of the Earth underwent a series of changes.   Some islands and even parts of continents changed their outlines, or disappeared altogether.

The continent, or large island, which was situated east from Yucatan, suffered from especially heavy blows : it was flooded with lava and covered by volcanic ashes and finally all the firm land sank into the Atlantic Ocean.

This terrible cataclysm had repercussions over the whole planet. But, when the tragic days were over, the spared mankind began to recover gradually from the effects of this cataclysm : the tribes who lived north of the most severely devastated region were the first to recover, then followed the nations who lived west from it, and finally those who lived south, the Mayas themselves being included in the latter.

During this catastrophe our present Moon made its first appearance in the sky and produced such a strong impression on the prehistoric peoples that they adopted the mixed solar-lunar calendar and deified our satellite.   The Egyptian priest, Manetho, tells us for instance that the forefathers of the Egyptians changed their former calendar during the *twelfth* millennium. This information is very precious : it indicates that some important reason forced the pre-Egyptians to introduce such a great reform. .... On the other hand, the date given by Manetho disagrees with the date of Plato, 9500 B.C. for the catastrophe of Atlantis : the difference between both dates is about 2000 years. But I must repeat that the chronology of various sources is very questionable and contradictory.

CHAPTER XIII

ERTAIN excavations in Ecuador have sometimes yielded vestiges of an enigmatical and at the same time highly-developed prehistoric culture. I have seen in the Guayaquil Museum stone arm-chairs of a type which often are found in the territory of this republic, and the local archæologists informed me that on the Colombian border there exists an entire field surrounded by such arm-chairs. The experts believe that this field must at one time have served for meetings of members of an unknown prehistoric nation. These arm-chairs, being arranged in a circle, remind one of the Celtic cromlechs and the ruins of Stonehenge. Do not these Ecuadorian monuments belong to the same mysterious race which left us the remarkable ruins of Tihuanaco in Bolivia?

I have heard that somewhere in Ecuador there exist monuments with hieroglyphïc and even alphabetical inscriptions, but Professor Uhle affirms that inscriptions of pre-Colombian times do not exist on the Pacific side of the continent anywhere south of Panama. I venture to contradict the venerable scientist: it is enough to mention the famous Stone of Chavin (see later for its description), or the portal of the Tihuanaco temple, containing some enigmatical hieroglyph-like drawings.

I saw in Ecuador several rich archæological collections. The largest, belonging to Señor Jijon in Quito, consists almost exclusively of objects of the Incaic period. Another interesting collection, belonging to Señor Ernesto Franco, consists almost exclusively of prehistoric objects and is unique of its kind.

Señor Franco accidentally found on the territory of his property in Esmeralda (on the northern shore of Ecuador) a series of ancient sepultures, and these finds awakened in him an interest in archæology. At present the rich collection of Señor Franco consists of about 12,000 objects, mostly belonging to some unknown culture. All the finds of this amateur-archæologist could be divided in four categories: 1, the few finds belonging

to the Incaic period ; 2, the pre-Incaic relics; 3, vestiges of
Paleolithic and Neolithic periods in South America; and 4,
vestiges of some very ancient and puzzling culture, which was
highly developed, although in time it preceded the Stone Age.

The first and second categories of exhibits are not of much
interest, the third contains some stone hatchets and maces,
remarkable for their massive size, but the last and the most rich
category contains objects which must give every archæologist
and historian much occasion to think.

Señor Franco observed that the number of finds grew in
the inverse ratio of their distance from the ocean: the closer
to the seashore, the more frequent became valuable finds. This
led him to the conclusion that the region of Esmeralda is nothing
else than the eastern side of a submerged area, and he tried
excavations offshore under the sea-waters, which are very
shallow there since many sand-banks diminish the depth. The
results were astonishing : Franco brought up from the sea-
bottom many artistic statuettes, several large busts and
numerous objects, strangely carved, and made of steatite. These
stone objects are, according to the opinion of Señor Franco,
nothing more than the personal seals of that unknown nation
which at some time inhabited Esmeralda. This hypothesis is
supported by the fact that among many hundreds of these
objects no two are identical. Each ' seal ' possesses the shape
of a rectangular four-sided prism, one base being smooth and the
other carved. The carvings consist of various conventionalized,
perhaps heraldic, animals and hieroglyphs, or hieroglyphoid
figures. Their existence contradicts the assertions of Professor
Uhle, unless it can be proved that these objects were brought to
Ecuador from Central America. These enigmatical objects are
identical with the personal steatite seals still in use in China,
although the Chinese seals lack animal motives. Perhaps the
Esmeralda carvings are simply the images of clan totems. In
any case it is evident that very long ago the inhabitants
of prehistoric Ecuador possessed individual seals for various
purposes. It is plausible to believe that these prehistoric seals
were used not for documents, but for tattooing, like the prehistoric seals found in the Canary Islands and in Puglia (Italy).

Most of the statuettes found in Esmeralda belong to the type
of bagatelles called in French *bibelots,* and served probably for the

adornment of homes, or as children's toys. In this collection are very numerous statuettes of women. Sometimes these are distinctly pornographic in effect. The type of the faces is neither Caucasian nor Mongolian, but is rather between the two : the eyes, for instance, are a little aslant and the cheek-bones a little more prominent than with the Caucasian race. Many statuettes resemble the ancient Egyptian style by their hairdress, clothes, and the breast-adornments on the statues of the priests. If we agree that the faces also are somewhat of Egyptian type, the idea of the American origin of the pre-Egyptians immediately comes to mind.

The work of these primeval sculptors is matchless and the technique does not differ at all from modern sculpture. The presence of pornographic statuettes indicates a certain degree of civilization, because primeval peoples rarely exploit this kind of sculpture. Such a degradation of taste is always the sign of a certain cultural decadence and, therefore, of a comparatively high previous culture. The Esmeralda culture is placed by the local scientists at about 20,000 years old.

In the collection of Señor Franco my attention was attracted particularly by what seems to be a school-collection illustrating various human races. In fact I found there busts of a Caucasian, of a Mongolian, of a Negro, of a Semite, and of a Mayan Indian. Besides these races some busts represent types of mankind which no longer exist. Among the latter one bust portrays a Japanese-like face, which seems to be a cross between Mongolian and Malayan types.

Señor Franco possesses in his collection a green-black obsidian mirror, about two inches in diameter, which arouses general admiration and amazement. It has the shape of a convex lens but is polished so irreproachably that it reflects the human face in a very reduced size with the correct proportion of all its details down to the tiniest hair. Everyone knows that the polishing of optical lenses requires a knowledge of mathematics and the use of very delicate and precise instruments. How would prehistoric opticians attain such perfection without proper equipment? The opinion of Señor Franco is that the unknown race which inhabited Esmeralda 20,000 years ago was connected with the highly-civilized Atlanteans.

I am of the opinion that the region of Esmeralda was at some time connected with certain regions of Central America, such as, for instance, Guatemala, where various ruins indicate that a highly-developed prehistoric civilization once existed.

*   *   *

In Bolivia, at the height of 12,500 feet above sea level, is situated the majestic and beautiful lake of Titicaca with an area of more than 9500 square miles. Several little islands adorn the surface of this lake and among them are the remarkable islands of the Sun and Moon. Both islands are sprinkled with the ruins of prehistoric buildings. Near the port of Huaqui exist the ruins of a prehistoric city, which probably are the most interesting in the whole world. This city is called Tihuanaco (' The City of the Dead ') and its age is many thousands of years. The unknown culture which left us these ruins is called ' the Tihuanaco culture.'

On the strength of certain data the city of Tihuanaco is thought to have been abandoned by its inhabitants and builders about 13,000 years ago, and the emperors of the dynasty of Incas, having invaded Bolivia in the second century A.D., found these ruins almost in the same condition as did the Spaniards thirteen centuries later. The new masters of the country found Tihuanaco absolutely deserted and only the beautifully paved streets and squares of the City of the Dead, the magnificent temples and statues and the remains of the aqueducts testified to the brilliance of the culture which once existed near Titicaca. Amongst the ruins of the cyclopic buildings were found also heaps of hewn stones, evidently provided ready for further construction.

When the Spaniards entered Tihuanaco, they were astonished by these giant cubic monoliths, prepared by unknown builders. The weight of these granite cubes varies from 60 to 200 tons, but the most astounding thing was that the enormous monoliths in the preserved buildings were riveted together by giant silver bolts, some of which weighed hundreds of kilograms. Naturally, the greedy adventurers of Pizarro made short work of these precious bolts, and soon the monoliths remained without ties. Thus, what had been spared by the millenniums and by the so-called ' savage Indians ' of Peru, was destroyed in a wink by the ' civilized ' subjects of His Catholic Majesty the King of Spain, of both Castillas, and of Aragon. The earthquakes, frequent in this part of the world, have shaken the colossal buildings, now deprived of their former supports, and the present aspect of the cyclopic constructions of Tihuanaco is quite different from that of the sixteenth century.

Having appropriated the silver bolts, the Spaniards turned their attention to the thousands of statues which adorned the streets and squares of Tihuanaco. Incited by their chaplain, the adventurers of Pizarro smashed to pieces countless works of prehistoric art, in their naïve fanaticism believing them to be idols. Miraculously one statue remained intact and still stands : it represents a man with a long beard and a face which resembles the faces of the enigmatical statues of Easter Island in the Pacific. This statue is called ' The Bearded Man,' and is an enigma for ethnologists, because there never was any bearded race in America. It is true that the enlighteners of the American peoples, such as Quetzal-Coatl, the Colombian Bochica, etc., all possessed long beards and one wonders whether they did not belong to the race represented by the statue of Tihuanaco ? As all enlighteners came from the east and apparently from Atlantis, may we not suppose that Plato's continent was at least partly populated by a bearded race ?

The area of the Tihuanaco ruins is equal to about three square kilometres and is covered by a series of prehistoric buildings. The most striking of them is the temple of the Sun with its beautiful and majestic portal. This temple is built on a gigantic truncated pyramid more than 120 feet high.

As the sign of the cross represents now a symbol common to almost the whole Aryan race, so was the sign of the swastika, at the epoch of the Tihuanaco culture, generally regarded by a considerable part of the American people. This South American swastika differs a little from the well-known Hindu one, consisting of two crossed rows of steps. Therefore Professor A. Poznansky (of La Paz in Bolivia) calls it ' *signo escalonado* ' (' the sign of stairways '). This prehistoric sign symbolized the idea of the gradual evolution of all beings, who little by little ascend to the Dèity, Who is the absolute perfection. I think that the existence of such profound mysticism at such a distant epoch is also a proof of the great age of the whole culture of mankind. Many great cultures had to develop and perish before humanity could attain such a high degree of philosophy as the idea of infinite evolution towards final perfection and immersion in God. The *signo escalonado* was spread throughout the whole of America, from Alaska to Patagonia, which fact is proved by ancient ceramics bearing this sign. Sometimes it varies in details, but generally it is represented as a stairway-like swastika, whose ends are terminated by the heads of various animals. The same, but somewhat modified, sign we also find on the Mayan monuments. The Tihuanaco culture is even supposed to be the originator of a peculiar style, called 'the epigonal style of Tihuanaco,' which is distinguished by the *signos escalonados* often found on the objects and pre-Incaic fabrics.

The city of Cuzco, situated at 12,000 feet above the sea level, was also founded many millenniums before the arrival of the Incas, but the latter embellished it and gave to it that aspect which still amazes tourists and scientists. Cuzco is a city of straight streets, vast squares, and beautiful buildings, and is quite different from any other city in the world : in Cuzco the tourist feels himself on another planet, like a stranger among entirely new conditions of existence. . . .

. In the centre of this prehistoric capital is situated the temple of the Sun, built of large round monoliths, a unique and incomparable edifice in the world. The powerful earthquakes which are so frequent in Peru could not destroy this cyclopic construction in the course of many millenniums. Some scientists suppose that the builders of this temple belonged to the same mysterious race as that which created the majestic monuments of Tihuanaco.

Near the temple of the Sun is lying the famous 820-ton monolith, called 'Piedra Cansada' ('The Tired Stone'). This nickname was given to the monolith because at one time it stood vertically, but later on, as if tired of standing, for some unknown reason it fell. This enormous stone doubtless belongs to the epoch of the Tihuanaco culture.

Everywhere in Cuzco can be seen ruins of Incaic and pre-Incaic buildings, but the most interesting fragment is the ruin of an aqueduct, built in unknown antiquity. The prehistoric engineers organized an ideal supply of water in this country of chronic drought. They rationally exploited the water of numerous torrents issuing from the glaciers of the Cordilleras, and ancient Cuzco was permanently provided with exceptionally good water. The remains of fortresses which can be seen around the former capital of the Incas prove that their unknown prehistoric builders were very good strategists and brilliant engineers. These fortresses scattered amidst the mountains were built, according to Professor Poznansky, by the mysterious race that constructed Tihuanaco. R. Mueller and Professor Poznansky, who visited some of these ruins, were astonished by the design of such ancient structures. These experts found within the age-old fortresses the vestiges of store-chambers for victuals provided for a possible siege, cleverly arranged aqueducts and enormous cisterns for the accumulation of water brought by mountain torrents and by rains. Professor Poznansky is convinced that the gigantic pre-Incaic buildings in Cuzco are also due to the activity of the race of Tihuanaco.

The valleys in the Andes are unsuitable for agriculture : therefore the race of Tihuanaco covered the mountain slopes with terraces, the total length of which is greater than the length of the whole equator-line.

Professor Arthur Poznansky has been studying the antiquities of Bolivia and Peru for more than forty years and has found ruins of an unknown highly-civilized race in Macchu-Picchu, Huaina-Picchu, Ollan-Taitambo, Pisac, and Plateriaio. Many of these ruins are surrounded by such precipices that they are inaccessible now and it is clear that at some time these mysterious structures were situated at a much lower level. Mueller and Poznansky had to study these with the help of a telescope. The ruins of Macchu-Picchu, situated on inaccessible summits in the mountains, are even more astounding than Cuzco itself : this group of snow-white edifices, palaces, and temples, which unexpectedly rises before the amazed traveller, produces the impression of something fantastic, of a tale in stone. The archæologists who are still discussing the question as to who were the builders of these magnificent structures, cannot explain how the prehistoric architects could have raised the materials and workmen to such a height. The only solution of these problems is given in the hypothesis of Poznansky to the effect that Macchu-Picchu, as well as Tihuanaco and other high-situated settlements in the Andes, were at one time on a much lower level. The citadel of Macchu-Picchu seems to be supported miraculously in the air : around it one can see only abysses and far below the rocks furiously swirls and foams the river Urubamba. It is necessary to mention that near Macchu-Picchu are also situated the ruins of a prehistoric astronomical observatory.

Eighty miles from Cuzco stretch the remarkable ruins of Intihuatan, where at present some archæological parties are working. Here the so-called *huacos*, or peculiar prehistoric ceramics, mummies, golden objects, and other adornments are often found. One German investigator has shown me a collection of small tubes, found by him in the ruins of Intihuatan : these tubes are made of some material, the chemical structure of which has not yet been established, but which resembles glass. Neither the prehistoric inhabitants of Peru and Bolivia, nor the subjects of the Incas, knew glass in our sense. Apparently the unknown aborigines of these countries invented some stuff of their own possessing the properties of our glass.

The Peruvian archæologist, Julio Tello, discovered near Trujillo in 1933 a prehistoric obelisk with multicoloured drawings. This find is considered one of the most remarkable made in the twentieth century.

*   *   *

Thanks to the researches of German scientists, it has now been established that the average height of the Andean ridge was at one time much lower than at present. We can even determine approximately the extent of its rise, at least for the district of Titicaca. Curt Bilau found that a 550-kilometre stretch of this district, together with the corresponding band of the seashore, were once 3500 metres lower than now. This assertion is based on a very interesting fact : this stretch is marked throughout its length by a horizontal white line at the height of 3500 metres. This line, resembling one drawn by chalk, was found to consist of the calcareous deposits of certain seaweeds, containing a great percentage of lime and covering a depth of no more than one to two yards. The presence of this white line at such a height is a proof that at some time the ridge and consequently the actual shore were much lower and immersed in the ocean. This idea is also supported by the discovery of the mouths of ancient rivers at the height of the ancient sea-level.

The astronomers of the Potsdam observatory, guided by certain hieroglyphs on the portal of the Sun Temple in Tihuanaco, established the position of the Sun at the epoch of the building of this sanctuary. They found that about 9,550 B.C. this building had not yet been finished. Near this temple are still to be seen the vestiges of an unfinished seaport, which prove that Tihuanaco at that epoch was situated on the ocean-shore. Everywhere in the surroundings are lying enormous monoliths and at the time of the discovery of Tihuanaco there were also found various builders' implements. By some signs it is evident that the builders were suddenly obliged to abandon the construction and hurry away.

Strangely enough the date of 9,550 B.C. coincides with the date of the Atlantis catastrophe given, according to Plato, by the priests of Sais. Solon visited Sais about 500 B.C. and the Egyptian priests told him that the catastrophe in question had occurred more than 9,000 years before his arrival at Sais. The coincidence of these dates shows that the causes of both events were probably the same : perhaps a phenomenon of cosmic importance occurred and provoked the simultaneous destruction of Plato's continent and the abandonment of Tihuanaco, following an unexpected heightening of the shore of South America to more than 10,000 feet. This supposition can be confirmed by another fact : in the neighbouring Colombia, near Bogotá, there exists on almost the same level the famous ' Giant's Field,' a vast plain covered by the petrified bones of mastodons. It is evident that these prehistoric elephants were surprised by the sudden elevation of their customary pasture-ground and perished from cold and the sudden rarefaction of air.

Professor Poznansky, who is at present one of the principal authorities concerning Bolivian prehistory, affirms in his numerous books that Tihuanaco was populated by a highly-cultured race at the time when this region was situated on the seashore. The epoch of the culmination of that prehistoric South American civilization can be placed at about 13,000 years ago.

The supposition that the heightening of the Andes occurred about 12,000 years ago coincides also with the data furnished by geology, which affirms that about 12,000 years ago some cataclysm occurred in this part of the world, heightening considerably the Pacific shore and, perhaps, contributing to the formation of the volcanic lakes of Titicaca and Poopo. Probably the same cataclysm provoked a phenomenon of inverse character in the neighbouring Ecuador, namely the above-mentioned lowering of the Esmeralda region together with the submersion of a comparatively vast area of firm land.

Professors Rudolph Mueller and A. Poznansky investigated the high Andean tablelands and found there many ruins of palaces and temples, situated sometimes on inaccessible rocky heights. The result of Mueller's calculations practically tallies with the conclusions of A. Poznansky: the German scientist decided that the Tihuanaco culture flourished about 14,000 years ago. Further, the investigations of both scientists proved that that nation possessed a profound knowledge of astronomy and mathematics, and used a peculiar alphabet and a calendar which was much more exact than ours. Professor Poznansky considers that the race of Tihuanaco was the most advanced of that time and played among prehistoric mankind the same role as the Aryan race plays in our day. He believes that the Tihuanaco culture was the source of other great American cultures such as the Toltec and Mayan. This prehistoric race of Tihuanaco spoke the Arowak language, which with some modifications is still spoken by some of the Indian tribes of Central and South America. The Tihuanaco race apparently came from the north, and the present tribe of Uru Indians in Bolivia represents, according to Professor Poznansky, the degenerate remainder of that once great civilized nation. The ceramics found in the ruins of Tihuanaco are adorned by drawings which sometimes represent the vanished animals of prehistoric epochs: this circumstance shows the great age of the Tihuanaco race and its culture.

* * *

In the vestibule of the National Museum in Lima stands a high stone slab covered with artistic carvings and symmetrical ornaments. It is the famous ' Piedra de Chavin ' (' The Chavin Stone '), whose origin is one of the most interesting archæological problems of modern times. The carvings and ornaments on this slab are not so deep as those on Central American monuments, but resemble rather the drawings of a skilled engraver. This slab was discovered among the ruins of Incaic buildings at Chavin de Huantara in 1840, which were built on doubtless still more ancient ruins belonging to the mysterious Tihuanaco culture. When the Incas conquered Peru and the region of the

Upper Marañon, they found in Chavin de Huantara very ancient ruins and used the ancient monoliths for the building of a new fortress. Thus the famous Stone of Chavin was found and fixed into the façade of the newly-built fortress, but when the Spaniards destroyed the latter the Stone of Chavin fell and, later on, was found again amongst the debris.

G. Hurley considers that the Chavin pre-Incaic ruins are 21,000 years old, but Bartholomeo Mitre believes that they are not older than 12,000 years. At any rate, the Stone of Chavin belongs to a very remote epoch and represents probably one of the oldest monuments in the world.

This diorite slab is 2 yards high and half a yard wide. In its centre is carved a human figure somewhat resembling Egyptian frescoes. Each hand of the figure holds a sceptre-trident, and both sceptres are enclosed in parallelograms with hieroglyphs, or at least hieroglyphoid drawings, as yet undeciphered. The feet of the figure are somewhat similar to tree-roots and the head is encircled by ten serpents resembling the head of Medusa. All around the figure are also seen serpents carved symmetrically on both its sides. On the head of the figure is seen a high tiara consisting of many small human heads and various ornaments.

Clements R. Markham finds in the central figure a resemblance to the drawings of the famous portal of the Sun Temple in Tihuanaco. G. Hurley believes that the mysterious design of the Chavin Stone represents the god of the Amazon, and the serpents surrounding the central figure symbolize nothing other than the numerous affluents and tributaries of the great South American river.

*   *   *

Geologists admit unanimously that the so-called ' Roosevelt's Tableland,' which is situated on the boundary between the Brazilian states of Amazonas and the Matto Grosso, has been above sea-level at least since the last Glacial Period and even probably since a much earlier epoch. This tableland is the natural continuation of the tableland of Goyaz and, geologically, the latter is one of the most ancient regions of the Earth's surface being, together with the so-called ' Angara Continent ' (the present Siberian provinces of Yakutsk and Irkutsk), the two territories of the earth-crust which apparently never have been submerged. This assertion is supported by a very interesting discovery made by the Russian entomologist, G. Bondar, of a species ' Brazilaphis Bondari,' a plant-louse which lives only in the above-mentioned Siberian provinces and on the tableland of Goyaz. It is known that plant-lice are some of the most ancient insects of the world and live always on the lowest parts of plants. Thus the slightest inundation would immediately kill these insects. The fact that ' Brazilaphis Bondari' is still preserved on two territories so distant from each other doubtless proves the geological antiquity of the ' Angara Continent' and of the Goyaz tableland, together with its continuation, the central Roosevelt Plateau of the Matto Grosso and Amazonas.

This plateau is remarkable for the complete absence of alluvial layers and consists of plutonic strata only. The climate of Roosevelt's Plateau is exceptionally healthy and perfectly suitable for man's existence. R. O. Marsh thinks that this tableland was populated at a very remote epoch by a highly-civilized race, connected apparently with the Atlanteans. The Indians who live near this plateau have informed various investigators that on this tableland at one time existed a mighty empire, ruling not only the tribes living in Brazil, but also those who inhabited the Pacific shores. In fact, amid the sumptuous growth of high grass, of lianas, orchids, bushes, and trees, the traveller sees sometimes the vestiges of prehistoric settlements, remainders of an unknown ancient civilization; and on the rocks overhanging the forest torrents and the so-called *cachoeiras* (rapids), inscriptions in enigmatical alphabets, strange drawings, hieroglyphs, and ideograms. Among the ruins of forgotten prehistoric cities are often found copper and bronze objects, arms, household articles, and pottery. Those fearless men who have dared to penetrate into the wilderness of the Matto Grosso report that they have seen there ruins of great cities with well-preserved streets and the remainders of majestic buildings.

R. O. Marsh considers that the Mayan and Incaic cultures derived from the culture of that unknown prehistoric empire. He proves that the race, who at a distant period inhabited Roosevelt's tableland, possessed an advanced knowledge of astronomy, knowing, for instance, the zodiacal constellations, and giving them the names which are preserved to-day. These names, entirely meaningless to us, had a profound meaning for those prehistoric astronomers. Later on, according to R. O. Marsh, this zodiacal terminology was inherited by the Toltecs, Mayas, Egyptians, Phœnicians, and Sumerians, and eventually was passed on to us. Thus, the elements of our own astronomy were evolved by the unknown prehistoric race of Roosevelt's tableland.

In 1923 I met the French Consul-General in Para (Brazil), the noted investigator, M. Lecointe, who has spent eighteen years in studies of the Amazonian basin and wrote a remarkable book, *L'Amazonie*. He told me that in his wanderings through the Amazonian jungle he sometimes found enormous stone disks, divided into sixteen sectors and covered by hieroglyphs. Each sector apparently had a symbol of its own. I saw M. Lecointe's photos of these disks, which he calls in his book, *pierres solaires* (solar stones), and I agree with him that they probably served the purpose of calculation tables and were used so by the prehistoric astronomers of Amazonia. Moreover, we find some resemblance between these disks and the famous ' Moctezuma's Clock ' in the National Museum of Mexico.

The archæological investigations in the Matto Grosso have been carried out by R. O. Marsh, General C. Rondon, Dr. Barbosa, Bernardo da Sylva Ramos, M. Lecointe, A. Frot, and others. B. Ramos and A. Frot have discovered on the rocks of the Matto Grosso many inscriptions in Phœnician, Egyptian, and even the Sumerian tongue, as well as texts in alphabets similar to those of Crete and Cyprus. These discoveries are certainly astounding, but R. O. Marsh has come to the conclusion that the Matto Grosso contains the vestiges of a culture much more ancient than the Phœnician or Carian. As I have said earlier, the Indian traditions tell about a great and powerful empire which flourished a long while ago in the western and northern Matto Grosso, and apparently these legends are well founded : there was a time, when in the territory of the present Great Forest there really existed an unknown, cultured nation. Following some unknown reason, perhaps calamities, or invasions, the prehistoric population of the Matto Grosso perished, or emigrated. But this occurred a very long time ago. . . . And later on, when men left the country, wild animals and giant reptiles settled within the ruins, and mighty tropical vegetation covered everything under its overpowering green blanket.

The whole area of Roosevelt's tableland is equal to 1,500,000 square miles and is the least-explored part of the world. There are rumours to the effect that in the rivers, forests, and swamps of this tableland are still living giant lizards, which have been extinct in other regions of the Earth for many millions of years.

*   *   *

Postscriptum

Not insisting on any particular date for the occurrence of that great prehistoric cataclysm which destroyed the political and cultural centre of the ancient world, I will try to paint an imaginary picture of this catastrophe. Although my picture will be rather a fantastic one, nevertheless it might reveal to my reader the possible circumstances of the tragedy of Atlantis.

. . . The happy and prosperous Atlanteans spent their days peacefully protected by Poseidon in his splendid temple towering on the summit of a three-peaked mountain. The dense population of the capital was busy with its extensive trade, the numerous priests and functionaries were preoccupied by the affairs of that immense state, the students and pupils filled the schools and, when the mild sun-disk disappeared behind the mountains, a cheerful crowd sallied forth into the streets. . . .

But the astronomers and magi of the observatory on Poseidon's peak were troubled : certain strange phenomena in the heavens worried them and gave them much to think about. That well-known little planet, Earth's only satellite, which shone every night in the sky of Atlantis, had become brighter. Simultaneously a strange luminosity had appeared on the horizon. From various points of the Atlantean empire had begun to come alarming news of earthquakes and volcanic eruptions. The sea was agitated and the tides reached an uncommon height. It was the first day of the fatal comet.

The next night this unexpected guest from Space appeared in the constellation of Cancer as a comparatively short and brilliant line of light, speedily growing in size. The population which filled the public gardens, squares, and streets, admired the comet.

They also wondered at a bright new star, which had suddenly arisen near the shining Hesper. The priests became silent; mysterious ceremonies were going on continuously within Poseidon's sanctuary.

By the third night the comet had become a large and shining band and its magnificent tail, like a great flaming fan, hid many familiar constellations. Earth's little satellite and the new star receded into small discs. The ocean heaved in a terrifying manner though the weather was calm and windless. Giant waves assaulted the shores of Atlantis and its signal-towers along the coasts. The earth-crust began to tremble and terrible earthquakes occurred in the vicinity of the capital. Many volcanoes burst into eruption and enormous streams of lava inundated the country. Hot geysers spouted everywhere; sometimes even in the streets of cities. While some lakes suddenly dried up, unexpected depressions occurred in the mountains and formed new lakes of crystalline transparent water. Numerous islands with little craters which spouted hot mud and salt water appeared in the ocean. The twilight took on an unnatural and ominous colour as a result of the masses of volcanic ash suspended in the atmosphere. Mighty electro-magnetic waves around the planet provoked phenomena in the sky analogous to the aurora borealis.

Very soon thundered the deep voices of all the volcanoes on the Earth's surface, greeting the mighty visitor from the depths of interplanetary Space. . . .

Bad news was coming to the Atlantean capital from everywhere : by means of a sort of optical telegraph various governors related that the volcanoes, which for a long time had been believed extinct, had begun to spout smoke, fire, and lava anew ; entire cities had been inundated by high tides or destroyed by earthquakes ; unprecedented heavy rains had devastated the fields and plantations ; everywhere the populace rushed panic-stricken into the mountains. . . . The governor of a distant province in South America reported that a new ridge had suddenly arisen there destroying the nearly-completed port and capital of Tihuanaco. The king of the Mediterranean province, vassal of the Atlantean emperors, sent a courier to say that the Iberian isthmus had given way and that his kingdom had been engulfed by the ocean, but the courier never arrived. . . .

By the next day the comet had attained gigantic dimensions ;

its fiery tail seeming to fill half the sky. The atmosphere became charged with electricity and to many it was as if malevolent radiations streamed towards the Earth from the comet's head. Soon the sky was covered with black clouds and a terrific storm burst. The deep rolling of the thunder was deadened by continuous subterranean and volcanic explosions. Streams of incandescent lava cut the communications between cities and villages. Everywhere were ominous flames and fires. They were very soon extinguished, however, by a torrential downpour of water, blackened with volcanic ashes, the coming of which cast the already terrified population into despair.

Reports from the provincial rulers and numerous Atlantean vassals became more and more alarming : they told of the destruction of entire districts, buried under the lava streams. Crowds of refugees flocked to the capital to find safety behind the walls of Poseidon's sanctuary. A nervous excitement seized mankind : cases of mass-madness became frequent and numerous fanatics and prophets appeared either ecstatically summoning the people to repent, or loudly blaspheming Poseidon and the gods. Men and women writhed in the streets with hysterical convulsions : some of them leapt into the streams of lava and were burned under the eyes of the crowd. Others climbed the shore-rocks and, bursting into mad laughter, jumped into the waves. The authority of the police melted away and hooligans broke into the taverns and eating places : drunken crowds danced among the burning houses, beat the priests and violated women under the eyes of the guardians. . . .

In spite of disorder and panic many of the population inertly continued its ordinary life : the markets and shops were open, idle people filled the sumptuous baths, the theatres and other establishments of entertainments were full, and even some schools continued their work. Civilization, established during thousands of years, continued much as usual ; neither hatred nor love disappeared : even facing a dreadful general calamity men have loved and hated. . . . Were it possible for us to ask ancient mankind what it thought about these menacing events, I am sure that the reasonable majority would have answered : ' certainly, the present calamities are great, but they will pass away. . . . The terrific cosmic forces will be appeased and life will again be as before. Therefore it would be ill-judged to abandon business and the gathering of money, or to act foolishly in any way.'

The emperor with his family, however, the members of the government, and the highest clergy, embarked on a ship, which was awaiting every minute the order to sail in the teeth of the raging hurricane; but the emperor, Noah, hoped that the calamities would cease before this became necessary, and delayed the departure. . . . Finally, being unable to overcome the fears of his courtiers, Noah ordered his ship to sail. . . . The population knew nothing about the flight of the ruler and his ministers,

The sky was covered with thick clouds and nobody could perceive the alterations in the positions of the familiar luminaries. Suddenly, in the middle of the common laborious day, while the streets of the capital resounded with the clamour of pedlars and were full of a variegated crowd of townsmen and newly-arrived provincials, while the alcohol-stores blazed in the outskirts and drunken crowds roared in delirium, the whole Earth's surface shook from a terrible blow. Into the remote western ocean there had fallen a giant meteorite, which some minutes earlier had shone in the sky as our ancient satellite. At the impact the old Earth shuddered.

Entire islands and large portions of land instantaneously sank and the waters immediately closed upon them. A giant wave, caused by the fall of the meteorite, encircled the globe many times at incredible speed, washing away shores, rocks, and cities.

The magnificent Poseidonis disappeared for ever and together with it vanished in the abyss the magnificent civilization of Atlantis. Palaces, temples, museums, and libraries, containing the age-old chronicles of mankind and all the most brilliant creations of human genius, were swallowed in a few minutes by the foaming waters.

And at the very moment when the waves began to cover the tops of the towers and the golden cupola of Poseidon's temple, while the screams of drowning people could still be heard on all sides, while mothers carrying their babies scrambled up the steep slopes of the three-peaked mountain of Poseidon, the ship of Noah, covered with thousands of frightened birds, speeded before the roaring hurricane and the terror, hurrying away under full sail eastwards, to the distant and half-savage Atlantean territories in Europe. . . .

The clouds which had covered the sky cleared away for a moment, and the passengers in the royal ship saw in the darkness of the night-heavens a new luminary, the enormous lunar disk. The human face, which was to be dimly seen shining on its surface, seemed to threaten the unfortunate prehistoric world with new calamities, like an unknown and menacing deity.

On the other horizon still shone the terrible guest of yesterday, the long-tailed comet. It had become much smaller and was returning to interstellar Space, because it had already passed its perihelium and, obeying the will of its Ruler, was running again with stupendous velocity towards the limits of the solar universe.

*   *   *

Millenniums passed rapidly by and the terrible cataclysm almost faded out of the memory of mankind. Little by little the very existence of the Atlanteans came to be forgotten, and gradually even the last offshoots of that mighty and cultured race, which once had been supreme on Earth, disappeared. Virgin forests grew over the ruins of its ultramarine cities in South America, its monuments decayed and crumbled into shapeless heaps. The ages accumulated upon them mighty layers of alluvium and hid them, seemingly, for ever from the eyes of men. Entire territories, once cultivated and full of laborious populations, became waste and unexplored deserts for the new mankind. The main portion of the Atlantean empire, the beautiful island of Poseidonis, rests now at a depth of many fathoms beneath the blue waves of the ocean and its temples and palaces are overgrown with seaweed. Multicoloured and unknown species of deep-water fauna swim between the stately columns of marble and porphyry and the spacious halls shelter the petrified skeletons of the men of 12,000 years ago. They are lying there awaiting the bold investigators of the twentieth century A.D. who, with the help of modern inventions, will dare to descend and see for themselves the vestigial proofs of the dark tragedy once staged by the cosmic forces. . . .

But the rhythm of Life continues as before its everlasting periodical replacement of old tribes with new, who settle upon the graves of their predecessors. The ancient waste lands, little by little, become peopled again with colonists, the descendants of ancient, barbarous races; the wood-chopper resounds in the virgin forests and new cities are born.

And occasionally the shovel of the venturesome archæologist discovers under the new settlements prehistoric signs and traces of the magnificent cities of old.

BIBLIOGRAPHY

ANCIENT LITERATURE

The Bible.

Saint Augustin's *De Civitate Dei.*

DIODORUS OF SICILY. *Historia.*

Plutarch's *Treatise about the Moon's Spots.*

AELIANUS. *Historia.*

HERODOTUS. *Melpomena.*

Vedas.

Bhagavat-Purana.

ENGLISH LITERATURE

WISHAW. *Atlantis in Andalusia.*

I. DONNELLY. *Atlantis the Antediluvian World.*

J. SHORT. *The North Americans of Antiquity.*

L. SPENCE. *Problem of Atlantis* and *The History of Atlantis.*

LORD KINGSBOROUGH. *The Antiquities of Mexico.*

LITERATURE IN PORTUGUESE

P. M. LIMA. *Iberos e Bascos.* 1902.

G. BARROSO. *Aquem da Atlantida.* 1932.

H. ONFFROY DE THORON. *Antiguidade da navega ção do oceano (Annaes da Bibliotheca e archivo publico do Para.* t. IV. 1905).

C. COSTA. *As duas Americas.*

L. SCHWENNHAGEN. *Antiga historia do Brazil.* 1928.

VARNHAGEN. *Historia Brasileira.*

G. CRULS. *A Amasonia que eu vi.* 1930.

J. HURLEY. *A Amasonia Cyclopica.* 1931.

B. DA SILVA RAMOS. *Inscripções e tradições da America prehistorica.* 1932.

LITERATURE IN GERMAN

A. POZNANSKY. *Die Osterinsel und ihre praehistorische Monumente. Die Alterthuemer von Tihuanaco.*

Praehistorische Ideenschriften in Suedamerica.

Kulturvorgeschichtliches und die astronomische Bedeutung des grossen Sonnentempels von Tihuanaco.

Der Mensch von vor 13,000 Jahren.

A. HERRMANN. *Die Erdkarte der Urbibel.* 1931.

LITERATURE IN FRENCH

MOREUX. *L'Atlantide a-t-elle éxisté?* 1924.

Où allons-nous?

La Science mystérieuse des Pharaons.

CHATEAUBRIAND. *Mémoires d'outre-tombe.*

LE PLONGEON. *Les Mystéres Sacrés.*

LECOINTE. *L'Amazonie.*

BERLIOUX. *L'Histoire des Atlantes.* 1883.

A. BESSMERTNY. *L'Atlantide.* 1935.

Atlantis—a review of PAUL LE COUR

LITERATURE IN ITALIAN

GENARO D'AMATI. *I documenti archeologici dell'Atlantide e le loro riper-
cussioni nel campo del sapere.* 1924.

LITERATURE IN SPANISH

M. TRIANA. *La Civilización Chibcha.*

HERRERA. *Décadas.*

R. MIMENZA CASTILLO. *La civilización de Yucatan.* 1929.

L. THAYER OJEDA. *Cuestiones relacionadas con la hypotesis de la formacion
del Mediterraneo.* 1919.

La Geografía Mediterranea. 1929.

La Cronología Mitologica.

La Prehistoria de España a través de los mitos. 1932.

A. POZNANSKY. *Un viaje en el lago Titicaca.*

Razas y monumentos prehistoricos del altiplanicie andino.

Monumentos prehistoricos de Tihuanaco.

Tihuanaco.

Breves reflexiones sobre el origen de los Incas.

El signo escalonado.

Una metropoli prehistorica en la America del Sur.

El gran Templo del Sol en los Andes.

La edad del genero humano.

Una ciudad prehistorica en el Beni.

Los Urus.

Y asi habla la Esfinge Indiana.

C. R. MARKHAM. *Los Incas del Peru.*

A. MEDIZ BOLIO. *Libro de Chilam Balam de Chumayel.* 1930.

E. VILLAMIL DE RADA. *Analogías Filologicas.*

DR. CHIL. *Obras sobre las Islas Canarias.*

N. R. COLMAN. *Nande ipi Cuera.* 1929.

INDEX

INDEX

LaVergne, TN USA
28 May 2010
184358LV00004B/64/A